CHOOSING SIMPLICITY

CHOOSING SIMPLICITY

A Commentary on the Bhikshuni Pratimoksha

by
Venerable Bhikshuni Wu Yin

translated by
Bhikshuni Jendy Shih

edited by
Bhikshuni Thubten Chodron

Snow Lion Publications
Ithaca, New York

Snow Lion Publications
605 West State Street
P. O. Box 6483
Ithaca, NY 14851 USA
(607) 273-8519
www.snowlionpub.com

Printed in Canada on acid-free, recycled paper.

ISBN 1-55939-155-3

Library of Congress Cataloging-in-Publication Data

Wu Yin, Bhikshuni, 1940-
   Choosing simplicity : a commentary on the Bhikshuni Pratimoksha /
by Venerable Bhikshuni Wu Yin ; translated by Bhikshuni Jendy Shih ;
edited by Bhikshuni Thubten Chodron.
             p. cm.
Includes bibliographical references.
         ISBN 1-55939-155-3 (alk. paper)
      1. Tipiṭaka. Vinayapiṭaka. Dharmaguptavinaya. Bhikṣuniprātimokṣa-
sūtra—Criticism, interpretation, etc. 2. Monasticism and religious orders
for women, Buddhist, Rules. I. Shih, Jendy. II. Chodren, Thubten, 1950-
III. Title.
         BQ2407 .W89 2001
         294.3'657—dc21
                                             00-011609

CONTENTS

FOREWORD

A Message from Lama Thubten Zopa Rinpoche

Homage to the Buddhas, the Dharma, and the Sangha.

The essential teaching of the kind, compassionate Buddha is the pure practice of the pratimoksha vows. Observing the pratimoksha precepts helps you keep purely the *bodhisattva* precepts of cherishing others and dedicating your life to them. This, in turn, facilitates keeping the tantric vows. As explained in the teachings, the pratimoksha vow is like a container. Into it, we pour the pure water of the bodhisattva vow, and on the water's surface, we see a beautiful reflection— the tantric vow. In this way, the latter vows are established upon the basis of the former ones.

Understanding the pratimoksha precepts is necessary for doing the essential Dharma practice. But simply understanding them is not enough. You must cherish them like a wish-fulfilling jewel and practice mindfulness to protect the precepts in your daily life. However, that, too, is not sufficient;

whenever a degeneration occurs, you must apply the antidotes and remedies as soon as possible. You should purify with confession, so your mental continuum does not become obscured and space and freedom exist for the path to enlightenment to manifest within you. Thus at the beginning, study of the pratimoksha precepts from learned masters and Vinaya texts is important.

To paraphrase Shantideva's *Guide to a Bodhisattva's Way of Life*: "What is the use of so many rules of conduct, if not for guiding the mind?" Thus, observing precepts helps you to take care of your mind and causes others to develop faith in the Three Jewels. The *sangha* has the responsibility to bring peace and happiness to the minds of people and to guide them toward liberation and enlightenment. Sangha members' inappropriate behavior can harm others' minds, and their observing the precepts and practicing the Dharma can bring incredible benefit to people in the world.

Education is important, but Dharma education alone will not bring satisfaction or fulfillment in life. Strong practice is needed as well. You must meditate on impermanence, death, and the sufferings of the lower realms for months and years. Meditating on emptiness and bodhichitta are important as well, but meditating on death and the lower realms is crucial in order to develop the realizations of emptiness and bodhichitta quickly, as well as to prevent future obstacles and to purify those already existing. The eight worldly concerns—which center around desire and aversion regarding material possessions, praise and blame, image and reputation, and pleasures of the senses—play a large role in preventing you from actualizing the path to enlightenment. Living with the fundamental practice of the *Lam Rim (Gradual Path to Enlightenment)* and meditating on the Four Noble Truths immediately cuts the evil thought of the eight worldly concerns. In this way, you immediately experience peace and satisfaction in your heart and life.

As mentioned in many teachings, realizing that following desire never leads to satisfaction is the first step in transforming your mind and opening the door to the holy Dharma. Following desire leads to many problems, which you can understand clearly by checking your own past and present experiences. You will see that desire is the basis of all problems and obstacles including anger, jealousy, and so forth. When desire and the evil thought of the eight worldly concerns arise, you seek external things for happiness. When you cannot get the pleasures of this life that you desire, anger arises. When others have more or better pleasures, jealousy torments you. All the manifold problems that you go through are the result of following the evil thought of the eight worldly concerns, the attachment to the happiness of this life.

Those who do even a little Dharma practice experience the benefits of giving freedom to themselves instead of being a slave to the evil thought of the eight worldly concerns. You give freedom to yourself by living with mindfulness of death, karma, and the sufferings of the lower realms. By relating these meditations to your life, you will find that being a sangha member and living in accord with ethical precepts will be a great protection and support in your life. Your ordination and precepts will become incredibly precious and important to you. With this understanding, attitude, and view, your life will become enjoyable. Peace, happiness, and fulfillment will exist in your heart because you know that you are benefiting others.

On the other hand, when you do not understand the disadvantages of desire, do not free yourself from it by applying the remedies of remembering death and impermanence, and continue to befriend the enemy of the eight worldly concerns, then ordination will seem like prison. You will feel claustrophobic because living in ethical discipline is not what the evil thought of the eight worldly concerns wants.

I observe that some people still feel something is missing in their heart although they have studied Mahayana Buddhism for years, received all the important teachings, have extensive intellectual understanding of the Dharma, and have lived in ordination for many years. Why does their heart still feel empty and dissatisfied? They say, "I am not finding satisfaction. All those nice things about the benefit of living in precepts are okay, but what about *me*? What about *my* happiness?"

This problem comes from the mind. It is not due to lack of Dharma study or lack of qualified teachers. It is due to your attitude. The chronic disease causing so much suffering is the attitude believing that the main goal of life is not liberation or enlightenment, but simply the happiness of this life. Feeling empty and dissatisfied despite living in ordination and studying the Dharma is due to following the attitude seeking only the happiness of this life; you are a slave to the eight worldly concerns. As soon as you change your attitude, making liberation your main goal, suddenly you will be free from obstacles. Your heart will be free from pain, and you find enjoyment in ordination. Then you will respect your precepts and those of others.

When your own mind is not stable in the Dharma and you lack deep understanding of death and renunciation, then continuously mixing with people can easily affect your mind, and you may lose your ordination. As Kadampa Geshe Kharag Gomchung said: "Until your mind is stable with realizations, physically mixing with people and serving others is a distraction and becomes an obstacle." Therefore, sangha members should try as much as possible to do retreat, especially in solitary places. The best retreat to do is on the *Lam Rim*. Even if you cannot continuously be in retreat, try to do retreat frequently to recharge your energy and deepen your understanding. Of course, if your mind is strong and stable in the Dharma, doing social work and being with many people will not be a problem.

Some sangha members who have studied for a long time and done solitary retreat have told me that retreat gives their hearts the best satisfaction. They discovered retreat's meaning and benefit. Although there are many things to study and do in this life, you must take care of your heart and fill it when it feels empty. Feeling satisfaction in the heart is important to Westerners and will give you the ability to continue living in ordination.

Thubten Zopa Rinpoche
New Delhi
February 4, 1996

Nuns praying together

EDITOR'S PREFACE

"Buddhism in the West." Nowadays, there are national and international conferences, books, audiotapes, and videos galore on this topic. Oprah has interviewed Buddhists; talk shows on *National Public Radio* and television news programs have hosted them, and major films have been made about them. Buddhism has been called the fastest growing religion in America.

In Asian societies where Buddhism has existed for centuries, the sangha—those who have taken full monastic ordination—are the ones principally responsible for the preservation and leadership of the Buddhist community. However, in the West, particularly in Protestant America, there is a certain skepticism about monastics, and lay Buddhists are the most prominent Dharma teachers in the public eye. Nevertheless, if we look deeper, we discover that monasticism is indeed relevant for the West and that Western monastics affect the spread of the Dharma in an important way. Having attended conferences of Western Buddhist teachers who are mostly laypeople and conferences of Western monastics, I have noticed a difference in emphasis. The conferences of predominately lay teachers emphasized topics such as the use and abuse of power, sex, and money by those in positions of authority; how to handle finances and earn one's living with right livelihood as a Buddhist teacher; and the transference of institutional power from Asian teachers to Western teachers who are their students. Sometimes heated discussion over these issues ensued, with people viewing their teachers and Asian Buddhism in general with a wary and critical eye.

At the conferences of Western Buddhist monastics, on the other hand, discussions centered on properly preparing people for ordination, working with the monastic precepts to train the mind, using community life as part of our practice, and subduing our own mind. At one conference, in a session entitled "Robes around the World," monastics from each tradition demonstrated how they wear their robes and explained the ancient symbolism. We talked of the variety of skillful means our teachers use to guide us and the need for consistent effort to go through the ups and downs of practice. These monastics were clearly intent on practice and on purifying their own minds. They were interested in teaching and helping others on the path, and in their own quiet way, they were westernizing the Dharma. The humility and self-confidence of those who had been ordained for many years was inspiring.

The Buddhist community includes monastics and laypeople. Both are necessary for the preservation of the Dharma. Cooperation between them is essential as Buddhism spreads in the West. But the differences in life styles must be noted and respected. While lay Buddhists may or may not live according to the five precepts of abandoning killing, stealing, unwise sexual behavior, lying, and taking intoxicants, monastics have voluntarily chosen to live by these and many other precepts regulating how they relate to the people and environment around them. Although some lay Buddhists remain single, the large majority live in family situations. With the exception of only a few, they work at jobs and by their outward life style differ little from the larger society: they have mortgages, car payments, staff meetings, sports games for their children, and active social lives. Monastics, on the other hand, choose a life of simplicity. They do not marry or have sexual relations. They have few personal possessions, as most property is owned and shared by the community in which they live. They work in their communities, doing jobs directly relating to the preservation and dissemination of the Dharma.

To spread the complete Buddha *Sasana* (doctrine) to the West, all Three "Baskets" (*Pitaka*) of the Buddha's teaching must be made available. These are the Vinaya Pitaka, which teaches the Higher Training in Ethical Discipline by describing the monks' and nuns' precepts; the Sutra Pitaka, which gives instructions on the paths and stages to develop the Higher Training in Concentration; and the Abhidharma Pitaka, which includes the teachings on the Higher Training in Wisdom. Of the Three Baskets of the Buddha's teachings, the first, the Vinaya, concerns monastic discipline. *Choosing Simplicity: A Commentary on the Bhikshuni Pratimoksha* describes the precepts and life style of *bhikshunis*, or fully ordained nuns. Although there are some differences between the precepts of monks and nuns, most of what is contained in this volume applies equally to *bhikshus*, or fully ordained monks. This volume explains the purpose of monastic ordination and the relationship of an individual nun to the monastic communities of monks and of nuns, to lay Buddhists, and to society in general. It discusses the major groupings of precepts—their meaning, the historical events leading to their creation, the boundaries of transgressing them, and the methods for purifying them.

Interest in the monastic discipline has increased in recent years, and this volume is the first to give a contemporary commentary on the nuns' precepts and life style. Given by Bhikshuni Master Venerable Wu Yin from Taiwan during *Life as a Western Buddhist Nun*, a remarkable three-week Vinaya training program for nuns in Bodhgaya, India, in 1996, this commentary can inform the spiritual practices of both monastics and lay practitioners.

The Gifts of This Book

Due to increased interest in Buddhism and the prominence of remarkable monastics, such as the Nobel Peace Prize winner, His Holiness the Dalai Lama, many people—monastics, lay Buddhists, and even non-Buddhists—want to learn about the Buddhist monastic life style and precepts. A multitude of reasons exist for this. Unlike other times in history, we now live in pluralistic societies. The general public sees Buddhist monastics—from His Holiness the Dalai Lama and Thich Nhat Hanh to a newly ordained monk or nun—on television, in airports, and on the streets in every major Western city. Therefore, people naturally would like to know more about these monastics' lives and the precepts that guide them. This book describes these.

In addition, with increased interreligious dialogue, people realize that knowledge of others' traditions enriches their own spiritual practice. For example, many Catholic monks and nuns have expressed interest in learning about the precepts and life style of Buddhist monastics. Since the Buddha did not prohibit others from learning the precepts of his monastics, anyone may study them. However, only the bhikshus and bhikshunis are allowed to attend the *poshadha*, the bimonthly ceremony for the purification and restoration of the monastic precepts.

Whether or not we are Buddhist monastics, knowing the precepts can make us more mindful of our behavior. For example, monastics have a precept not to watch entertainment with the motivation of attachment or distraction. Even if we do not have this precept, it is nonetheless valuable to become more aware of the role entertainment plays in our life. Do we turn the radio on every time we get into the car? Do we spend hours channel surfing on the television? How valuable is this in our life? What is a healthy way to relate to entertainment, and how do we differentiate entertainment from gaining relevant and necessary information on current events? Such questions are important for everyone to contemplate, and learning the precepts can spark introspection and discussion on such matters.

Moreover, although university scholars have examined the Vinaya, little has been written about it in a style suitable for the nonspecialist. Although a certain amount of technical vocabulary is unavoidable when discussing the Vinaya, this book is readable and informative. Full of stories describing the activities of the Buddha's disciples that led to his establishing the precepts, it makes evident that although the social environment has changed since the Buddha's time, basic human nature has not. Our own foibles and bad habits come to life in these stories, and we come to understand the necessity of ethical discipline for a harmonious society and a happy mind.

This volume presents the Vinaya as a living tradition. It shows how to interpret it in the context of modern society and how to implement it in daily life. This is helpful for practitioners and for scholars alike, for the Buddha's teachings do not exist in a static, dry form in books. The evolution and application of the precepts to people's lives in each generation is a living process.

Further, as lay practitioners learn more about monastic life style through this book, their faith in sincere monastic practitioners will increase, for they will see that monastics can help and inspire them along the path. The Buddha established a system whereby the lay and monastic communities depend on each other, and thus mutual understanding and respect between the two are extremely important for the existence and spread of the Dharma.

In addition, through reading this book, people considering taking ordination will gain a better understanding of monastic life and will therefore be able to make well-informed and thoughtful decisions about ordination. Those who are novices, or shramanerikas, will know the full precepts and be able to train in them before actually receiving them. Doing this, in fact, is one of the main purposes of the novice ordination. By knowing this commentary, those who are fully ordained will understand what to practice and what to abandon on the path, thus enabling them to keep their precepts purely and progress on the path. Ignorance about the precepts is not a valid reason for transgressing them, so learning the precepts is essential.

Although the bhikshuni sangha is not present in many Buddhist countries, a new opportunity exists for it to spread and flourish now. For this to happen, both monks and nuns must understand the bhikshuni precepts, and this book is an excellent guide for this. Currently, the bhikshuni sangha is vibrant in countries such as China, Taiwan, Vietnam, and Korea. However, due to political upheavals, it died out in Sri Lanka and India many centuries ago. Due to difficulties in travel and other factors, the bhikshuni sangha never was established in Tibet, Thailand, and other Southeast Asian countries. The possibility now exists of reviving or introducing the bhikshuni lineage in these countries. This is an exciting prospect for Asian as well as Western women who aspire to the monastic life, as demonstrated by nearly 150 women receiving bhikshuni ordination in Bodhgaya in February, 1998, in an ordination ceremony organized by Master Hsiung Yun from Taiwan. While a scattering of Western women, a few Tibetans, and a handful of Sri Lankans had taken the bhikshuni ordination prior to this from Chinese, Vietnamese, or Korean masters, this was the largest ceremony in recent times that included ordainees outside of these communities.

Venerable Wu Yin, a Chinese bhikshuni from Taiwan gave these teachings to an international audience at *Life as a Western Buddhist Nun*. Thus, this volume illustrates the inter-traditional learning that, due to geographical and language barriers, did not widely exist until now, and it reflects the international and cooperative nature of the bhikshuni sangha nowadays.

While nuns practicing in the Tibetan tradition have received teachings on the *Bhikshuni Pratimoksha Sutra* as individuals or in tiny groups before, as far as I know, this was the first time they did so as a large group. Thus, their receiving this commentary at *Life as a Western Buddhist Nun* was an historical event.

About the Title of this Book

In the West, we sometimes think that discipline means unwelcome restrictions. But monastic precepts are taken voluntarily and function to simplify our life. Especially in the twenty-first century, when advertising and social and economic pressures pull us in multiple directions, our lives have become complicated and stressful. Taking monastic precepts is choosing simplicity. While living on automatic and acting out any impulse that arises leads us to a dead-end, a simple and ethical life style is an excellent support for becoming more aware, thoughtful, and loving. Living according to the precepts subdues our physical actions and our speech. To do this, we have to pacify our mind. The more our body, speech, and mind become gentle, flexible, and appropriate, the more joyful and peaceful our life becomes. Of course, this takes time and effort. Our life is not instantaneously transformed by shaving our head and putting on robes! Transformation comes through gentle, consistent discipline.

We may wonder, "If the goal is simplicity, why are there so many precepts? Learning them is complicated and living according to them can be artificial!" Yes, initially, monastic life may seem complex, but the more we are familiar with the monastic form, the more we see how it simplifies our lives. For example, when we first learn to drive, all the rules in the driver's manual may seem difficult to learn. But when we are on the road, we understand their purpose in facilitating movement and preventing harm. In fact, sometimes we even wish there were more of them! Similarly, precepts protect us from involvement in actions that create disharmony and mistrust among people. They regulate our behavior so that we know what to expect from others, thus reducing actions motivated by whim or ever-changing personal preferences. For example, the Vinaya indicates how juniors in ordination treat their seniors and vice-versa. In this way, a junior knows that anyone senior to her will help her and guide her, and a senior overcomes personal likes and dislikes to help equally those junior to her. This builds trust among the members of the sangha. Similarly, a senior knows that she can ask for reasonable help from any junior and receive it, because the junior will look beyond her whims and preferences and work to benefit the community.

An Historic Event

On February, 4, 1996, the day of the opening ceremony for *Life as a Western Buddhist Nun,* the *stupa* marking the site of the Buddha's enlightenment at Bodhgaya, India, shone in the setting sun. Gathered near the gate were nuns, monks, laypeople, teachers, participants, and staff. Drawing nearly one hundred participants from all over the world, *Life as a Western Buddhist Nun* was a grass-roots endeavor whose principal aim was to help the first generation of Western nuns practicing in the Tibetan Buddhist tradition learn the Vinaya, the monastic discipline. We invited two principal teachers to educate us in Vinaya: Venerable Bhikshuni Wu Yin from Luminary Temple in Taiwan, and Venerable Geshe Thubten Ngawang from Sera Je Monastery in India and Tibet Center in Hamburg, Germany.

Together teachers and students circumambulated the Enlightenment Stupa feeling the cool marble of its inner walkway under our feet. Then we sat under the Bodhi Tree with its sprawling branches and offered prayers for the success of the program and for its benefit to ripple forth to bring happiness to all beings. We entered the small sanctuary inside the stupa, and in the presence of the Buddha statue and with nuns, monks, and lay practitioners crowded around her, Venerable Wu Yin said:

> Over twenty-five hundred years ago, the Buddha's stepmother, Mahaprajapati, and five hundred women from the Shakya clan went through incredible difficulties to request bhikshuni ordination from the Buddha. In giving them permission to enter the order, the Buddha affirmed women's ability to practice the Dharma, to liberate themselves from cyclic existence, and to become enlightened. For over twenty-five centuries, women have practiced the Dharma and achieved the beneficial results. Now we are reaping the benefit of their practice and of the Dharma that they preserved and passed down. It is our privilege and responsibility to learn and practice the Dharma not only to attain spiritual realizations, but also to benefit others by preserving and passing on these precious teachings to future generations.

Venerable Bhikshuni Wu Yin's care and respect for the sangha is illustrated by her talk to this international gathering of nuns on the Lunar New Year:

> Early this morning I went to the Enlightenment Stupa and prayed for peace to fill our world and for Dharma to be sustained. I prayed that the Buddha's wisdom and light go with each bhikshu and bhikshuni, shramanera, shramanerika, and layperson, so that you will bring the *Buddhadharma* to each corner of the world you visit, sharing it in skillful ways according to the dispositions of the people and culture of the place. Each of you preserves the Dharma within yourself, and by practicing the Buddha's teachings and observing the Vinaya, you will tame your body, speech, and mind. For that reason, take

care of yourselves, not out of selfishness, but in order to cultivate your wisdom, accumulate positive potential, and benefit all beings.

For three weeks, our teachers taught us for many hours each day, passing on what they had learned from their teachers, guidelines for practice going back to the time of the Buddha himself. Three volumes will record these teachings. The first, *Blossoms of the Dharma: Living as a Buddhist Nun* (North Atlantic Books, Berkeley, 2000,) is an anthology of the talks the Western nuns gave at the program. This is the second volume, containing the Vinaya teachings of Venerable Bhikshuni Wu Yin, and the third will comprise the teachings of Venerable Geshe Thubten Ngawang and other monks.

Venerable Wu Yin

Born in Taiwan in 1940, Venerable Wu Yin received the shramanerika, or novice, vows in 1958 from Venerable Ming Tzung and bhikshuni vows in 1960 with Venerable Pao Shen as her preceptor. She graduated from the Chinese Cultural University with a degree in Chinese Literature and from the five-year Buddhist studies program at the Chinese Buddhist Threefold Training Seminary. Then she resided at the Hsin Lung Temple, headed by the distinguished Bhikshuni Tien Yee.

After World War II, people in Taiwan were struggling to survive. They were trying to recover from the Japanese occupation, deal with the huge influx of refugees from mainland China, and rebuild their political and economic infrastructure. At that time most Buddhist temples in Taiwan engaged in agriculture or depended on ritual services for the deceased in order to support themselves. Very few could afford to offer in-depth teachings on the Buddhadharma, nor did the monastics have time to engage in social work. Most laypeople were unable to distinguish Buddhism from folk religion. Saddened by the condition of Buddhist education and practice and inspired by the examples of past monastics who upheld the Buddha's teachings, Bhikshuni Wu Yin made a vow: she would establish Buddhist institutes and temples to train nuns so that they would have the necessary knowledge and skills to transmit the Dharma to the greater society. Her goal became to help Buddhist nuns in Taiwan, China, and the West so that they could establish sangha communities and use their talents and wisdom to help humanity.

In 1980 she became the abbess of Hsiang Kuang Temple (Luminary Temple) in Chia-I Country, Taiwan, and began the Buddhist Institute of Hsiang Kuang Temple. Most of the institutes' students—nuns or those preparing for ordination—came from universities and colleges. By 1994, over eighty nuns had graduated, each being capable of teaching the Dharma and of offering spiritual leadership and guidance. To engage monastics in social education, she founded a Buddhist Studies School for laypeople in 1984. This was the first time in Taiwan that structured and organized materials were designed and used to teach Buddhadharma to the public. At present, under Venerable Bhikshuni Wu Yin's guidance, three such schools have been founded in southern Taiwan. They offer a three-year program of study to the public, and each year over eight hundred people graduate from this program.

In 1985 Bhikshuni Wu Yin initiated the magazine *Glorious Buddhism,* and in 1992 she established Hsiang Kuang Publishers. At present her ordained disciples translate and edit Buddhist texts and are preparing a Vinaya dictionary. In 1989, the Luminary International Buddhist Society was founded to encompass these various projects, with Bhikshuni Wu Yin as its abbess and leader.

About this Book

Before we study the bhikshuni precepts, understanding reasons for and benefits of living according to the precepts is helpful. Therefore, as an introduction to this volume, we begin with "The Benefits and Motivation for Monastic Ordination," an edited version of an article by Bhikshuni Tenzin Kacho and Bhikshuni Thubten Chodron that originally appeared in *Preparing for Ordination: Reflections for Westerners Considering Monastic Ordination in the Tibetan Buddhist Tradition.*

Venerable Bhikshuni Wu Yin's discourses form the majority of this volume. She begins by describing the importance of monastic precepts and giving an overview of the Vinaya. From there she goes on to talk about the requirements for ordination, the way to purify and restore the precepts when they are transgressed, and the boundaries for remaining a monastic. Then she begins a more detailed explanation of the precepts. Generally, the precepts are taught in the numerical order and according to the categories of severity presented in the *Pratimoksha Sutra*. In the present teaching, however, Venerable Wu Yin discusses the precepts according to the type of behavior they regulate. Some precepts concern sexual and/or physical contact, others deal with being stubborn and not accepting admonition, procuring and using resources, or daily activities such as eating, dressing, lodging, and travel. This way of explaining the precepts gives us a better understanding of each behavior. Finally, she discusses the way a Buddhist community is organized and life in a monastic community. A glossary contains the meanings of basic terms, and a list of recommended reading and other resources at the end directs the reader toward further learning.

Because these teachings were given during the three weeks of *Life as a Western Buddhist Nun,* Venerable Wu Yin was not able to comment on each precept individually. The essential points are here, however. Hopefully, more comprehensive commentaries will be taught and translated in the future.

The Sanskrit, Chinese, and sometimes Tibetan terms are numerous, and to make for easier reading they have been written without diacritical marks. Also to allow for easier reading, commonly used Sanskrit terms—those designating the various members of the sangha, the categories of

precepts, and the offenses—are italicized on their first occurrence only.

As this is a teaching primarily on the Bhikshuni Pratimoksha, the pronoun "she" has been used although most of
the information equally applies to monks. It is my hope that
this volume will be of aid to both female and male monastics,
as the majority of our precepts are held in common.

Appreciation

First and foremost, I thank the lineage of bhikshunis beginning with the Buddha's aunt and stepmother, Bhikshuni
Mahaprajapati, who have practiced and preserved the Bhikshuni Vinaya throughout the centuries. I express my deep
gratitude and respect for Venerable Bhikshuni Wu Yin, who
accepted our request to teach at *Life as a Western Buddhist
Nun.* This was the first time she had taught Westerners, and
I had to go to Luminary Temple the year before to convince
her personally of the importance of teaching us. During the
program, she had to deal with our numerous blunders in
etiquette as well as with the poor living conditions in India.
We are indebted for her kindness. Her three disciples,
Bhikshunis Jendy Shih, Jen Chin, and Jen Ker, who accom-
panied her also are worthy of many thanks. Bhikshuni Jendy
Shih joined the sangha in 1980 and acted as her translator.
She also painstakingly went through this manuscript, an-
swering my questions, checking for errors, and adding new
material where appropriate. Both Venerable Bhikshuni Wu
Yin and Bhikshuni Jendy Shih have been consistently encouraging and supportive of Western nuns as we endeavor to
bring the Dharma and the Vinaya to Western countries. Bhikshuni Jen Chin joined the sangha in 1990 and is compiling a
dictionary of Vinaya terms. Bhikshuni Jen Ker also joined
the sangha in 1990 and translates Dharma books at Luminary Temple. Under Venerable Bhikshuni Wu Yin's guidance,
Bhikshuni Jen Chin gave the discourse on the sangha and
the interrelationship of its members, and Bhikshuni Jen Ker

gave the discourse on the regulations for joining the sangha. The chapters on those topics include their talks as well as Venerable Bhikshuni Wu Yin's comments. All errors are my own.

I also thank the co-organizer of *Life as a Western Buddhist Nun*, Bhikshuni Jampa Chokyi. Together we want to express our appreciation to His Holiness the Dalai Lama, Tenzin Geyche Tethong, Bhikshu Lhakdor, Venerable Master Bhikshuni Wu Yin, and Bhikshuni Jendy Shih who have been continuously supportive of our endeavors and helpful in accomplishing them. We also thank Venerable Sonam Thabkye, Bhikshuni Jampa Tsedroen, Bhikshuni Lekshe Tsomo, Bhikshuni Tenzin Kacho, Shramanerika Tenzin Dechen, Shramanerika Paloma Alba, Mary Grace Lentz, Margaret Cormier, Bets Greer, Lynn Gebetsberger, Kim Houk, Lydia Kaye Maddux, Sarah Porter, Angel Vannoy, and Karen Shertzer for their tireless efforts before or during the program. We are grateful to Dharma Friendship Foundation in Seattle for enabling us to organize *Life as a Western Buddhist Nun* under their auspices, Luminary Temple in Taiwan, and many other kind benefactors who made this program possible, and to all the participants, who made this program successful.

May the Dharma and the Vinaya flourish in all places and may all sentient beings derive temporal and ultimate benefit directly and indirectly from the existence of the sangha!

Bhikshuni Thubten Chodron
Seattle
June 16, 2000

A CONTEMPORARY CULTURAL PERSPECTIVE ON MONASTIC LIFE

by Bhikshuni Thubten Chodron

"How do you explain the precept that a nun who has been fully ordained for even one hundred years should rise and respectfully greet a monk even if he was ordained only that day? This contradicts our current cultural values," an American man exclaimed. A day later, another man asked me, "Why do the nuns sit behind the monks? Since the Buddha said that all sentient beings could become enlightened, it seems that monks and nuns should sit side-by-side. Some great Buddhist leaders, such as His Holiness the Dalai Lama, affirm women's equality in the Dharma. Why, then, don't they change these outmoded customs?" Another questioned, "How do you live in our modern world with so many precepts? Some of them don't seem to fit in with modern society. Can they be adapted or must you keep them literally?" As someone who has been happily ordained for over twenty years, I will attempt to share some of my thoughts on the issues of adaptation, gender, and hierarchy with the Buddhist monastic tradition.

Adaptations: the Same and Yet Different

To paraphrase His Holiness the Dalai Lama: "Although our external environment has changed over the centuries, especially due to the impact of science and technology, our human mind remains more or less the same. People from all cultures and all historical periods have the same fundamental wish to be happy and not suffer. They also have the same obscurations that impede their attaining this—ignorance, anger, and attachment." Thus, over twenty-five centuries ago in India, the Buddha established the Vinaya to guide people so they can subdue the same ignorance, anger, and attachment that are present now and actualize the same remarkable human potential that is present today. The situations the monks and nuns in ancient India faced may have differed in some respects from those that contemporary monastics face, but the lessons gleaned from their experiences apply equally to us today.

But, how and when do they apply? All religious traditions face a similar challenge: to maintain the continuity of the tradition from the past while at the same time making it relevant to the present. Within each religion, people have different approaches. Some rely on the literal meaning of the scriptures, while others leave room for interpretation. But when do interpretations of the scriptures cross the line to become the reflection of one's own views and not of those who wrote the scriptures? No religious tradition has reached internal consensus on this matter, and I consider the variety of responses within each tradition to be healthy. It keeps each tradition alive and forces the individuals within it to think about the meaning of the teachings.

The tension created by differing interpretations and ways of practice has existed for centuries. For example, during the Buddha's time, monastics received their food by collecting alms in the village, and many monastic precepts related to this were set up. The Buddha wanted the laypeople and monastics to have a mutually dependent relationship, with the laypeople caring for the monastics' requirements and the monastics caring for the laypeople's spiritual education. Monastics were therefore prohibited from activities such as cutting whole vegetables, cooking, and doing agricultural work. These restrictions prevented them from accidentally killing insects and from spending many hours attending to their own livelihood. Thai Buddhist monastics have strictly adhered to these customs and precepts, and the weather and culture in that country favor this.

Chinese monastics, on the other hand, could not adhere to these precepts. The Chinese culture considered collecting alms repugnant and looked down on Buddhist monastics who did it. In addition, many monastics preferred to live in isolated areas so they would not be drawn into the politics of the cities. Therefore, they began to grow their own food and prepare their own meals. In Tibet, the monasteries were similarly located far from the towns, and the cold weather and long distances made going on alms rounds impossible. Laypeople brought food to the monasteries, and the monastics prepared it themselves. Although Chinese and Tibetan monastics today do not adhere literally to the method of procuring sustenance prescribed by the Buddha, the changes were made to facilitate their Dharma practice given the cultural and climatic conditions they faced.

Now with Buddhism coming to the West, each sangha community has its own way of keeping the precepts in accordance with the culture, climate, location, and dispositions of its members, as well as the customs of the particular Buddhist tradition it follows. Once developed, this way may again be altered as conditions change. Tolerance of differing ways of observing the precepts is valid as long as the precepts are used to subdue our disturbing attitudes and negative emotions. For example, the style of monastic robes varies from place to place, but no matter which style a community wears, the purpose of each member wearing the same clothes is the same: to lessen our attachment to appearance and to subdue our wish to assert our individuality by dressing differently from the rest of the community.

Nevertheless, the danger of stretching the boundaries of the precepts beyond reasonable limits remains, and the monastics within each tradition must be vigilant to prevent this. For example, strictly speaking, monastics should not have physical contact with those of the opposite sex. Thus Western monastics in the Theravada tradition do not shake hands with people of the opposite sex, nor do monastics from the Chinese Mahayana tradition. However, both Tibetans and Westerners in the Tibetan tradition often shake hands as a way of conforming to Western culture. Doing so prevents an unknowing layperson who extends his or her hand from being embarrassed. Or, to offer comfort, they may touch an ill person on a hospital visit. However, giving casual hugs to members of the opposite sex is considered by all traditions to be beyond the limits outlined in the Vinaya.

Gender Issues

Gender equality has been a prominent topic in Western cultures for decades, and Western Buddhist practitioners bring their perspectives to their Dharma studies. People may angrily rail against discriminatory practices or remain oblivious to them. Gender discrepancies disturbed me for many years, but they also forced me to look at my own anger and pride. After many years of struggling with both my own negative emotions and external prejudice, I arrived at several conclusions.[1] First and foremost was that it was essential for me to look at my own mind and calm my anger, hurt feelings, and pride. Second was that losing faith in the Dharma because of gender inequalities was harmful. I came to see that Buddhism does not exist independently of culture. The Buddha spoke in relation to the Indian culture of twenty-five hundred years ago, which had differing roles and expectations for men and women. By merely allowing women to leave the household to ordain, he was already

going against established social norms. Making the two
sanghas equal in all ways would have been more than both
the men and women of that time could have handled. Not
being as educated as the men and not having had the opportunity to develop their own skills and assertiveness before
ordination, Indian nuns of that time had to rely on monks
for spiritual guidance, although they were responsible for
operating their own communities. In addition, for the sake
of ease in public situations and gatherings, the Buddha
stipulated that monks sit in front, enter first, and be shown
respect by nuns. At that time, such arrangements accorded
with existing social conventions and were acceptable to both
men and women.

While both men and women may have felt comfortable
with these arrangements in ancient India, in Western cultures we do not. With a calm mind that understands the historical background, when appropriate I ask questions or raise
points for discussion regarding gender issues. The points and
the methods of raising them differ depending on whether I
am with Asians or Westerners. For example, in large public
gatherings of the Tibetan community in India, I hold the
philosophy, "when in Rome, do as the Romans do." However, privately, I discuss my concerns with Tibetan friends
and teachers. Although it is not for me to insist that Tibetan
culture change, sharing varying cultural perspectives is important. The recent improvement in the Tibetan nuns' education has in part been due to Westerners raising their
concerns about the nuns. However, sustained change of attitudes and customs in any culture occurs slowly, not by the
decree of a leader. However strongly His Holiness the Dalai
Lama may wish attitudes and habits in the Tibetan community to change, he does not have the power to legislate them
and must walk the delicate line between encouraging change
and not offending those who hold more traditional views.

Similarly, when I am in a procession in Taiwan, for example, where the nuns walk behind the monks, I take my

place according to the Chinese custom. I do not feel denigrated or angry, for I am a guest in their country. Once I raised this issue with a highly esteemed abbess after she walked behind a junior monk in a procession, and she responded, "If I show him respect, he will learn to respect himself." Thus, through her behavior, she was acting as his mentor on the path. This monk, of course, had great respect and admiration for the abbess's accomplishments, even though she followed him in the procession.

Nevertheless, in similar situations with Western monks, this approach does not feel comfortable to the nuns, and often to the monks as well. Most of us prefer to sit as separate groups side-by-side, and this is the custom in our gatherings. When in Western-organized Dharma events, I speak more forthrightly about gender bias. For example, many Western translators and Dharma students still use gender-biased language. Politely pointing this out so that it can be corrected is important. Despite the West's progress in gender equality, many Westerners still show more respect for monks than for nuns. This, too, needs to be pointed out in a polite way, so that people can become more aware of their behavior and counteract subtle discriminatory attitudes they may still have.

Some people say it is unfair that bhikshunis have more precepts than bhikshus. However, I do not see it that way. Each precept was made in response to some misbehavior on the part of a monastic. The bhikshus' precepts arose due to improper conduct on the part of monks. Bhikshunis follow most of these precepts as well as precepts that arose due to the wrong actions of the nuns. However, bhikshus do not follow precepts that arose due to the misbehavior of nuns. Precepts are the ornaments of a monastic. We voluntarily undertake them in order to train our minds. As nuns, having more precepts only makes us more aware and scrupulous in our actions.

Some Western monks and nuns advocate integrating the bhikshu and bhikshuni precepts to form a joint standard followed by all fully ordained monastics, with the exception of specific precepts that depend on the different anatomies of the two sexes. A council of elders would have to agree formally to change the listing of the precepts, and this is unlikely to occur at present. Nevertheless, since each monastery has its own internal rules in addition to the pratimoksha precepts followed by all monastics, new interpretations and guidelines could be followed in individual communities.

Full Ordination

Yet another sensitive issue is the fact that within many Buddhist traditions, full ordination is not available to women. To understand this situation, knowing its background is essential. Several years after the monks' order was established in India in the sixth century B.C.E., the Buddha set up the nuns' order. Three levels of ordination exist for nuns: *shramanerika* (novice), *shikshamana* (probationary), and *bhikshuni* (full ordination). These are taken gradually in order to prepare and accustom one to keep the full precepts and to assume responsibility for the well being and continuation of the monastic community. Lineage is an important issue, for one becomes a nun by taking the ordination from those who have themselves received it, and in this way the purity of the transmission is traced back to the Buddha himself. Women are to receive bhikshuni ordination from a community of at least ten bhikshunis, and, at a separate ceremony later the same day, from a community of at least ten bhikshus (fully ordained monks). In lands where such a large number of monastics does not exist, communities of four or five can give the ordination.

The bhikshuni lineage flourished in ancient India and in the third century B.C.E. spread to Sri Lanka. From there it went to China in the fourth century C.E. Due to warfare and political problems, the lineage died out in both India and Sri Lanka in the eleventh century C.E., although it continued to spread throughout China and to Korea and Vietnam as well. The bhikshuni lineage was not established in Tibet due to the difficulties of crossing the Himalaya Mountains. A sufficient number of Indian bhikshunis did not go to Tibet, nor did a sufficient number of Tibetan women go to India to take the ordination and return to Tibet to pass it on to others. However, monks in the Tibetan community give the shramanerika ordination. In Southeast Asia, women receive eight precepts and in Sri Lanka they receive ten precepts. Although they live in celibacy and wear robes demarcating them as religious women, their precepts are not regarded as any of the three pratimoksha ordinations for women.

As Buddhism spread in ancient India, various Vinaya schools developed. Of the eighteen initial schools, three are extant today: the Theravada, which is widespread in Sri Lanka and Southeast Asia; the Dharmaguptaka, which is popular in Taiwan, China, Korea, and Vietnam; and the Mulasarvastivada, which is followed in Tibet. All of these schools have spread to Western countries in recent years. Considering that the Vinaya was passed down orally for many centuries before being written down and that the various schools had little communication with each other due to geographical distance, it is amazing that the Vinaya is so consistent among them. Slightly different variations of the listing of the monastic precepts exist, but no major, glaring differences appear. Of course, over the centuries, the schools in each country have developed their own ways of interpreting and living the precepts in accordance with the culture, climate, and social situation of each place.

Given recent improvements in communication and transportation, the various Buddhist schools now have more contact with each other. Some women who have trained in the countries where the bhikshuni sangha does not exist wish to receive this ordination. In 1997, eight women from Sri Lanka received the bhikshuni ordination from a Korean sangha in India, and in 1998, twenty women from Sri Lanka received it in Bodhgaya, India from Chinese bhikshunis and bhikshus. The bhikshuni ordination was given in Sri Lanka in 1998, and while some opposed this, many prominent Sri Lankan monks supported it. Since the early 1980s, a number of Western women trained in the Tibetan tradition have gone to Taiwan, Hong Kong, Korea, or in more recent years to the USA, France, or India to receive the bhikshuni ordination. As far as I know, only one Thai woman has received it and only a handful of Tibetan women.

These women would like the support of the monks in their traditions to introduce or re-establish the bhikshuni lineage. Some monks have expressed various concerns about this: (1) Has the Dharmaguptaka lineage been passed on without interruption up to the present day? (2) Has the bhikshuni ordination in China and Taiwan consistently been given according to procedures indicated in Vinaya? The bhikshuni ordination should be given by bhikshunis and bhikshus, and for some time in Chinese history it was given only by the bhikshus. The Pali Vinaya followed by the Theravada allows for this, but sufficient research has not yet been done in the Dharmaguptaka and Mulasarvastivada Vinayas regarding this point. (3) How will the ordination be given once new bhikshunis return to their own countries? Now these women receive the ordination from Chinese, Korean, or Vietnamese masters, but after twelve years when they are qualified to give the bhikshuni ordination themselves, can they do so together with the bhikshu sangha of another school which is present in that country?

These Vinaya concerns are important, but I feel that some other, unspoken, issues are also at play regarding the introduction or re-establishment of the bhikshuni ordination. For example, how does one tradition feel about taking on a lineage from another, thus acknowledging that their own tradition was lacking in some way? How do political issues on a governmental level influence attitudes on this matter? With both the male and female sanghas coming to exist in one place, how will the economic conditions of the monasteries be affected? How will the relationship between monks and nuns change when both are fully ordained? Will nuns be able to receive proper training from monks and support from the laypeople when they return to their own countries as newly ordained bhikshunis?

The existence of the sangha community establishes a place as a "central land," one where the Dharma is flourishing. Both monks and nuns can contribute in myriad ways to the well-being of a society and its citizens, for tremendous value exists in receiving and observing precepts for the benefit of all beings. Thus, many of us hope that full ordination will be available to both men and women and that everyone will work together to meet whatever challenges arise.

Hierarchy Issues

Some Westerners see monasticism as too hierarchical and advocate more democratic and egalitarian structures. Often they form their opinions based on a few incidents without having studied the Vinaya. In fact, when studying Vinaya, we discover that the sangha was set up as a democratic community with regular meetings. As Venerable Wu Yin explains in chapter sixteen of this book, the Vinaya scriptures set forth the various types of sangha meetings and the procedures to be followed in them. The most prominent of these ceremonies, the twice-monthly confession ceremony on new and full moon days, is also a time for people to share their ideas and to discuss community affairs.

However monastic institutions may have evolved in various countries, theoretically they are based on egalitarian principles. For example, unless they are ill or doing important work for the community, all fully ordained monastics must attend sangha meetings so that everyone's voice is heard. Almost all formal decisions in a sangha community are made by consensus. The positions in a monastery—from abbess on down—are changed on a regular basis, so that no one becomes entrenched or too powerful in his or her job. It is true that while all fully ordained members have a vote, novices do not, but the reason for this is sound. Learning the Vinaya and becoming accustomed to monastic life takes time. New members are not yet sufficiently grounded in the Dharma and Vinaya to make decisions affecting the future of the community. They need to focus on building a solid foundation in their practice and subduing their minds before assuming increased levels of responsibility in the community. They are, however, included in the decision-making processes concerning the daily operations of the monastery.

Unfortunately, because many Westerners have authority issues, we misunderstand the purpose of respecting and following the guidance of those senior in ordination to ourselves and think these practices set up a rigid hierarchy. Rather, this system is based on compassion. Although we may be adults capable of running our own lives in the world, when we ordain, we still need guidance and instruction to learn how to be monastics. To help junior members in this regard, seniors give guidance, instruction, and admonition so that the juniors will develop their talents and abilities. This eases the pressure on junior members for they are not expected to be experts or to do everything correctly. By being open to guidance from senior monastics, they can relax and rely on the accumulated wisdom of previous generations. In addition, by serving their seniors, they have a first-hand view of how others integrate the Dharma into their daily lives. They have role models from whom they can learn skills such as dealing with conflict, illness, and so forth. Personally speaking, I have benefited greatly from situations in which I could serve my seniors. In addition, doing so enables us to develop humility, an important quality for monastics.

Chinese nuns chanting prayers

THE MOTIVATION AND BENEFITS OF MONASTIC ORDINATION

by Bhikshuni Thubten Chodron and Bhikshuni Tenzin Kacho

The Motivation for Ordination

Our mind is the creator of our happiness and suffering, and our motivation is the key to our actions and their results. Therefore, the motivation for receiving monastic ordination—the determination to be free from cyclic existence and to attain liberation—is of great importance. We generate this motivation by reflecting continuously on the disadvantages of cyclic existence. The method to free ourselves and attain nirvana is to practice the Three Higher Trainings: Ethical Discipline, Concentration, and Wisdom, as explained in the Three Baskets of the Buddha's teachings. The Higher Training in Ethical Discipline is explained in the Vinaya Pitaka, the Higher Training in Concentration in the Sutra Pitaka, and the Higher Training in Wisdom in the Abhidharma Pitaka. To develop the wisdom that liberates us from cyclic existence, we must be able to concentrate. Otherwise we will not be able to meditate on the nature of reality—emptiness of inherent existence—in a sustained manner. Developing concentration requires us to subdue the manifest disturbing attitudes in our mind. A firm foundation for doing this is created by pacifying our gross verbal and physical actions motivated by these disturbing attitudes. Ethics—living according to precepts—is the method to harmonize our physical and verbal actions, and thus to subdue the gross disturbing attitudes. Thinking that we can ignore our bad habits and how they manifest in our daily life and yet still develop spiritual realizations by meditating is erroneous.

Ethical discipline challenges us to live the Dharma in our daily interactions, that is, to integrate what we experience in meditation into our relationships with other people and with our environment. The Higher Training in Ethical Discipline is developed by taking and keeping one of the various types of pratimoksha (individual liberation) vows: the lay vow with five precepts or one of the monastic vows. The latter is comprised of the novice vow (shramanera/shramanerika) with ten precepts, or the full vow (bhikshu/bhikshuni).[1] For women, there is an intermediate ordination (shikshamana) between novice and full ordination with six additional regulations.

Since there are different levels of ordination and each successive level requires greater mindfulness and awareness due to the increased number of precepts, it is advisable to progress gradually, rather than immediately receiving the full ordination. In this way, we are able to adjust to the commitment required at each stage. Such a gradual approach allows a solid foundation to be built and sustained and joyful practice to ensue.

Ordination is easy to take, but difficult to keep. In order to remain as monastics for our entire life, we must cultivate a strong motivation before ordaining and continuously develop it afterwards. If we do, living as a monastic will always be a joy. When we are aware of the preciousness and rarity of this human life and our potential to attain higher

spiritual states in order to benefit others, then living in accord with precepts brings much happiness. In comparison,
the happiness of family, career, relationships, and pleasure
are seen as unsatisfactory and interest in them pales. We have
a long-range and noble spiritual goal, and this makes our
mind strong and courageous so that we can go through the
ups and downs of life. Being stable in Dharma practice enables us to keep the ordination once we have taken it.

The disadvantages of cyclic existence are many: in addition to birth, sickness, aging, and death, while alive we face
not getting what we seek, being separated from what we like,
and encountering undesirable circumstances. All these problems are caused by our internal disturbing attitudes and the
actions (karma) that they fuel. Householders must do many
things for the sake of their families, and easily find themselves in situations where they must create negative karma
by lying or cheating. Distractions to spiritual practice abound:
the media, career, and social obligations. It is easy for disturbing attitudes to arise and more difficult to accumulate
positive potential because life is so busy with other things.
In lay life, people face the difficulty of finding the right life
partner and then the difficulty of making the relationship
last. At the beginning they have the problem of no children,
and later the problems of raising the children.

As a monastic, we have more freedom from such distractions and difficulties. On the other hand, we also have great
responsibility. We have decided to be more aware and not to
act according to whatever impulse arises in our minds. Initially this may appear as a lack of freedom, but in fact such
awareness frees us from our bad habits and the difficulties
they create. We have voluntarily chosen to keep precepts,
and so we must slow down, be aware of our actions, and
choose what we do and say wisely.

However, not all monastics are enlightened Buddhas,
and there will be times when we do not keep our precepts
perfectly. The reason that we take precepts is that our mind,

speech, and actions are not subdued. If we were already perfect, we would not need to take precepts. Therefore, we should do our best to live according to the precepts, but when our disturbing attitudes or negative emotions are too strong and the situation gets the better of us, we should purify and restore our precepts and determine how we would like to act in the future. In that way we will learn from our mistakes and become stronger practitioners.

Monastics are representatives of the Three Jewels. Laypeople will be inspired or discouraged from learning and practicing the Dharma depending upon our behavior. For example, if they see monastics who are kind to others and are happy living ethically, they will try to do the same. If they see monastics who act brashly or manipulate others to get what they want, they may lose faith in the Dharma. Because monastics cherish the Three Jewels and cherish other beings, they should joyfully act in a responsible way that inspires others to have confidence in the Dharma.

If we become a monastic with strong conviction in the path to liberation, willingness to persevere and to face our problems, confidence in our potential, and patience with ourselves and others, we will be able to live as monastics happily and for a long time. However, if we wish to ordain because we have a romantic idea of living a holy life, or seek an easy way out of our personal or financial problems, we will be unhappy as a monastic because what we seek will not be actualized. By understanding what a crucial role our mind plays in keeping ordination, we see that keeping the pratimoksha (individual liberation) precepts makes not only our words and deeds peaceful, but calms our mind as well.

Joining the Sangha Community

Ordination is not only about living ethically; it involves being a member of a community, the Buddhist sangha, the monastics upholding the precepts and principles established by the Buddha. This is a virtuous community of people who practice the Buddha's teachings and assist others in taking refuge. As members of the sangha we focus on developing the quality of not retaliating in four situations: when someone harms us, is angry with us, insults or criticizes us, or abuses or beats us. The root of non-retaliation is compassion, the wish that others be free from suffering. Thus the main quality of the spiritual community stems from compassion.

The Buddha's ultimate goal for establishing the sangha is for people to attain liberation and enlightenment. The manifest goal is to create a harmonious community that enables its members to progress along the path. To accomplish this, the Vinaya Pitaka explains six harmonies towards which members of the monastics community should diligently work:

1. Physical harmony: we live together peacefully
2. Harmony in communication: there are few arguments and disputes, and when they occur, we remedy them
3. Mental harmony: we appreciate and support each other
4. Harmony in the precepts: we have a similar life style and live according to the same precepts
5. Harmony in views: we share similar beliefs
6. Harmony in welfare: we equally use and enjoy what is given to the community.

New monastics commonly focus on the benefit ordination brings to them as an individual and may consider the compromising of their individual styles or the reforming of their habits that community life entails as at best an inconvenience and at worst an unnecessary infringement of their freedom. While in some respects the individualistic concern for one's own practice is to be expected, it also reflects a certain self-centeredness and narrow-mindedness. With time, new monastics should hopefully expand their motivation from just forwarding their own practice to also working together with the community for the benefit of all its members. This motivation, too, with time, should be extended to also preserving the

Dharma and Vinaya for future generations, thus enabling so many beings to benefit from the Buddha's teachings.

The Benefits of Ordination

Living in accord with the precepts spurs our spiritual growth. The simplified life style of a monastic enables us to be content with little and gives us the time to practice the Dharma in a deep and committed way. As we practice, we will become more mindful and restrain ourselves from getting caught up with endless wants and desires. We will develop greater awareness of ourselves and others. We will have a method to deal with our problems and will cease reacting strongly to things that disturb us. Rather than acting on impulse, mindfulness of our precepts will help us to reflect before acting. We will develop greater tolerance, will not get emotionally entangled in unhealthy relationships, and will be of greater assistance to others. We will become calmer, healthier, and more content by living in the conducive circumstances that precepts create. By living according to the precepts, we will become ethical, trustworthy, and thus more confident.

Maintaining precepts purifies stores of negative karma and creates great positive potential (merit). This acts as a basis for obtaining higher rebirths in the future so that we can continue to practice the Dharma and attain liberation and enlightenment. Living in accord with the precepts will protect us from harm, and through our subdued behavior, the place where we live will become more peaceful and prosperous. We will become examples of individuals who are content with little and of a community that can work together and resolve its problems in a healthy way. Our mind will be peaceful and calm, and distractions in meditation will arise less often. We will get along better with others. In future lives, we will meet the Buddha's teachings and circumstances conducive to practice, and we will be born as a disciple of Maitreya Buddha.

Living in accord with the precepts directly contributes to world peace. For example, when we abandon killing, all living beings who contact us can feel secure. When we abandon stealing, everyone around us can relax and not fear for their possessions. Living in celibacy, we will relate to others more honestly, free from the subtle and not-so-subtle games between people. Others can then trust us because we are committed to speaking truthfully. In this way, each precept influences not only ourselves, but also those with whom we share this world.

In the *Lam Rim Chenmo* by the Tibetan sage Lama Tsong Khapa, the Higher Training in Ethical Discipline is described as the stairway to all other virtuous practices. It is the banner of all Dharma practice, the destroyer of all negative actions and unfortunate rebirths. It is the medicine that cures the disease of harmful actions, the food to eat while traveling the difficult road of samsara, the weapon to destroy the enemy of the disturbing attitudes, and the foundation for all positive qualities. Seeing the value in living in this and preserving this tradition for others in the future, we seek to learn the Vinaya from wise and compassionate spiritual masters. Thus, we are fortunate to have here Venerable Bhikshuni Wu Yin's oral teachings on the Bhikshuni Pratimoksha.

Venerable Bhikshuni Wu Yin

CHAPTER ONE

The Importance of the Precepts

I make obeisance to all the Buddhas, the Dharma, and the Sangha. The Dharma in the Vinaya will now be ex pounded so the true Dharma will abide forever.

The Dharma and the Vinaya are traced back to our teacher, Shakyamuni Buddha, who lived in the sixth century B.C.E. Having initially spread throughout Asia, his teachings are now found all over the world and have benefited millions of people throughout history.

Shila, or ethical discipline, means freedom from emotional disturbance and is an attitude of non-harmfulness. Training ourselves in ethical discipline, in conjunction with training in other aspects of the Dharma, extinguishes the three poisonous attitudes of ignorance, attachment, and anger and leads us to liberation. The main body of teachings on ethical discipline are found in the Vinaya Pitaka or "basket." Thus the term "Vinaya" refers to the collection of scriptures teaching ethical discipline as well as to the process of subduing infractions.

Among the various Vinaya scriptures, the most essential ones are the *Bhikshu Pratimoksha Sutra* and the *Bhikshuni Pratimoksha Sutra*, which detail the precepts of the fully ordained monks and nuns respectively. Pratimoksha means "self-liberation," and refers to the goal of practicing the Vinaya: one's own liberation from the bondage of cyclic existence and the attainment of nirvana. Pratimoksha can also refer to means of attaining one's own liberation, that is, the eight types of pratimoksha vows: those of the bhikshu, bhikshuni, shikshamana, shramanera, shramanerika, *upasaka*, *upasika*, and the one-day vow. In addition, in a general sense, pratimoksha may be used to refer to all the guidelines and precepts explained in the Vinaya.

Precepts are the specific rules established by the Buddha to help his disciples avoid misdeeds and wrongdoings. The scope of the precepts' influence includes our conduct, habits, character, and mental states. Precepts are not commandments, but guidelines to help us subdue our physical and verbal actions, become more aware of our mental motivations, and live harmoniously with those around us. The precepts are not an external ideal being forced upon us, but points for training that we voluntarily undertake.

As Buddhadharma spread from place to place in ancient times, different Vinaya traditions arose. Chinese Buddhists follow the Dharmaguptaka Vinaya, while the Tibetans follow the Mulasarvastivada Vinaya, and Buddhists in Sri Lanka, Thailand, Cambodia, Burma, and so on follow the Theravada Vinaya. The number of precepts in these traditions varies. For bhikshunis, the Dharmaguptaka Vinaya has 348 precepts, Mulasarvastivada has 364, and the Theravada 311. The bhikshus in those traditions respectively have 250, 253, and 227 precepts. The Vinaya of the various schools are remarkably consistent in the meaning of the precepts considering that each tradition was passed on orally in its own geographical area for many centuries before being written down. Nevertheless, a detailed analysis of this is beyond the scope of this book.

I have put the bhikshuni precepts into categories according to topic, for example, those concerning sexual conduct, listening to admonition, methods for procuring the requisites for daily life, and so on. In this way, the various areas of a nun's life will become clear, as will the Buddha's guidelines for relating to those areas in a healthy and pure way. The basic topics to be explained are: members of the sangha, joining the sangha, the poshadha to purify and restore our precepts, basic requirements for remaining a monastic, precepts dealing with sexual contact, stealing, and other *parajika*, accepting admonition, right livelihood, resources for monastic life, organization in the Buddhist community, and community life.

Any sincerely interested person—whether he or she is a monastic or not—may study the monastic precepts. However, when the bhikshus or bhikshunis do their bimonthly poshadha ceremony, only the bhikshus or bhikshunis may attend. If one has not taken the full precepts, he or she has no need to purify them through the poshadha rite. In addition, the sangha members may want to discuss privately issues relating specifically to their community at that time.

As Buddhism has spread from one country to another, certain elements have changed according to different environments and cultures. In this regard, we must consider some important issues. For example, what adaptations can and should be made in different communities? How should monastics from various cultures, ethnic groups, and backgrounds be trained? How do the climate, geography, society, culture, and times in which we live affect how we practice Vinaya? I will not go into these questions at this moment, but keep them in mind as you study and practice the Vinaya. In exploring these issues, we must be open-minded and not expect to find one "right" answer.

Because the geography, climate, customs, culture, political situation, and economics have changed since the time of the Buddha, the circumstances in which we currently practice have to be taken into account. Some people advocate following every precept set up by the Buddha literally. Do you think this is possible? On the other hand, if we do not follow the Buddha's precepts, are we the Buddha's disciples? What does it mean to follow the Buddha's precepts? Are there different ways of doing so? These are serious questions to reflect upon, and people will come to different conclusions.

In investigating this, we must distinguish the fundamental from the secondary teachings of the Buddha. I will explain the original teachings in the Vinaya Pitaka and then sometimes discuss how the bhikshuni sangha at the Luminary Temple in Taiwan practices them. In this way, you will see one example of how the Chinese monastic community connects the tradition to the modern situation. With this as a background, Westerners will have some tools for bringing the Vinaya into their own cultures in a pure, yet practical, way.

Bhikshunis are religious practitioners and are part of the sangha. The life style of a bhikshuni is one of spiritual practice. Since most bhikshunis live in a community, spiritual practice and community life are related. Joining the sangha is a voluntary act; we are willing and choose to live our lives as religious practitioners. Because this is our wish, we want to receive proper and complete training in the life style we have chosen, and having done that, we are committed to implement it in practice. If we decide not to be a serious monastic practitioner, we can return our vow. No one forces us to become or to remain a bhikshuni. We are free to decide. The commitment to monastic practice comes from within us.

When we choose to join the sangha, we have to make some changes because we are entering a community. The bhikshuni sangha as a whole is our community, whether or not we live in a particular monastery. To be part of the bhikshuni sangha, we need to adapt and follow its way of life. Some actions are prohibited while others are prescribed. Doing prohibited actions, such as engaging in sexual contact, killing, stealing, lying, and so forth, violates the precepts. Similarly, neglecting to do prescribed actions, such as ordination, poshadha, rains retreat, and so on, violates the precepts. These practices are done in a community with a certain number of people and the procedure has to be legal, that is, done in the manner the Buddha described. New nuns should realize that monastic ordination is not just between them and their teacher. Rather, they are entering a community of nuns and will be guided, supported, and trained by the bhikshunis.

In *The Path of Purification (Visuddhimagga)*, the bhikshuni precepts are put into four categories:

1. Moral behavior for human beings
2. The method to discipline our senses
3. The livelihood of a monastic
4. Daily encounters with people, etiquette, and interactions with people

Understanding the origin of each precept—the circumstances under which the Buddha established it—is necessary to categorize them according to importance or according to topic. The meaning of a precept is not always clear from its wording. For this reason, examining the incident triggering that precept is important.

For example, in the Buddha's time, a group of bhikshus was bathing in a pond. Beginning before sunrise, they continued for many hours, enjoying the water and helping each other put medicine on their bodies. Meanwhile, King Bimbisara waited until nightfall for the bhikshus to finish so that he could bathe. By the time the king had finished his bath, the gates of the city were locked for the evening, and he had to sleep outside. The Buddha heard about the situation and established the following precept, which for bhikshunis reads:

> *Prayascittika* 41: A healthy bhikshuni may take a bath once every half month. If she bathes more than that, she is commits a prayascittika, unless it is done at an allowable time. The allowable times are when the weather is hot, when she is sick, when she works, when it is very windy, when it rains (and she gets wet), and when she is traveling. These are the times.

According to this precept, all healthy bhikshus and bhikshunis should not bathe more than once every half a month. However, when certain situations occurred and the Buddha was consulted, he made exceptions to this precept. For example, if monastic is sick, if the weather is hot, if a monastic has done manual labor or walked for a long time, he or she is exempt and may bathe. Nowadays, if we bathe only twice a month, what will the laypeople say? By paying close attention to the circumstances under which this precept was established, we will see the Buddha's real purpose and will be able to adapt it to our present circumstances.

The Importance of Learning the Precepts

By ordaining, we join a sangha, a community of practitioners. A sangha is not made of only one person; four or more fully ordained monastics are necessary for a sangha to exist. Pratimoksha precepts are guidelines for living and practicing together harmoniously with our fellow practitioners, so learning them is important. Beginners' ignorance of the precepts is understandable, but if we continue to live with the sangha and do not learn the precepts we make our own life difficult as well as commit the offense of being ignorant of our precepts.

> Prayascittika 56: If a bhikshuni, at the time of reciting the precepts says, "Elder Sisters, what is the use of these trivial precepts? Reciting these precepts only makes one annoyed, ashamed, and suspicious," due to slighting and denigrating the precepts, she commits a prayascittika.

> Prayascittika 57: Suppose a bhikshuni, at the time of reciting the precepts says, "Elder Sisters, I have just now come to

know these precepts from the *Pratimoksha Sutra*, which is read once every half month," and other bhikshunis know that this bhikshuni has attended the recitation of the precepts two or three times, or even more. Even if she is without knowledge and understanding, if she commits an offense, she should be properly dealt with, and more so for the offense of not knowing. They say to her, "Elder Sister, you are not benefited and not good because you were not mindful during the recitation of the precepts and did not listen with undivided attention. Due to not knowing (the precepts), she commits a prayascittika.

In the Buddha's time some bhikshus were lazy and said, "Why should we go through so much trouble to learn these burdensome precepts?" They did not pay attention when the precepts were recited every half-month in the poshadha ceremony to purify and restore the precepts. In response, the Buddha established these two precepts to stress the importance of learning the precepts. If a bhikshuni ignores learning the precepts and ignorantly transgresses a precept, she commits the offense of whatever precept she transgressed as well as these two additional offenses. Therefore, monastics in the Chinese Buddhist community primarily study the pratimoksha for the first five years after ordination. With that as a foundation, we learn the Dharma and meditation in depth. In this way, we can continue our spiritual journey in an effective way.

The Vinaya deals with many of our daily life activities, for example, how to procure and use food, clothing, and lodging. It also discusses how to interact with other nuns and laypeople, how to live together as a community, and so on. Since the Vinaya deals with so many practical topics of our daily life, we learn it first. Doing so enables us to live together with others harmoniously, increases our mindfulness, and enhances our care and consideration for others.

The moment we join the sangha, don the robes, and shave our head, we become monastics, regardless of our age or gender. People see us as monastics and expect us to be religious practitioners. If we do not learn the precepts, people will say, "This person looks like a religious practitioner but does not act like one. She acts like a regular person, but does not look like one." Then we will be a stranger in the world.

Just after the Buddha's enlightenment, he encountered two merchants on the road and taught them the Dharma. At that time, only the Buddha and Dharma refuges existed. The Sangha refuge came into existence later when the Buddha taught the five bhikshus in Deer Park, near Varanasi. At the beginning, Buddhist monastics were of very high quality. They behaved well and earned people's respect. Because of their good qualities, they did not need precepts to regulate their behavior, and thus initially, the Buddha instructed and guided the monastics, but no precepts existed.

Because society trusted and supported the monastics, many people followed their example and joined the sangha. However, not all of them had the proper motivation. At first, beggars and practitioners of other religions followed the sangha to receive leftovers after the monastics had completed their meal. But as time went on, some of these people joined the sangha simply so they could receive the food and clothing offered to the sangha. Other people joined the sangha to avoid paying their debts. Their relatives treated them well, but ignored serious practitioners. As the sangha grew, problems such as these inevitably arose. Because some monastics acted improperly, the Buddha began to establish precepts to regulate their behavior.

Although some people take ordination with the wrong motivation, in my experience, most people join the sangha with the bodhichitta motivation. However, people do go through ups and downs in their practice. In the Chinese community we say that during the first two years after ordination, the Buddha is still in front of us. In the third and fourth year, the Buddha is in the air; and from the fifth year onwards, the Buddha has gone to Sukhavati, the Western Paradise, so keeping our initial inspiration becomes difficult! Since we are not enlightened, our disturbing attitudes arise, and we have to deal with them. In addition, we face aging, illness, and balancing service for others with meditation practice and study. Further, a community must discuss and decide which of its members will study, teach, do administrative jobs, and engage in advanced meditation. All these issues come up in our lives, and working with them is part of our spiritual practice. The Vinaya is rich with stories of similar situations, giving us many examples and much advice about how to resolve them.

The Ten Advantages of Establishing Precepts

The Buddha did not make all the precepts before creating the sangha. Rather, each precept was established following a specific incident. Many of the bhikshunis' precepts arose in response to actions done by bhikshus. In addition, other precepts were created due to bhikshunis' actions.

The Buddha established the precepts gradually. The first were the *shikshakaraniya*, the training rules. Initially these were sufficient guidance for the Buddha's disciples. Later, a few monastics did more serious negative actions and the other precepts came into existence. The first incident prompting the establishment of a major precept occurred twelve years after the Buddha's enlightenment when Bhikshu Kalandaka went back to his family and had sexual relations with his former wife. When monastics misbehaved, the Buddha did not beat them. Rather, he scolded them and established a precept to discourage others from acting similarly in the future.

Before establishing each precept, the Buddha mentioned the ten advantages of precepts. Each precept has these ten advantages, and they clarify the Buddha's reasons for setting up precepts. The first three reasons are to promote harmony in the sangha:

1. To direct the monastics

When we take full ordination, we are the newborns of the sangha, and sangha is pleased to have us. However, like newborns, our good qualities need to be developed. This comes about through kind yet firm discipline. By observing the discipline of the precepts, our physical, verbal, and mental behaviors are directed in positive ways, and our good qualities are shaped and made steady.

2. To foster peace and happiness among the monastics

The monastic community rests upon a sound foundation of discipline, and serious implementation of the precepts acts as the centripetal force holding the sangha together.

3. To protect the monastics

Generally speaking, equality is the basis for harmony. Thus to make the first and second advantages possible, sangha members must be equal in sharing similar views, following the same precepts, and caring equally about the welfare of each member. By living harmoniously together while practicing the Dharma and Vinaya, monastics can focus their attention on individual progress. They will not, intentionally or unintentionally, destroy the Dharma or create disturbance in the sangha. In this way, following precepts naturally protects the monastics and makes their life together comfortable.

Although the Buddha often asked kings, ministers, and Dharma protectors to guard the Three Jewels, the real responsibility to protect the Three Jewels lies with the monastics. The Buddha often said he is one member of the sangha, and that he, together with all the other monastics, must work to improve the world and the environment. In this way, these first three advantages contribute to the harmony of the sangha.

The next two advantages of the precepts transform society:

4. To inspire those who have no faith in the Dharma

5. To advance the practice of those who already have faith

The sangha exists in relationship to society: new sangha members come from the general public; our support comes through the kindness of the laypeople; and we exist within the context of society. For these reasons, the sangha should contribute to the welfare of laypeople in return. Even if we meditate in solitude, we still depend on others' kindness. At every stage of our practice we need the support of both the sangha and the lay community. Ignoring or quarreling with laypeople shows a lack of compassion and has negative repercussions. For example, Tsantuo, a very argumentative bhikshu during the Buddha's time, provoked the dislike of the laypeople who, in turn, refused to support him. This, of course, made him even angrier!

The relationship between laypeople and sangha is an interactive one. As religious practitioners, we cultivate not only our internal spiritual capacities, but also our ability to help others learn and practice the Dharma. The sangha fulfills its responsibility to the larger society by inspiring people who at first did not see the value of the Dharma and by advancing the spiritual welfare of sangha members and laypeople who already have faith.

Working for the spiritual welfare of others not only includes teaching the Dharma, leading ceremonies, and guiding meditations, but also involves offering service to the lay community and to the monastic community. For example, sangha members distribute among themselves the work required to oversee the temple's operations and the coordination of its Dharma events. Our focus in observing precepts is not just our individual benefit, but the welfare of the community as well.

The following four advantages bring about our individual liberation:

6. To restrain the restive
7. To stabilize those who have a sense of integrity

These two advantages speak of resolving monastics' wrongdoings and conflict. According to their degree of severity, we purify our mistakes and transgressions of precepts by a variety of means. Simple lapses are confessed to either another bhikshuni in private or to the community during poshadha, our bimonthly confession ceremony. Transgression of a *sanghavashesha* entails temporary suspension of a monastic's rights in the community, and full transgression of a parajika means the person is permanently expelled from the sangha. As sangha, our main purpose is not to pretend to be pure. We are not yet *arhats* or bodhisattvas, so naturally we will err. Therefore, our main purpose is to recognize our mistakes, know the methods to purify them, and apply these methods. In this way we maintain the sangha's purity. The point of our spiritual journey is not never to commit any offenses, but to purify them when we do. Without our first being immature monastics, we could not grow to become mature ones.

8. To eliminate present defilements

9. To prevent defilements from arising in the future

We initially join the sangha in order to tame our mind, eliminate our defilements, and prevent new defilements from arising. Through this, we will be able to offer service to others with the bodhichitta motivation, and eventually, we will liberate ourselves from cyclic existence. As we progress in this direction, our attachment, anger, and other defilements will grow thinner, and our good qualities will increase. These last four advantages are for the purpose of our individual liberation.

While the first nine advantages are a detailed explanation of the advantages of precepts, the tenth states their ultimate purpose:

10. For the Dharma to be forever sustained

This is the ultimate goal of all the previous advantages and is contained in our opening prayer, "I make obeisance to the Buddha, the Dharma, and the Sangha. The Dharma in the Vinaya will now be expounded so that the true Dharma may abide forever." Some of the previous founding

Buddhas—those who first turned the Dharma wheel when Buddhism was unknown in the world—did not teach Vinaya elaborately while they were alive. As a result, after their *parinirvana*, their Dharma declined because no model existed for practitioners to follow. Shakyamuni Buddha, with great compassion, established the Vinaya extensively so that his Dharma could last forever. Interestingly, the ultimate goal is not our own enlightenment; it is preserving the Dharma and causing it to flourish so that others can learn and practice it.

The advantage of establishing precepts can be summarized as follows:

In detail:

1. To promote harmony within the sangha
   * To direct the monastics
   * To make monastics peaceful and happy
   * To protect monastics

2. To transform the society
   * To inspire those without faith
   * To advance the practice of those with faith

3. To bring about individual liberation
   * To restrain the restive
   * To stabilize those with a sense of integrity
   * To eliminate present defilements
   * To prevent defilements from arising in the future

In general:

1. The ultimate goal
   * For the Dharma to be forever sustained

By repeating these ten advantages before establishing each new precept, the Buddha encouraged us to actualize them by keeping the precepts as purely as possible. Observing each precept has an effect on the individual, on the relationships among individuals, on the relationship between the individual and the community, and on the relationship between the sangha and society.

The Buddha created each precept for the benefit of common practitioners like us, as is evident from the following story. Once, many Brahmins in a village repeatedly requested the Buddha to accept their support for the sangha for the three months of the summer retreat. The Buddha accepted. However, due to famine in the land, the Brahmins forgot their promise, and the sangha did not have food. When a group of horse traders passed by, the Buddha's disciples had no other choice but to ask them for food. All the horse traders had to offer was grass for the horses, and out of respect to the Buddha, they gave him double the amount given to the other bhikshus.

The Buddha's attendant, Ananda, ground the grass into powder, mixed it with water, and offered it to the Buddha. Because many bhikshus experienced indigestion after eating the grass, one monk who was famous for his superhuman powers thought to use them to go to another place and collect better alms. The Buddha asked him, "You have the superhuman power to do this, but what will happen to those who do not?" He replied that he would take a few monks with him each time so that they could have better food as well. The Buddha questioned him further, "How about those disciples in the future who have neither superhuman powers nor you to help them?" Here we see that the Buddha's primary focus was the welfare of ordinary practitioners. Similarly, he established the precepts for the benefit of us common practitioners, not for those with superhuman powers or those who are *aryas* or arhats.

The ten advantages of establishing precepts are for us to implement and realize. Although we are not yet liberated, we are protected by the devoted practitioners of the past. Our present opportunity to practice the Dharma is due to their kindness. They worked hard to observe the precepts and practice the Dharma, so that society and the individuals in it would benefit and have faith in the Dharma. It is now our time. We have the responsibility to observe the precepts and practice the Dharma, so that the Buddhadharma will exist for those in future generations. Through our efforts, we can bring purity to the world and become the hope of others. We can prolong the existence of Three Jewels in the world. This is our responsibility.

CHAPTER TWO

An Overview of the Vinaya

Eight different versions of the *Bhikshuni Pratimoksha Sutra* are still extant, and here we will use the *Pratimoksha Sutra* of the Dharmaguptaka, the predominant one in the Chinese Buddhist community. This sutra was translated into Chinese in 410-412 C.E., during the Yiao-Chin Dynasty, by Tripitaka Master Buddhayasa from India and Chu Fo-nien from Liang Zhou, China.

Five versions of the Vinaya Pitaka (the Vinaya scriptures) are preserved in the Chinese language.[1] Initially, the Chinese Buddhist community used the Sarvastivada Vinaya for bhikshu and bhikshuni ordination. However, the Dharmaguptaka Vinaya was widely taught after 709, when Venerable Tao-an, a disciple of Vinaya Master Tao-hsiun, brought it from northern China to southern China. Its popularity is due to its ordination procedure and precepts being consistent with the Mahayana teachings practiced in China.

The first bhikshunis in Buddhist history were Mahaprajapati, the Buddha's aunt and stepmother, and the five hundred women from the Shakya clan who ordained with her.

In China, the first bhikshuni was Bhikshuni Ching-chien, who was ordained in 357 C.E. Since that time the bhikshuni lineage has existed in China, and nowadays the bhikshuni sangha flourishes in Taiwan and several other Asian countries. I hope it will also flourish in the West.

The Dharmaguptaka Vinaya was compiled by the Master Dharmagupta according to Aryasthaviranikaya's Vinaya, especially the Samgika Vinaya of the Sarvastivadins.[2] Because he presented it orally in four lectures, which became the four sections of the Dharmaguptaka Vinaya, it is also called the *Four-part Vinaya* in China. These four parts of the Dharmaguptaka Vinaya comprise sixty volumes. Of these sixty, Part One has volumes 1-21, containing the bhikshu pratimoksha. Part Two has volumes 22-36 with the bhikshuni pratimoksha, ordination rite, and poshadha. Part Three, with volumes 37-49, contain sixteen of the twenty *skandha*. Part Four, volumes 50-60, discuss the other skandha, the two councils, issues arising in the sangha and methods to settle them, and a review of the previous precepts with some additional explanation.

The Vinaya Pitaka may also be divided into three classifications: the *Sutra-vibhanga* (also known as Pratimoksha), the Skandha, and the *Parivara*. The Sutra-vibhanga contains principally the bhikshu and bhikshuni pratimoksha, which describe the precepts prohibiting certain actions in detail. The Chinese Vinaya masters call the Sutra-vibhanga the "gate of the don'ts."

The Skandha contains the various practices and rituals that the monastic community should perform. It is called the "gate of the do's" by the Chinese Vinaya masters and contains twenty sections:

1. *Pravrajya-vastu*:[3] the procedure of ordination
2. *Poshadha-vastu*: (also called *uposatha*) the recitation of the *Pratimoksha Sutra*
3. *Varsha-vastu*: the rains retreat (summer retreat) and related issues

4. *Pravarana-vastu*: regulations, formalities, and related issues regarding the confession ceremony held at the end of the rains retreat

5. *Carama-vastu*: usage of things made from hides

6. *Civara-vastu*: the making and wearing of robes, etc.

7. *Bhaisajya-vastu*: usage and retention of medicine, etc.

8. *Kathina-vastu*: the receiving and giving away of the "robe of merit"

9. *Koshambaka-vastu*: living in harmony, proceedings in case of dissension

10. *Karma-vastu*: the carrying out of sangha proceedings in a legal fashion

11. *Pandulohitaka-vastu*: the handling of quarrelsome monastics

12. *Pudgala-vastu*: purification of the sanghavashesha transgression

13. *Parivasika-vastu*: consequences for concealing the commitment of a sanghavashesha

14. *Poshadhasthapana vastu*: handling those who have committed transgressions and are not allowed to attend poshadha

15. *Sanghabheda-vastu*: handling cases of ruining the harmony of the sangha

16. *Shamata-vastu*: procedures for ending disputes

17. *Bhikshuni-vastu*: matters related to bhikshuni ordination and recitation of the *Bhikshuni Pratimoksha Sutra*

18. *Acara-vastu*: manners for different situations

19. *Sayanasana-vastu*: usage of housing, beds, and clothing

20. *Kshudraka-vastu*: extensive explanations on all skandhas.

The twenty skandha discuss what is prohibited as well as what is prescribed. Of them, five are the most important for the monastic community to implement: the vastus on ordination (1), the purification and restoration of precepts, poshadha (2), the summer retreat (3), the ceremony at the end of the summer retreat (4), and the *kathina* robe (8). Some *skandha* describe manners and how monastics should conduct themselves in various situations, such as walking, standing, sitting, or lying down. Other skandha deal with aspects of monastics' personal life and possessions, such as the use of leather, medicine, clothing, sitting cloths, and bedding.

The Parivara is like an appendix supplementing the material in the Sutra-vibhanga and the Skandha. Amassed around the third century B.C.E., it discusses the compilation of the Vinaya at the first and second councils—at Rajagriha and Vaishali respectively. Another section, observance, contains explanation of extraordinary circumstances and clarifies doubts regarding the precepts, and the section on suspension of the pratimoksha further explains the meaning of the precepts.

The *Pratimoksha Sutra* is also known as the *Sutra of Discipline* because it details the precepts. Pratimoksha can mean "the best," "individual liberation," and "liberation from individual wrongdoing." It is the root of all virtues, for following it will free us from the bondage of the disturbing attitudes and the unpleasant results of wrongdoings. Sutra means "thread," like the thread in a flower garland connecting the flowers so the wind cannot blow them away. Similarly, the *Pratimoksha Sutra* has a certain sentence structure and sequence, acting as threads which have enabled it to be preserved and transmitted in oral and written forms for over twenty centuries.

The Origin of the Pratimoksha

Volumes 22-30 of the Dharmaguptaka Vinaya contain the bhikshuni pratimoksha. However, since many of the precepts held by bhikshunis arose due to wrongdoings originally committed by bhikshus, we have to study the bhikshu pratimoksha in volumes 1-21. In both pratimoksha, three major elements appear:

1. The incident which brought about the creation of a specific precept
2. The linguistic formation of that precept
3. The discussion of each transgression and its type

1. The incident which brought about the creation of a specific precept

For each incident, five factors are described:

1. The place where the misdeed was done
2. The person who did it
3. The incident itself
4. The offense
5. The defilement that provoked the transgression

The incidents and explanations of a particular precept are not always laid out together. Some precepts were amended according to circumstances that arose later. For example, the precept to avoid eating in the absence of the assembly was amended seven times, and the Vinaya mentions three reasons for each exception.

2. The linguistic formation of that precept

The written language of each precept is simple and concise, so that reading it does not always enable us to understand its purpose. Further explanation, including definition of the terms and narration of the circumstances triggering its establishment, is often needed. The description of each precept contains these, and knowing them enables us to understand the kind of person involved, his or her mental state, the details of the situation, and the kind of offense created. Knowing these will make us more conscientious in guarding our precepts.

3. The discussion of each transgression and its type

There are various degrees of transgression, from minor to major. In general, a precept falls in one of the following two categories:

1. The natural precepts. These regard actions that are negative by nature, regardless of whether or not one holds a
precept to abandon that action. Killing, stealing, unwise
sexual behavior, and lying fall in this category.

2. The preventive precepts. These prohibit actions which are
not naturally negative, but which, if done, may lead the
person down the path to committing a naturally negative
action. For example, the precept against taking intoxicants
falls in this category. Although taking intoxicants is not
naturally negative, people are more likely to violate other
precepts while intoxicated. In addition, they incur public
criticism.

Outline of the Dharmaguptaka Vinaya

Part One	21 vols.	bhiksu pratimoksha (1-21)
Part Two	15 vols.	bhiksuni pratimoksha (22-30)
		ordination (31-35 first half)
		poshadha (35 second half -36)
Part Three	13 vols.	rains retreat (37 first half)
		pravarana (37 second half - 38 first half)
		hides (38 second half - 39 first half)
		robe-material (39 second half - 41)
		medicine (42 - 43 first half),
		kathina, kosambaka (43 second half),
		karma (44 first half)
		probation (44 second half - 45 first half)
		people (45 second half)
		accumulation of offenses and schism (46)
		settlement (47 - 48 first half)
		nuns (48 second half - 49 first half)
		manners (49 second half)
Part Four	11 vols.	lodgings (50 - 51 first half)
		miscellaneous skandha (51 second half -53)
		the Council of Rajargha, the Council of Vaishali (54)
		observances (55 - 57 first half)
		suspending the pratimoksha (57 second half - 60)

The discussion of each transgression and its type demarcates a transgression from that which is not a transgression and distinguishes a major offense from a minor one. The seriousness of a violation depends upon the type of person involved, his or her motivation, and the results. For example, an action done voluntarily is very different from one done under coercion. An action done intentionally brings different results than one done accidentally. Knowing this enables us to prevent wrongdoings or to mute their force should they occur. This section also relates exceptional and/or problematic cases regarding parajika and sanghavashesha offenses. Let me give some examples regarding the types of transgression.

> Prayascittika 88: If a bhikshuni, over some trivial matter, makes a oath (i.e. swears) to fall into the three negative states of rebirth and not be born (in a place) with the Buddhadharma, saying, "If I did such a thing, may I fall into the three negative states of rebirth and not be born in (a place with) the Buddhadharma," or "If you do such a thing, may you fall into the three negative states of rebirth and not be born (in a place) with the Buddhadharma," she commits a prayascittika.

When frustrated over trivial occurrences, one bhikshuni often exclaimed, "If I did this, may I be reborn as a hellish being, a hungry ghost, or an animal and never be born in a place where the Buddhadharma exists. If you do such an action, may that happen to you as well." Do you think this bhikshuni seriously meant what she said? Did she like the Dharma or not? I do not think she really meant what she said, but swore like that due to dissatisfaction or frustration. As result, her action is a prayascittika offense, which is not as serious as a sanghavashesha.

> Sanghavashesha 16: If a bhikshuni becomes angry and unhappy over some small thing and says, "I forsake the Buddha, the Dharma, and the Sangha. It is not only with Buddhist renunciants that we can cultivate pure conduct. We can cultivate pure conduct with Brahmin renunciants who cultivate

pure conduct too," then a bhikshuni should admonish that bhikshuni saying, "Elder Sister, you should not get angry and unhappy over some small thing and say, 'I forsake the Buddha, the Dharma, and the Sangha. It is not only with Buddhist renunciants that we can cultivate pure conduct. We can cultivate pure conduct with Brahmin renunciants who cultivate pure conduct too'." If, when admonished by a bhikshuni, that bhikshuni persists in her misconduct and refuses to repent, the bhikshuni should admonish her three times. If the bhikshuni gives up her misconduct upon the third admonition, good. If she does not, she commits a sanghavashesha requiring repentance on the third admonition.

This bhikshuni spoke out of resentment. Do you think she wants to be a bhikshuni or not? One's bhikshuni vow and one's commitment as a monastic can terminate in various ways. One is by saying, "I renounce the Buddha, the Dharma, and the Sangha. I renounce my master." If a person intentionally says this to another person who can understand her, and if she means what she says, she has given back her vow. Should a bhikshuni with a bad temper frequently utter this kind of statement, how do we know if she is serious in her commitment to be a bhikshuni? Her fellow sangha members have to reach out and help her clarify her intention and commitment. They need to find a means to help her. For example, they may speak with her privately if that seems more skillful. Or, they may ask her in front of the sangha if she is serious about her statement, if she is serious about being a nun or not. The pratimoksha helps us clear up this kind of issue and thus to maintain the purity of the sangha.

As religious practitioners, we must not only know ourselves, but also help our fellow practitioners to understand their motivation and commitment. Some people say that behavior and speech are the essential aspects of being a monastic. However, our deeds and words do not arise on their own; they come from our motivation. To maintain our precepts we must constantly be aware of our motivation and purify it if it is polluted.

The Vinaya records other instances that demonstrate the importance of one's motivation to be a monastic. Once a group of bhikshus accepted many young boys as *shramaneras*. During the night these children cried because they were hungry. The bhikshus comforted them, saying, "At dawn, we will go on alms round. Please don't cry." But the young shramaneras would not cooperate and continued to cry, awakening the Buddha by their wails. In a separate event, some bhikshunis accepted a very young girl as a shramanerika. Having no idea about men's desires or evil intentions, this naive, lovely girl was raped by a man. In both these cases, their young age made it difficult for these children to observe precepts, and this led to the Buddha stipulating that youths be a certain age to become shramaneras. A person must by physically and mentally mature in order to have the proper motivation and sufficient capability to be a monastic.

Even in an adult, motivation is important to determine whether an action is positive or negative, or whether it contradicts the precepts or not. For example, when an act of stealing was reported to him, the Buddha asked, "What motivation did that person have when he did that? Was he sleeping? Was he mentally ill?" Do not think that the precepts simply say do not do this or that. They are much more subtle and make us examine our mind and its motivation. In doing so, they guide us in a new direction and indicate beneficial ways of being.

CHAPTER THREE

The Members of the Sangha

Sangha is an assembly of Buddhist monastics. Within the general sangha, five types of members are found: bhikshus, bhikshunis, shikshamanas, shramaneras, and shramanerikas. Sometimes four subgroups are listed: bhikshus, bhikshunis, shramaneras, and shramanerikas. Other times, we speak of two subgroups: bhikshus and bhikshunis. The term "sangha" is sometimes extended to include laypeople as well, making seven subgroups in the sangha: bhikshus, bhikshunis, shikshamanas, shramaneras, shramanerikas, upasakas, and upasikas.

The various members of the sangha have different roles, responsibilities, and stages of observance of precepts. This hierarchy is designed to help people grow and progress along the path by enabling them to practice at various levels. In that way they train and gradually refine their mindfulness of their physical, verbal, and mental activities. It also enables them to accept gradually more responsibility. Expecting junior members to have the knowledge of Dharma and Vinaya, the skill, and the level of practice of more senior members would be unfair. Each person needs the time and opportunity to grow and to learn from those who are more experienced in the Dharma. Among all these followers of the Buddha, bhikshus and bhikshunis, as the core members of the sangha, are the most essential.[1] The terms "bhikshu" and "bhikshuni" have three meanings:

1. Alms person or religious mendicant. Bhikshus and bhikshunis seek the Dharma from the Buddha for their spiritual development and seek alms from laypeople to sustain their lives.

2. Terrifier of Mara.[2] By practicing the Dharma, a bhikshu or bhikshuni can end the cycle of rebirth and Mara will no longer be able to disturb him or her under any circumstances. Mara is terrified because he is losing another child.

3. Foe destroyer. By observing the precepts, a bhikshu or bhikshuni will eliminate negative actions committed physically and verbally. Through continued Dharma practice, he or she also will destroy the foes of the disturbing attitudes and karma—the causes of cyclic existence—and thus will attain liberation.

Bhikshus and bhikshunis follow the precepts in the bhikshu and bhikshuni pratimoksha respectively, and they have the same responsibilities: to lead the sangha, to teach Buddhist followers, and to guide the minor members of the sangha— shikshamanas, shramaneras, and shramanerikas. Mentally sound and physically healthy shramaneras and shikshamanas between the ages of twenty and sixty are the primary candidates to become bhikshus and bhikshunis. Having trained as minor members of the sangha, they are prepared to assume the responsibilities that full ordination entails.

A shikshamana is a probationary nun who, in addition to the ten shramanerika precepts, observes the six regulations: to avoid killing, stealing, sexual contact, lying, taking intoxicants, and eating at improper times (that is, from midday to the following dawn). Although the six regulations are similar to six of the ten shramanerika precepts, a shikshamana must keep them without any fault for two years in order to qualify to receive the bhikshuni ordination. The primary candidates to become shikshamanas are shramanerikas over eighteen years old.

The meaning of "shramanera" and "shramanerika" is to eliminate negativity and practice compassion. The primary candidates are those younger than twenty, those older than sixty, and those whose bodies are partially impaired. The shramaneras and shramanerikas follow the ten precepts: to avoid 1) killing, 2) stealing, 3) sexual contact, 4) lying, 5) taking intoxicants, 6) singing, dancing, and playing music, 7) using cosmetics, ornaments, or perfumes, 8) sitting on high or expensive seats or beds, 9) handling precious substances or money, and 10) eating at improper times.

Shikshamanas, shramaneras, and shramanerikas are probationary members of the sangha. Because they are learners, not core members, their responsibilities are different from those of the fully ordained. They serve as attendants to their teachers and help in the daily operation of the sangha's activities, for example, by taking care of the prayer hall and classrooms. Through service and by listening to teachings, they prepare to become bhikshus and bhikshunis.

The existence of the sangha is important for the Buddhist community in general, because the sangha is principally responsible for preserving the Dharma so it will be sustained and endure forever. To realize this ideal, we need to establish the operation of monasteries as well as the interpersonal relationships of its members in a constructive way. On that basis, each person's spiritual practice can advance, and the goal of liberation from suffering can be achieved. If monastic operations and sangha relationships are not well established or are forever being debated, much time and energy will be consumed in constant repetitive discussion.

We must maintain a healthy balance between the Dharma and the Vinaya. If they are developed equally, the individual, the community, and the Buddhadharma will grow in a healthy, wholesome manner. If we value the Dharma over the Vinaya, ethical discipline will decline, and the sangha will have a mixture of good and bad members. When the Vinaya is not universally followed, difficulty in the transmission of the Dharma will result. On the other hand, if we value the Vinaya over the Dharma, we will not correctly grasp the essence of our practice. That is, the Vinaya discipline is a preparation for the actual mental transformation that the Dharma brings about. If we focus disproportionately on the preparation, the sangha may become rigid and legalistic in its keeping of the precepts, and neglect the development of concentration and wisdom. Only if the sangha's training is well rounded and completely developed can the Dharma be preserved.

The ultimate purpose of the precepts is the attainment of nirvana, and the temporary purpose is to create a harmonious community facilitating its members' progress along the path. Harmony, as the key to a healthy sangha, has six aspects:

1. Harmony in the body: living together peacefully
2. Harmony in oral communication: avoiding disputes
3. Harmony in the mind: appreciating and supporting each other
4. Harmony in the precepts: observing the same precepts
5. Harmony in views: sharing the same beliefs
6. Harmony in welfare: enjoying benefits equally

While the first three describe harmony, the last three are the essence of equality and make harmony possible. With these six aspects, the sangha's development will be healthy and balanced, and for this reason, we strive to develop them within ourselves.

Becoming a Monastic

When one becomes a monastic, one undergoes many changes marking the difference between living as a monastic and as a layperson:

1. Change in appearance.
2. Change in name: one should be addressed by one's Dharma name.
3. Change in livelihood or occupation.
4. Change in dress: monastics wear robes, the wearing of lay clothes being prohibited.
5. Change in diet: monastics receive their food as alms from others, eat only at allowed times, and should be attentive and aware while eating.
6. Change in lodging: bhikshunis are not allowed to live with bhikshus or with laypeople. They should not sleep alone, nor should they reside in the forest or other dangerous places.
7. Change in responsibility toward the Buddhist community and society: monastics assume the responsibility to improve the Buddhist community and the society in general.

Change in appearance and dress

When we become a nun, we shave our head and abandon wearing makeup, ornaments, perfume, and jewelry. Wearing monastic robes, we avoid the attractive clothing that women usually like. Lacking conscientiousness in this regard can have pitfalls. During the time of the Buddha, Bhikshuni Sthulananda went to a layman's house to visit his wife, who was a good friend of hers. When the bhikshuni arrived, the woman said, "I am very glad to see you, but I was just about to take a bath. Please wait for me." The woman took off her beautiful clothes, rings, necklaces, and earrings, put them on her bed, and went to bathe. While waiting for her friend, Sthulananda suddenly forgot she was ordained. Attracted to her friend's beautiful clothes and jewelry, she thought to put them on for a few minutes just for fun. Then, since she was tired, she laid down on the woman's bed to rest. While she was sleeping, the woman's husband returned home. Opening the door, he thought his beautiful wife was lying on the bed and embraced her. But when he touched her head, he exclaimed, "What! No hair!....Oh no, you are not my wife! You are a nun!" Because he was a Buddhist and respected bhikshunis, the man was upset by what happened. When this incident was brought to the Buddha's attention, he asked the bhikshuni, "Why did you wear a laywoman's dress and lie down on her bed? This is not right." Since the Buddha had already told his disciples not to wear lay clothes, he now set up another precept:

> Prayascittika 115: If a bhikshuni sits or lies down on a couch or bed in a layperson's house, she commits a prayascittika.[3]

Change in livelihood or occupation

A monastic should not work as a servant or be involved in trading or in business. Nor should we tell fortunes or meddle in laypeople's private affairs. Rather we want to use our time for spiritual pursuits and service that benefits others.

> Prayascittika 113: If a bhikshuni works as a servant for lay-people, she commits a prayascittika.

Six bhikshunis worked as servants at a layman's house, cooking and doing the housework. When other laymen saw them, they said, "My wife cooks and cleans for me. Since the bhikshunis do the same work, I don't need to respect them because they are just like my wife." Since women's position in ancient India was inferior to that of men, most men had such an attitude toward their wives. If bhikshunis did the work of laywomen, people would not respect the bhikshuni sangha. The Buddha established this precept because he wanted the public to respect bhikshunis and he did not want bhikshunis to be distracted from their spiritual endeavors by working as servants.

Change in lodging

> Sanghavashesha 7: If a bhikshuni crosses water alone, enters a village alone, sleeps, lives, or walks alone, she commits a sanghavashesha unless she refrains from her misconduct after the first admonition.

For safety reasons, a bhikshuni should not sleep alone, but should sleep in a room with other bhikshunis. Bhikshunis are not allowed to sleep in a room with laypeople, but the reasons for this are different, as will be explained. Nor should they sleep in a room with a bhikshu.

> Prayascittika 4: If a bhikshuni sleeps overnight in the same room with a man, she commits a prayascittika.

The incident triggering this precept concerned a bhikshu, but the precept applies to bhikshunis as well. While walking from Shravasti to Kosala, Bhikshu Aniruddha needed a place to stay the night. Not finding a bhikshu's *vihara*, he asked some local people where he could stay. They told him that a prostitute provided space for travelers under the eaves of her house. Aniruddha went to the woman, obtained permission to stay there overnight, arranged his seat, and began to meditate one-pointedly.

Meanwhile a group of respected citizens from Kosala also asked the woman if they could stay the night. She agreed but told them to ask the monk if that was agreeable to him. It was, so the citizens settled in. However, since there were so many of them, the space became crowded. Seeing this, the woman thought, "Aniruddha came from a wealthy family and is used to comfort. He will not be able to bear such crowded quarters." "Honorable One," she said to Aniruddha, "You can sleep inside," and the monk gratefully moved into the house.

During the night, he sat upright and meditated mindfully. However, twice the woman tried to persuade him to take her for his wife. And twice Aniruddha, without looking at her, rejected her advances by his silence. After the second rejection, she undressed and came to touch him, but using his superhuman powers, he flew into the air. Seeing this, she was ashamed of her behavior, and putting her clothes back on, she repeatedly begged for his forgiveness and asked him to return to his seat. When Aniruddha came down, she bowed to him. He then expounded the Dharma and the various aspects of the path to her, and she attained the first stage of liberation, stream-enterer.

When Aniruddha later returned to the monastery, he mentioned this incident to his fellow practitioners. The pure bhikshus who practice diligently were uneasy about the fact that a monk stayed overnight with a woman and reported this to the Buddha. After verifying the details with Aniruddha, the Buddha explicitly explained the inappropriateness of this conduct to the assembly and established this precept.

> Prayascittika 5: If a bhikshuni sleeps overnight for more than three nights in the same room with a woman who has not received the (full) precepts, she commits a prayascittika.

One day the Buddha gave a Dharma talk to his monastic and lay disciples, and that night all the disciples together slept in a big hall. One bhikshu was careless, and while he slept, turned this way and that, so that his robe opened and the laypeople saw his naked body. They felt embarrassed and mocked the bhikshu. Even though another monk put a cover on the sleeping bhikshu, he kept turning while he slept. Again his body was exposed, and again the laypeople ridiculed him. When the Buddha came to know of this incident, he said that a bhikshu should not sleep in a room with people who are not fully ordained, including shramaneras and upasakas. He wanted to protect the laypeople from embarrassment and the bhikshus from ridicule should a bhikshu accidentally expose himself while sleeping.

Due to another situation, the Buddha later amended this precept. Rahula, the Buddha's son who was at that time a young shramanera, sought a place to sleep with some bhikshus. The bhikshus said that they could not sleep in the same room with a shramanera and asked him to leave. Having nowhere to sleep, the young Rahula went to the washroom and cried. Hearing his sobs, the Buddha came out and took Rahula into his room. The next day, the Buddha scolded the monks for having no compassion and making a young child sleep outside. He then modified the precept so that bhikshus could not sleep in a room with shramaneras more than three nights. Thus, in special cases, when a shramanera has nowhere to sleep, he can sleep in a room with a bhikshu. Although this precept was set up due to an incident concerning a bhikshu, bhikshunis also follow it.

Relationships among Sangha Members

Some of the above precepts concern the relationship between those with full ordination and the junior members of the sangha—shramaneras, shramanerikas, upasakas, and upasikas. Other precepts concern the relationship between monastics and non-Buddhists, and still others the relationship between bhikshus and bhikshunis. While studying the precepts, noting the specific relationships involved in each one will guide us to have suitable interactions with others. We will know how a bhikshuni should behave in situations involving various types of people.

Of the precepts regulating interactions between bhikshus and bhikshunis, the most important are the eight *gurudharma*,[4] which the Buddha asked the first bhikshuni, Mahaprajapati, to accept in order to be ordained. All but two of the gurudharma relate to precepts in the *Bhikshuni Pratimoksha Sutra*. The gurudharma reflect the fact that ancient Indian society viewed women as inferior to men. This is illustrated even by the way laypeople rebuked the bhikshus and bhikshunis when they did not act well. The monks were censured by saying they were acting like kings, high ministers, or Brahmins, while the nuns were criticized by saying they were like cunning women, wives, or prostitutes.[5]

> Gurudharma 1: Even if a bhikshuni has been ordained for a hundred years, she must show respect even to a bhikshu who has just been ordained.[6]

This corresponds to prayascittika 175: When a bhikshuni sees a newly ordained bhikshu, she should rise, pay respect to him, greet him, and ask him to sit down. If she does not, she commits a prayascittika unless she has a particular reason for acting this way.

> Gurudharma 2: A bhikshuni may not slander a bhikshu.

This corresponds to prayascittika 145: If a bhikshuni scolds a bhikshu, she commits a prayascittika.

> Gurudharma 3: A bhikshuni may not raise a bhikshu's offense.

This does not have a corresponding precept.

> Gurudharma 4: A bhikshuni must request ordination from bhikshus.

Prayascittika 139 illustrates this: If a bhikshuni, having already given someone full precepts, waits until the next day to bring her before the bhikshu sangha, she commits a prayascittika.

> Gurudharma 5: When a bhikshuni violates a sanghavashesha, she must undergo *manatta*[7] for half a month. After that, a ceremony of rehabilitation should be held in the presence of both the bhikshu and bhikshuni sangha.

Although this is not in the form of one precept, it is mentioned at the end of the bhikshuni sanghavashesha precepts and applies equally to all of the precepts in that category.

> Gurudharma 6: Bhikshunis should seek teachings from bhikshus every half month.

This corresponds to prayascittika 140: If a healthy bhikshuni does not go to receive instruction (from the bhikshu sangha), she commits a prayascittika. It also relates to prayascittika 141: A bhikshuni should go to the bhikshu sangha every half-month to request instruction. If she does not, she commits a prayascittika.

The bhikshunis at my monastery in Taiwan go to the bhikshu sangha for instruction during the summer retreat. At other times, we collect questions, and when a sufficient number have accumulated, we request bhikshus who are expert in certain areas of the Dharma or the Vinaya for their answers or ideas. In addition, we study with other bhikshunis and professors of Buddhism.

> Gurudharma 7: A bhikshuni may not do the rains retreat in a place where there is no bhikshu.

This is illustrated by prayascittika 143: If a bhikshuni stays the rains retreat in a place where there is no bhikshu, she commits a prayascittika.

> Gurudharma 8: After the rains retreat, bhikshunis should visit bhikshus to report what has been seen, heard, and suspected,[8] and to clarify issues and doubts.

This corresponds to prayascittika 142: At the end of the rains retreat, the bhikshuni sangha should go to the bhikshu sangha to report three things: what has been seen, heard, and suspected. If they do not, they commit a prayascittika.

Other precepts also regulate the interaction between bhikshunis and bhikshus:

> Prayascittika 144: If a bhikshuni, knowing that bhikshus are in a monastery, enters without making an announcement, she commits a prayascittika.

At the time of the Buddha, a learned bhikshuni passed away in Shravasti, and many bhikshunis built a memorial stupa in her honor in a bhikshus' monastery. Bhikshunis would occasionally go to pay their respects at the stupa, and while there, some talked or laughed, while others chanted or cried. These sounds disturbed the bhikshus who were meditating. One day, after the bhikshunis had come and gone, Kapila, a senior monk who liked to meditate, destroyed the stupa and put the remains outside the monastery. Hearing the news, many angry bhikshunis rushed to the monastery and tried to hit that monk with sticks and rocks. However, Kapila, with his superhuman powers, flew into the sky. When hearing about the commotion, the pure bhikshunis who practice diligently reprimanded the other bhikshunis for trying to strike

Kapila. The news spread and came to the Buddha's attention. After examining the story, he made the precept: If a
bhikshuni enters a bhikshus' monastery, she commits a
prayascittika. The precept was later revised several times due
to various situations, until it became the above precept. Here,
"making an announcement" means letting the bhikshus
know that she is entering their monastery.

> Prayascittika 172: If a bhikshuni asks a bhikshu to explain the
> meaning of something without asking his permission first,
> she commits a prayascittika.

Anwen, an intelligent bhikshuni in Shravasti, often asked
Dharma questions to the bhikshus. Not able to answer, many
bhikshus were embarrassed. Hearing this, the pure bhikshunis who practice diligently criticized Anwen, "Why do you
still ask bhikshus questions when you have great wisdom
and can answer them yourself? You embarrass them by pos-
ing questions that they cannot answer." Because of this incident and other similar situations, the Buddha established the
above precept.

> Prayascittika 174: If a bhikshuni builds a stupa in a monas-
> tery where she knows there are bhikshus, she commits a
> prayascittika.

After a learned bhikshuni in Shravasti passed away, other
bhikshunis built a memorial stupa inside a bhikshus' monastery. A guest monk stopped by the monastery, and not
knowing that the stupa belonged to a bhikshuni, he bowed
to it. When hearing this, the pure bhikshunis who practice
diligently reprimanded the bhikshunis who built the stupa,
"How could you build a stupa there, which misleads unknowing monks to bow to it?" Due to this incident, the Buddha established this precept.

> Prayascittika 75: If a bhikshuni gives water to a healthy bhik-
> shu or fans him, she commits a prayascittika.

This incident concerns a married couple who joined the
sangha. One day after alms round, the bhikshu went to the

bhikshunis' temple to have his meal. His former wife, who is now a bhikshuni, offered him water, and because he was sweating, began to fan him. He became upset and said, "You are a dirty woman. Stay away from me." Puzzled, the bhikshuni said, "What happened to you? In the past you liked when I did this for you. Why are you so angry now?" Offended and angry, she hit the bhikshu, her former husband, with the fan and spilled the water over him. When the Buddha heard about this, he created this precept.

Monastics do not live removed from other people. Although our identity and role have changed, we still live with others, and so after ordination we have to redefine our relationships with them. Our previous position, status, and way of relating to others have to change. Because the bhikshu and bhikshuni in this incident had not clarified their relationship and were acting more like husband and wife than like bhikshu and bhikshuni, this disturbance occurred. They must abandon their previous ways of relating to each other and interact according to their new positions as monastics.

Sometimes after a woman who was previously married joins the sangha, her ex-husband asks her to carry out her duties as a wife. We see such cases from time to time in Taiwan. The sangha's senior members have to help resolve this issue. Before ordaining a woman, we must know her background and be sure that she has clarified her relationship with her ex-husband and that he understands this well. In addition, she must learn the role of a bhikshuni—a bhikshuni's responsibilities, work, and relationship with other bhikshunis, bhikshus, shramanerikas, and laypeople.

Women and the Sangha

When the Buddha accepted women into the sangha, he confirmed their ability to attain arhatship and enlightenment. Therefore, nuns are religious practitioners; they are no longer ordinary women under the control of their parents, family, or husband. As female religious practitioners, we have to know our potential, opportunities, and limitations and to act accordingly with dignity and restraint.

The above precept does not imply that bhikshunis do not offer service to bhikshus. On the contrary, when necessary and appropriate, bhikshunis serve the bhikshu sangha. However, we do not do so with a subordinate attitude indicative of low self-esteem. Nor do we serve them because we are their former relatives. We must know to what extent we should serve bhikshus, and when offering service, do so to the whole community, rather than to one or two specific monks.

When the bhikshu sangha needs assistance, they should first ask laypeople or shramaneras for help. Within the monastic community, the junior members usually serve their seniors. In this way, the juniors accumulate merit and have the opportunity to be around those who practice well and whom they can emulate. Such service is not regarded as a burden, but an opportunity.

Many of the limitations regarding women practitioners found in the Vinaya are related to women's position in ancient Indian society. Women were manual laborers, working in the fields and in the house. Their role was in the family, giving birth to children and taking care of the household. They were largely uneducated and dependent on their families economically, emotionally, and so on.

Nowadays women have higher education and wider opportunities. When women further their intelligence and skills, the entire sangha benefits. Female practitioners should not passively wait for others to tell them what to do. We must understand our own potential and capabilities and then act, using our compassion and wisdom.

In ancient times—and even now—women work mainly behind the scenes, and in general, they are more patient and willing to serve. I see these as positive qualities in women. However, nuns should not be limited to being supporters but should also be independent, making decisions and acting as leaders themselves. We should preserve in ourselves the good qualities that women have traditionally had, as well as develop other good qualities that enable us to practice better and benefit more beings.

In former times, people said women were dirty because they menstruate, and women were not allowed to approach a Buddha statue or sit on a Dharma throne to teach when they had their period. Many times women, too, thought themselves incapable because of their body. For example, when I first joined the sangha, another bhikshuni and I had the task of climbing high ladders to hang banners and decorations in the shrine room prior to large Dharma gatherings. Whenever the other bhikshuni had her period, she refused to climb the ladder. One time she told a bhikshu, "I have a bad stomach ache. Please hang the banners for me." The bhikshu did, and gradually, that work became his, and the bhikshunis told themselves, "We aren't supposed to hang the banners." One day this bhikshu got smart and refused to climb the ladder to hang the banners. When that bhikshuni asked him why, he replied, "I have a bad stomach ache."

Bhikshu and bhikshuni precepts are not identical. The creation of many of the bhikshuni precepts was influenced by our biological makeup. For example, women are more vulnerable than men to sexual harassment, assault, and robbery. While the Buddha allowed bhikshus to live under trees, in caves, or in forests, he did not allow bhikshunis to live alone, go out in a village alone, or live outdoors in forests. He did this not because he thought women were incapable, but because he wanted to ensure their safety.

Because men were better educated and ancient Indian society regarded them as leaders, the Buddha required bhikshus to provide teachings and guidance to bhikshunis. While initially one could think that the eight gurudharma indicate that bhikshunis were seen as inferior, from another angle, one sees that the Buddha put responsibility on the bhikshus to aid and support the bhikshuni sangha. The bhikshus are not to ignore bhikshunis, but to help them to actualize the path.

Women tend to be more emotional than men. This may account for the fact that bhikshunis have more sangha-vashesha precepts than bhikshus, and that all of the sangha-vashesha emphasize the necessity of listening to the admonition of other bhikshunis.

The Buddha affirmed women's potential to attain arhatship and therefore accepted them into the sangha. However, the scriptures record him as predicting that having women in the sangha would shorten the existence of the Buddhadharma. Accepting this as true means accepting pre-determination. If we think that it is fate and we cannot change it, then practicing the Dharma becomes senseless. We do not have to do anything because the future is already determined.

In my thinking, having both men and women in the sangha made the situation more complex. Because of that, the Buddha warned us that if we do not practice Dharma with commitment, the existence of the Dharma will be shortened. We must find means to work with this more complex situation so that it will have a positive, not a negative impact on the existence of the Dharma. For this reason, the Buddha affirmed the bhikshus' leadership of the sangha in the gurudharma. For example, bhikshuni ordination is complete only after the new bhikshuni has come to the bhikshu sangha and received ordination from them as well as from the bhikshuni sangha.

In ancient times women were not well educated and lacked the skills to organize and educate themselves and to serve the society. The bhikshu sangha was also new and not well organized. On top of this, if another group—the bhikshuni sangha—was added, it could be difficult to sustain the Dharma. In fact, in the early days, bhikshus found it difficult to organize the bhikshuni sangha and to teach the nuns so many details. For this reason, the Buddha said if women join the sangha the true Dharma will be shortened by five hundred years. His main concern was not women's spiritual capabilities. Rather, he knew that if the interrelationship between the two sanghas was not healthy, the Dharma would be the victim. His warning enables us to be careful and to preserve the Dharma.

Bhikshunis have many talents that they should actively develop. For example, we should teach the Dharma to other bhikshunis, shramanerikas, and the public. In Taiwan many temples are headed by bhikshunis who have a large circle of monastic and lay disciples. In addition, bhikshunis are active in propagating the Dharma, counseling laypeople, publishing Dharma books and magazines, and organizing Dharma events. When bhikshunis are responsible, confident, well organized, and harmonious, I believe bhikshus are also more comfortable.

As stated in the Vinaya, a bhikshuni who becomes a teacher must care for her disciples materially and spiritually, teaching them as well as providing food and lodging for them. If her disciples become sick, she has to see that they receive medical care. Bhikshunis are responsible for their own community affairs, organization, discipline, and activities. Although they seek guidance from bhikshus and may learn the Dharma and Vinaya from them, the two communities function separately.

We have to know our opportunities and potentials, as well as our limitations. Understanding purity and impurity in guarding our precepts is also essential. Similarly, we must differentiate between the fundamental teachings of the Buddhadharma and cultural customs and taboos. Confusing cultural traditions with pratimoksha precepts leads to big problems. To be clear on all these issues, we must continuously study and discuss the teachings.

New nun, just after ordination

CHAPTER FOUR

Joining the Sangha

Maintaining the sangha in this and future generations is important so that the Dharma can be upheld forever in the world. To do this, the present sangha must be nourished, and qualified new members admitted. The quality of the sangha as a whole depends upon the characteristics of its individual members. If the new members are intelligent, open-minded, and sincere, without much difficulty they will evolve into capable bhikshus and bhikshunis who have the responsibility to lead the sangha and to teach and guide junior sangha members and Buddhist followers. Thus, ordination is the first checkpoint for the quality of the sangha. The topic of regulations for joining the sangha has three sections:

1. The applicants should be eligible
2. The preceptor should be qualified
3. The bhikshunis' ordination procedure should be legal

The Applicants Should Be Eligible

By screening applicants, the sangha helps an individual discern if monastic ordination will be beneficial for her spiritual progress. In addition, screening applicants ensures that people who understand the purpose of precepts and monastic life will be welcome new participants in the sangha. In this way, the sangha can guide its own development. For these reasons, the Vinaya speaks of various obstacles that inhibit joining the sangha. These are listed as the thirteen major hindrances, the sixteen minor hindrances, and additional hindrances for women requesting ordination.

The thirteen major and the sixteen minor hindrances are the same for bhikshus and bhikshunis. Those who have any of the thirteen major hindrances are not permitted to be ordained in this life. Those who have any of the minor hindrances are not allowed to be ordained as long as that hindrance exists. When the minor hindrance ceases, he or she can be ordained in this life. According to the list of thirteen major hindrances, the following are not allowed to ordain in this life:

1. Those who have committed a parajika
2. Those who have sexually violated a bhikshu or bhikshuni
3. Those whose intention is for personal benefit or to "steal" the Dharma

   Once, during the Buddha's time, the populace suffered from a severe famine. Nevertheless, the Buddha and bhikshus still managed to receive food when they went for alms. Seeing this, one man thought, "Being a sangha member is good for getting lots of food," so he put on robes and shaved his head by himself. Taking a bowl and going for alms, he met a bhikshu on the way who asked him his Dharma name. The man replied that he did not know. When the bhikshu asked him who his preceptor was, he could not respond to that either, nor could he say when and where he was ordained. It became clear that he was "stealing" the appearance of a monastic and using the Dharma for his own personal benefit. After this event, the Buddha set up this regulation.

4. Those who had joined the sangha but later left to join another religion

During the Buddha's time, a non-Buddhist practitioner named Busa challenged any disciple of the Buddha to debate with him. Shariputra, who excelled in debate, accepted and responded quickly and easily to the five hundred questions that Busa asked. However, unable to respond to Shariputra's questions to him, Busa thought, "The disciples of the Buddha are very intelligent. I want to be a bhikshu." Going to a temple to seek ordination, he met a bhikshu named Ballanta. Thinking that Ballanta was more intelligent than Shariputra, he asked Ballanta to accept him as his disciple, which he did. However, later when Ballanta was unable to answer some of Busa's questions, Busa became upset and quit the sangha to join another religion. Due to this event, the Buddha said that before someone from another religion joins the sangha, he or she has to live with the sangha for four months first.

Then, someone from another religion came to join the sangha, and after living with the sangha for four months, he became a bhikshu. When Busa heard this, he changed his mind again and said, "Maybe all the sangha members are intelligent, so I want to be a bhikshu again." Because Busa's refuge was unstable, the Buddha said that those who join the sangha and later convert to another religion are not allowed to be ordained again in this life. The point of this regulation is to ensure that applicants have firm belief in the Three Jewels and a strong determination to be a Buddhist monastic.

5. Those who are eunuchs, that is, their sex organs have been removed

6. Those who have committed patricide

7. Those who have committed matricide

A man who practiced in a non-Buddhist group intentionally killed his father. (In another, similar case, a non-Buddhist intentionally killed his mother.) Troubled and ashamed of his evil deed, he looked for someone to remove his sense of guilt and thought, "Since the monastics following the Buddha practice virtuous deeds, my becoming a bhikshu may get rid of my evil karma." When he asked to be ordained, the Buddha said that those who have committed heinous actions such as killing their father or mother cannot develop and benefit from the Buddhadharma as a monastic member. Such a person can still learn and practice the Buddhadharma, but due to his heavy karmic obscuration, he is not suitable to be a monastic in that lifetime.

8. Those who have killed an arhat

9. Those who have ruined the harmony of the sangha by causing schism

10. Those who have shed the Buddha's blood

11. Those who are non-human beings

12. Those who are animals

13. Those who are hermaphrodites, that is, they have both male and female organs

    The reason for not ordaining hermaphrodites is a practical one: if they were ordained, would they receive the bhikshu or the bhikshuni vow? Would they live with the bhikshu sangha or the bhikshuni sangha? Because of this difficulty, they are not allowed to become monastics in this life. However, anyone possessing any of the thirteen hindrances can learn and practice the Dharma and will benefit from doing so.

From the thirteen major hindrances, four main points emerge:

1. The person's intention to become a bhikshu or bhikshuni must be pure. Ordination should not be taken for personal, worldly benefit, for choosing an intelligent preceptor, or for getting rid of one's sense of guilt arising from a brutal and merciless action. One's intention should be to attain liberation from cyclic existence.

2. The person's gender must be specific. If the sex organs have been removed or if both male and female organs are present, it is difficult to decide whether that person would be a bhikshu or a bhikshuni.

3. The person must not have done a serious negative action, such as committing a parajika, sexually violating a bhikshu or bhikshuni, killing an arhat, creating schism, shedding the Buddha's blood, and so forth.

4. The person must be able to practice the Buddhadharma properly and receive its benefit. Animals and non-human beings, such as *nagas*, cannot do this. In addition, the person must be mentally and physically healthy in order to keep up with the rigors of ordained life.

Those who have any of the sixteen minor hindrances are not allowed to be ordained until the hindrances no longer exist. These sixteen are:

1. Being a slave

Slavery is prohibited now, but at the time of the Buddha, society accepted it. A slave once joined the sangha to escape his bondage. One day on his way for alms, he met his former master. Grabbing him, the master cried, "You are my slave. How can you be a bhikshu?" The bhikshu tried to escape, but the master held him tightly. Many people gathered around, and some told the master, "You must free the bhikshu because King Bimbisara said that everyone must support the sangha. If you hold onto him, you will be punished." Although the master freed the bhikshu, he was very angry and exclaimed, "All the sangha members are slaves! All of them want to escape their obligations." To prevent the recurrence of such a scene, the Buddha set up this regulation.

2. Being a thief

This requirement for ordination is directly mentioned in the *Bhikshuni Pratimoksha Sutra* and a bhikshuni who ordains a thief commits an offense.

Sanghavashesha 5: If a bhikshuni, knowing that a woman is a thief and is known to have committed a crime punishable by death, without consulting the king or a high official and without inquiring about the woman's family background, ordains her and allows her to receive full precepts, that bhikshuni commits a sanghavashesha unless she refrains from her misconduct after the first admonition.

Many women, wearing their fine ornaments, attended a special event in Vaishali. A thief stole many of their jewels and escaped to a neighboring land. Hiding in a temple, she shaved her head, donned robes, and was ordained as a bhikshuni. Since King Bimbisara had prohibited the arrest and trial of bhikshus and bhikshunis by the civil government, when the police found her the king simply scolded her, "You are a thief and a prostitute. You are ignorant." The citizens did not consider this treatment just, and angrily accused the sangha, saying, "All the bhikshunis are criminals who hide in the sangha." From that time on, they did not respect the sangha, refused to support them, and gave up listening to the Buddhadharma. In this case, who do you think should be reprimanded, the person who ordained the thief or the thief herself? Even nowadays sometimes criminals seeking to hide their illegal financial dealings escape to another country and request ordination. A preceptor who does not implement his or her responsibility to examine the applicant properly errs. A criminal must serve his or her sentence first. Only when her obligation, sentence, or social responsibility has been fulfilled can she join the sangha.

3. Being in debt

This too is designed to prevent people from joining the sangha in order to avoid their responsibilities in society. The *Bhikshuni Pratimoksha Sutra* says that a bhikshuni who gives the full precepts to someone in debt commits an offense.

Prayascittika 168: If a bhikshuni gives the full precepts to someone who is in difficulties due to sickness or debt, she commits a prayascittika.

4. Being under the age of twenty

Some young boys who became bhikshus cried at night because they were hungry, awakening the Buddha and other monks. Since those under twenty are not able to endure cold, heat, hunger, thirst, and discomfort due to insects, the Buddha said they should not be fully ordained. In addition, young people are not mature enough to understand serious instructions.

5. Having scabies

6. Having ringworm

7. Having a carbuncle

8. Being afflicted with a disease that makes one emaciated

9. Being mentally deranged

At the Buddha's time, these five illnesses—scabies, ringworm, carbuncles, emaciation, and mental imbalance—were common in Magadha. Some people suffering from them went to see the famous doctor Jivaka, but since Jivaka had promised to attend ill sangha members, he asked them to wait. The sick people discussed amongst themselves, "The sangha receives good food, good beds, and Jivaka treats them for illness. Let's become bhikshus too." They joined the sangha, but when they recovered from their illnesses, they disrobed and returned to their families. On the way, they met Jivaka, who queried, "Aren't you the bhikshus I treated?" These people explained the situation to him, and Jivaka was very upset. After he told the Buddha about it, the Buddha stipulated that anyone suffering from one of these five diseases cannot be ordained until he or she recovers. The particular diseases are not important; in general, a very ill person should not be ordained until he or she recovers. This regulation is not meant to deny treatment to the ill. Rather it emphasizes that one should have a pure motivation in joining the sangha.

10. Not having obtained permission from one's parents

The Buddha accepted Rahula, his own son, as a shramanera. Afterwards, the Buddha's father was sad and said,

"Before ordaining someone, you should obtain permission from their family." The Buddha agreed that because parents' affection for their son or daughter is very deep, having their permission before ordination is given is wise.

Prayascittika 134: If a bhikshuni fully ordains a woman in spite of the opposition of the latter's parents or husband, she commits a prayascittika.

After the Buddha gave bhikshunis permission to ordain new renunciants, a bhikshuni ordained some women who had not obtained the permission of their parents or husband. As a result, after they were ordained, their families came to take them back home. The pure bhikshunis who practice diligently criticized this bhikshuni's action, and in response, the Buddha established this precept.

11. Being a royal servant

Since royal servants—be they in the military or civil service—are needed by the government, especially at times of crisis, they cannot be ordained until their term of duty has finished.

12. Not having a bowl and robes, or having a bowl and robes that are borrowed

One man who wanted to ordain did not have robes or a bowl, so he borrowed them from a bhikshu. After ordination, the owner of the robes asked that they be returned, and consequently the new bhikshu sat naked on the side of the road. Because laypeople complained, the Buddha set up this regulation.

13. Motivated by defilement, refusing to say one's own name during the ordination ceremony

14. Motivated by defilement, refusing to say the name of one's preceptor during the ordination ceremony

15. Motivated by defilement, refusing to request ordination

These three regulations came about due to the insincerity of some applicants. Dominated by arrogance, they refused to answer even simple questions or to say that they wanted to be monastics, even at the time of the ordination ceremony.

16. Wearing the clothes of laypeople or of people from other religions, or wearing ornaments

The sixteen minor hindrances can be summarized in five points:

1. Before joining the sangha, one should deal clearly with his or her relationship with society. Someone should not join the sangha to avoid her responsibilities. For example, someone who is a slave, thief, debtor, or royal servant cannot join the sangha until her duties have been fulfilled. Also, before joining the sangha, a candidate should communicate with her family and have their consent.

2. One should be sincere in learning the Dharma and the Vinaya. At the time of receiving ordination, a sincere candidate will not refuse to say her own name or the name of her preceptor, nor will she refuse to request ordination.

3. One's garments must be sufficient; that is, one has robes and a bowl.

4. One's intention to ordain is pure. One is not ordaining to get free medical treatment, food, and so forth.

5. One is mature enough—that is, over twenty years old—to endure the monastic life style.

Nine additional hindrances apply to women who seek ordination and correspond to precepts in the bhikshuni pratimoksha. The following may not ordain:

1. Those who are pregnant

> Prayascittika 119: If a bhikshuni, knowing a woman is pregnant, gives her the full precepts, she commits a prayascittika.

Pregnant at the time of ordination, a woman was a bhikshuni when she gave birth. She carried the baby with her when she went for alms, and the laypeople were shocked, "This bhikshuni had sexual relations and has a baby!" After that, the Buddha said those who are pregnant cannot ordain.

2. Those who are breast-feeding their babies

Prayascittika 120: If a bhikshuni, knowing a woman has a nursing child, gives her the full precepts, she commits a prayascittika.

If a woman is nursing her baby, she should take care of the child first. The Buddha insisted that applicants fulfill their social and individual responsibilities before being ordained. Once those are fulfilled, sincere people are then free to commit themselves to spiritual practice. The Buddha also was concerned with the image of the sangha, and thus its members should be mature and responsible in their behavior.

3. Those who have not learned and practiced the six regulation of a shikshamana for two years

To ensure that candidates for bhikshuni ordination are mature and are not pregnant, they must first keep the shikshamana precepts purely for two years. The six shikshamana precepts are to abandon sexual conduct, stealing, killing, lying, taking intoxicants, and eating at unregulated hours.[1]

Prayascittika 122: If a bhikshuni does not give the two years training (i.e. the shikshamana precepts) to an eighteen-year-old virgin but gives her the full ordination when she is twenty years old, she commits a prayascittika.

Prayascittika 123: If a bhikshuni teaches the discipline to a woman over eighteen, but does not give her the six regulations and then, when she is twenty years old, gives her the full precepts, she commits a prayascittika.

In the latter case, the bhikshuni thought that because the candidate was already twenty, it was sufficient for her to learn the discipline, i.e. to learn Vinaya in general, but it was not necessary for her to keep the six regulations of a shikshamana for two years before becoming a bhikshuni. The Buddha, however, said that this is necessary.

4. Unmarried women under the age of twenty or those who have been married but are under the age of twelve.

Prayascittika 121: If a bhikshuni, knowing a woman is under twenty years old, gives her the full precepts, she commits a prayascittika.

Prayascittika 125: If a ten-year-old girl who has been married has had two years of training in the precepts, a bhikshuni can give her the full precepts when she is twelve years old. If she gives her the precepts when she is younger than twelve, she commits a prayascittika.

I have not come across an explanation of why the Buddha allowed a twelve-year-old married girl to become a bhikshuni, but only allowed an unmarried girl to do so when she was twenty.

5. Prostitutes

Prayascittika 127: If a bhikshuni gives the full precepts to someone she knows to be a prostitute, she commits a prayascittika.

Once a prostitute ordained, and when going for alms, she encountered a man who called out, "There's the woman who had sex with me." Naturally, the bhikshuni was very embarrassed. The Buddha then said that when someone who used to be a prostitute ordains, she should live far away from the place where she worked before.

6. Those who do not have permission from their husbands

Prayascittika 134: If a bhikshuni gives the full precepts to a woman despite the disapproval of the woman's parents, husband or guardian, she commits a prayascittika.

The reason for this was explained above.

7. Those who are in love with a man and are prone to melancholy and resentment

Prayascittika 135: If a bhikshuni knows a woman is in love with a boy or man and prone to depression or resentment, yet allows her to leave the household life and gives her the full precepts, she commits a prayascittika.

If a girl who is in love wants to be ordained, she should wait until her emotions have settled. When she is in a calmer and more balanced state of mind, she will be able to consider her decision more carefully.

8. Those who lose control of the discharge of urine and excrement

Prayascittika 165: If a bhikshuni gives the full precepts to a woman whom she knows often loses control of the discharge of urine or feces, or of mucus from the nose and of saliva, she commits a prayascittika.

If a bhikshuni has lost control over these bodily functions, she will unavoidably dirty the places she goes, thus upsetting others.

9. Those who have the same outlet for both urine and excrement

Prayascittika 167: If a bhikshuni gives the full precepts to someone whom she knows discharges urine and excrement from one orifice, she commits a prayascittika.

This deformity happened after a woman had a baby. Today, the condition could be medically remedied.

The Importance of Proper Screening and Preparation

The two-year period of a shikshamana tests if a woman is pregnant. In ancient times no medical means were available to test for pregnancy, so they simply had to wait. Although she may have become pregnant before receiving ordination, if a bhikshuni gives birth, the image of the sangha is damaged because people will think she broke her precepts. I believe the two-year period as a shikshamana addresses other concerns as well. Before making a lifelong commitment, an applicant needs time to consider if monastic life is what she really wants. These two years enable her to examine and reflect, "How do the nuns live? Is this life style suitable for me?" Knowing this, she will be able to make a wise decision.

In our monastery, young women go through various examinations before they are permitted to join the sangha. I ask them, "What kind of person do you want to be in thirty years' time? Do you want to become like me? Like your mother? What qualities do you want to develop?" Although the Buddha often said that life is short, nevertheless trying to imagine one's life thirty years from now can be helpful. By doing this, an applicant will become clear regarding her direction and the actions she must take to accomplish her goals. She will determine if she is serious about making a lifetime commitment as a bhikshuni by examining deeply, "Can I remain celibate for the rest of my life? Can I live without an intimate emotional relationship? Can I sustain this kind of solitude?" In addition, an applicant must consider how she can serve the sangha community as well as society as a whole. Thinking seriously about such topics before being ordained will prevent obstacles arising afterwards.

Studying the requirements for ordination, we see the Buddha's concern and compassion for each member of the sangha. He wanted people to be happy and safe as sangha members. For example, every so often, the Buddha would walk around the monastery to inspect the living quarters. One day, from far away, he smelled something terrible, and in a room he discovered a very sick bhikshu lying in his own excrement. "What happened?" the Buddha asked. The bhikshu responded, "I am very sick and cannot take care of myself." "Why don't other bhikshus take care of you?" The bhikshu replied, "When I was healthy I never paid attention to my fellow practitioners. Now when I'm sick, no one cares about me." The Buddha then set up a precept saying that we have to take care of each other. When a bhikshuni has a problem or becomes sick or old, we must take care of her.

However, if we do not properly screen prospective members and allow many elderly or ill people to join the sangha, who will take care of them? In Taiwan, some old people seek ordination but lack the proper motivation. They want to live in a quiet place, be financially supported, and have someone take care of them in their old age. While their wishes are understandable and the sangha wants them to be happy, being ordained for these reasons is not appropriate. The focus of the monastery would shift from learning and practicing the Dharma to being a nursing facility. The old and sick need care, but the monastery is not the appropriate place for the care they need. Their needs, as well as those of the sangha, are better met if these people are directed toward appropriate facilities. For these reasons, the bhikshuni in charge of examining applicants must be very sagacious. Once we accept someone into the sangha, we assume the responsibility to teach and take care of her.

Some masters express their kindness and compassion by receiving everyone into the sangha. However, most Chinese masters have concluded that the quality of monastics is more important than their quantity. If the sangha does not screen applicants carefully, the devoted, talented monastics will spend most of their time taking care of the elderly, ill, and handicapped and little time will remain for them to practice and teach the Dharma. If we really care about the old and infirm, we will let them remain laypeople and establish a nursing facility with the professional help they require. This is more efficacious than allowing them to join the sangha and does not adversely affect their spiritual development. Individuals who join the sangha should be mentally and physically healthy, as well as emotionally mature.

If we know that an applicant to become a shramanerika or bhikshuni is mentally unstable, we have the responsibility to tell the preceptor who is considering ordaining this person. Doing so demonstrates our concern for that individual as well as for the community and the public.

The entire assembly should know the procedure for screening applicants. A teacher is responsible for teaching the students, enabling them to practice the Dharma, liberate themselves, teach the Dharma to others, and serve society.

In this way, the Dharma will be sustained. Although we may feel sad refusing ordination to those who are not qualified, we must be clear. Of course, we do not want to discourage these people from learning or practicing the Dharma. However, we do want to preserve the purpose and function of the sangha, and therefore paying close attention to the screening of applicants is essential.

The Preceptor Should Be Qualified

Several precepts either directly describe or indirectly correspond to the qualities of a preceptor. A qualified preceptor is:

1. One who does not accept too many disciples, who teaches her disciples the discipline for two years, and who takes care of her disciples by providing Dharma teachings, food, clothing, and medicine

   Prayascittika 128: If a bhikshuni ordains many disciples, yet does not teach them for two years or provide them with the two things (Dharma and the requisites[2]), she commits a prayascittika.

   Although Bhikshuni Anwen accepted many disciples, she did not teach them. As a result, they did not know the way to wear their robes or to eat properly, and they lacked good manners. Therefore, the Buddha said that when a bhikshuni accepts a disciple, she must teach her the Dharma and support her with food, clothing, lodging, and medicine.

2. One who instructs her disciples to follow the *bhikshuni-upadhyayini* (preceptor) for two years after being ordained

   Prayascittika 129: If a bhikshuni does not follow her bhikshuni-upadhyayini for two years (after being ordained), she commits a prayascittika.

   After being ordained, some new bhikshunis left their preceptors, and no one taught them. Thus they did not practice or behave well. For that reason, the Buddha said that for two years after ordination, a bhikshuni should follow her bhikshuni-upadhyayini, or preceptor, who should teach her conscientiously.

3. One who is permitted by the sangha to give full ordination

Prayascittika 130: If a bhikshuni gives the full precepts to someone despite the disapproval of the sangha, she commits a prayascittika.

Prayascittika 132: If a bhikshuni has been ordained twelve years and gives the full precepts despite the disapproval of the sangha, she commits a prayascittika.

4. One who has been ordained for at least twelve years

Prayascittika 131: If a bhikshuni gives the full precepts before she has been a bhikshuni for twelve years, she commits a prayascittika.

The preceptor should be experienced, wise, stable, and capable of training a disciple. Such qualities are developed by observing the precepts for many years oneself.

5. One who, being prohibited by the sangha to ordain others, does not say, "The sangha are filled with partiality, hatred, fear, and ignorance"

Prayascittika 133: If a bhikshuni has been prohibited by the sangha from giving the full precepts and says, "Partiality, hatred, fear, and ignorance exist in the sangha. If they like something, they approve it; if they do not like something, they do not," she commits a prayascittika.

The sangha checks the eligibility of the applicants as well as the qualifications of a preceptor. The sangha community, not one individual, ordains a disciple, thus only the sangha has the authority to determine who is suitable to be ordained. If the entire sangha community does not accept a certain candidate and only the preceptor does, what will happen? How can the applicant learn in the future? For this reason, a bhikshuni may not ordain someone without the approval of the sangha.

6. One who has ordained someone more than a year after having ordained another

Prayascittika 138: If a bhikshuni fully ordains someone less than a year (after ordaining someone else), she commits a prayascittika.

Bhikshuni Anwen accepted so many disciples that she could not give them individual guidance or teach them well. As a result, they did not behave well. Thus the Buddha set up this precept.

The Bhikshunis' Ordination Procedure Should Be Legal

Volume 27 of the Vinaya Pitaka describes the ordination procedure in detail. The bhikshunis' ordination procedure is somewhat different from that of the bhikshus, and for an ordination ceremony to be performed properly, the following characteristics must be present:

1. The candidate should obtain permission from her teacher; the teacher should inform the assembly that she wishes to accept the applicant as a monastic disciple; and the assembly should agree.
2. The candidate should have received the shramanerika precepts.
3. The candidate should have trained in the six regulations of a shikshamana for two years.
4. The full ordination should be given by both bhikshu and bhikshuni sanghas.

Prayascittika 139: If a bhikshuni, having already given someone full precepts, waits until the next day to bring her before the bhikshu sangha, she commits a prayascittika.

Points 3 and 4 do not pertain to bhikshus. To be ordained as a bhikshu, a man does not need to train in the six regulations for two years, and a novice monk is given full ordination by only the bhikshu sangha. To become a bhikshuni, one should gradually receive the various levels of precepts, becoming an upasika (a laywoman holding the five precepts), a shramanerika, a shikshamana, and then a bhikshuni.

5. The candidate must be questioned about both the major and minor hindrances.
6. The formal act (karma) of ordination consisting of an announcement and a proclamation repeated three times in the assembly should have been passed.
7. The candidate should be asked if she can observe the precepts.
8. The method of procuring and using the four resources necessary for living—food, clothing, lodging, and medicine—should be explained to the candidate.
9. The ordination procedure, including the general features of the bhikshuni precepts, should be explained to the candidate.

The ordination ceremony is not done secretly. Rather, the preceptor will publicly invite the sangha to examine the qualifications of the applicant. Once the sangha approves of an applicant, the sangha as a whole accepts her as a new member.

The final process of making a bhikshuni ordination official depends on the bhikshu sangha. It is there that the actual giving and receiving of the precepts is completed. In general, both the bhikshu and bhikshuni sanghas granting ordination come from the same Vinaya lineage. However, in the future, they may be from different lineages. In that case, they should agree beforehand which version of the bhikshuni precepts the new bhikshunis will receive.

Our preceptor must be someone who is alive at the time of our ordination. Although an applicant may prefer to choose the Buddha or Mahaprajapati as her ordination preceptor, this is not permitted. The preceptor should have the ability to judge if the person is acceptable as a sangha member. In addition, the preceptor must be able to provide teachings, guidance, and care so that the disciple will progress. A trusting relationship between the preceptor and the disciple is important. Such conditions can only be met by a living preceptor.

A bhikshuni should not promise to ordain someone and then neglect to do so. Once a candidate is eligible and has been properly trained in preparation for bhikshuni ordination, the preceptor should make the necessary arrangements for her ordination.

> Prayascittika 136: If a bhikshuni says to a shikshamana, "Younger Sister, renounce this and study that, and I will give you the full precepts," and then does not use expedient means to give her the full precepts, she commits a prayascittika.

> Prayascittika 137: If a bhikshuni says to a shikshamana, "Bring a robe and give it to me, and I will give you the full precepts," and then does not use expedient means to give her the full precepts, she commits a prayascittika.

The three conditions for joining the sangha explained in this chapter are important. Applicants must be mentally sound and physically healthy; the preceptor should be qualified; and the ordination procedure should be properly done. If all of these circumstances are complete, the Dharma can be preserved forever.

Shramanerika Ordination

Shramanerikas are ordained by bhikshunis. At least two bhikshunis are needed to perform this ceremony. The preceptor must be a bhikshuni for at least twelve years, and the instructor must be one for a minimum of five years.

Sometimes lay women ask me how to prepare for ordination. Most important is to cultivate the proper motivation. Reflect on the Four Noble Truths and the disadvantages of cyclic existence. See that the causes for suffering and the causes for happiness are both created by the mind, and make a determination to abandon the former and create the latter in order to attain liberation. Engaging in practices such as prostrations, making offerings, reciting mantras, and reading the sutras is helpful for purifying the mind and creating positive potential to be ordained. If you have any of the minor hindrances to ordination, do what is necessary to clear them up. Also, be prepared for the questions and doubts your friends and family may pose: "Why do you want to become a nun? Will we still be able to see you, or are you leaving the family forever? What will you do after you are ordained?" In this way, think about and prepare for ordination from many angles.

After ordination, shramaneras and shramanerikas in the Chinese community study *A Brief Introduction to Shramanera Precepts and Manners*, a text written by a master during the Ming Dynasty. Consisting of twenty-four chapters, it describes proper behavior for novices and deals with topics such as living in a community, entering the meditation hall, travelling, writing letters, and speaking with others. If a monastic is busy offering service to the temple and has little time to study the Vinaya, she should learn this text well. In this way, she will know suitable monastic behavior and appropriate ways to interact with others in the Buddhist community. To illustrate its importance, the shramanerikas at my monastery recite their precepts and this text when they meet together on poshadha days.

CHAPTER FIVE

Poshadha: Purifying and Restoring Our Precepts

Poshadha is the ritual for purification and restoration of precepts that the sangha does every half-month. Although the recitation of the *Pratimoksha Sutra* and the precepts is the central part of poshadha, the ceremony also involves confessing our wrongdoings and helping others by pointing out theirs. A bhikshuni who has seen, heard, or suspected a wrongdoing can bring it up for discussion at this time.

Since the precepts of bhikshus and bhikshunis are not the same, they conduct their poshadha ceremonies separately. A bhikshuni does not confess to a bhikshu. Many women's issues cannot be mentioned to or dealt with by men, and the bhikshunis handle these themselves. A bhikshuni who committed a sanghavashesha offense does the ceremony of rehabilitation (*abbhana*) after manatta in the presence of both the bhikshu and bhikshuni sanghas to get rid of the delinquency of her mistake. However, she does not reveal the details of the wrongdoing to the bhikshus.

Similarly, bhikshunis should examine the qualifications and preparation of applicants to the bhikshuni sangha. A bhikshu cannot do this well. Bhikshunis are responsible for observing the candidates closely, checking their motivation, seeing if they are overly dependent or independent, and determine if they will be able to adapt to the community's life style. Bhikshunis must teach other bhikshunis and guide women practitioners, both lay and ordained. We need the bhikshus' instructions and teachings on the Dharma and the Vinaya, but we must manage our own community affairs as well as teach and guide future generations of bhikshunis and women practitioners.

While everyone may study the *Pratimoksha Sutra*, those who are not fully ordained cannot participate in poshadha. The sangha's affairs should be determined by the sangha themselves. It is not suitable for those who are not fully ordained to listen. Thus, shramanerikas and laypeople are not permitted to attend poshadha. Depending on the type of offense committed, a shramanerika should confess her transgressions to a group of bhikshunis, to an individual bhikshuni, or to herself. A ceremony which is a similitude of poshadha exists for shramanerikas. In our monastery in Taiwan, shramanerikas meet as a group with a bhikshuni to confess and review their precepts. In the Tibetan tradition, shramanerikas now attend parts of the bhikshus' ceremony and confess to them. In the future, if a bhikshuni sangha is nearby, those shramanerikas could attend part of the bhikshunis' ceremony and declare their purity to the bhikshunis. A shramanerika who lives alone should do self-examination, confess any wrongdoings, and recite her precepts by herself every half-month.

After receiving precepts, we should safeguard them as best as we can as well as learn the methods for purifying them. By developing our conscientiousness, mindfulness, and introspective alertness concerning the precepts, our Dharma practice will progress well.

The Buddha emphasized poshadha as the principal way to maintain the purity of the sangha, and thus required every qualified sangha member to attend. Mahakashyapa, one of the Buddha's most famous disciples, spent most of his time meditating in a cave alone. Although he seldom went out to join the monastic community, the Buddha required him to participate in poshadha every half-month.

Nowadays, bhikshunis from various Vinaya schools are in contact with each other. Because the precepts as found in each school were set up by the Buddha, hard and fast distinctions among the Vinaya schools is lacking. No matter in which Vinaya school a woman's ordination occurs, she becomes a bhikshuni and can do poshadha together with bhikshunis from any other school.

Many bhikshus and bhikshunis recite the precepts as part of their daily practice. If a bhikshuni lives alone in a city or the countryside, she should try to find other bhikshunis with whom she can do poshadha on new and full moon days. Otherwise, she can confess any wrongdoings and read the *Pratimoksha Sutra* herself. Many of the precepts are violated only in a community setting, and those who live alone are sometimes not sure if they have violated them. For that reason, meeting and discussing with other bhikshunis whenever possible is helpful for refining their understanding of the Vinaya.

Because of the lack of nuns' communities in Western countries, many Western bhikshunis live on their own. They are very courageous pioneers. They should teach students and gradually form a bhikshuni community and do poshadha together.

Two people are appointed by the assembly to perform specific roles during poshadha. One is the reciter, the bhikshuni who recites the *Bhikshuni Pratimoksha Sutra* while her sisters in the assembly listen and reflect upon it. The other is the respondent, another bhikshuni who responds on behalf of the assembly to questions the reciter asks. Sometimes the reciter will ask a question and everyone in the assembly answers by remaining silent to indicate their consent.

To prevent the sangha from transgression, the poshadha must be held within a boundary set up by the sangha before beginning the recitation of the sutra.[1] The bhikshunis confess their wrongdoings and praise the Buddha. Then, the recitation of the sutra begins. The *Bhikshuni Pratimoksha Sutra* has three sections:

1. The introduction: homage and preparatory motions
2. The body of the precepts: listing of the precepts
3. The conclusion: dedication and final encouragement

In this chapter, we will discuss the introduction and the conclusion. Since the body of the precepts is lengthy, it will be discussed in the upcoming chapters.

The Introduction

The introduction has two sections:

1. Showing the importance of the pratimoksha
2. Convening the assembly before the actual recitation of the precepts

The first part of the introduction—showing the importance of the pratimoksha—consists of verses added by Dharmagupta, the founder of this school. This too has several sections:

1. Praising, paying homage to the refuge, and stating the purpose of poshadha

This is done in the first verse:

> I prostrate and pay respect
> To all the Buddhas, the Dharma, and the Sangha.
> I will now proclaim the regulations (dharma) of the
>   Vinaya
> So that the correct Dharma will last forever.[2]

2. Characterizing the benefits of having precepts and
   encouraging the assembly to observe them

The only purpose for reciting and learning the pratimoksha
is to enable the true Dharma to abide forever. This expressed
in the second verse:

> The precepts are as limitless as the ocean,
> Like jewels that can be sought tirelessly.
> In order to protect the sacred treasure of the
>   Dharma,
> The assembly is gathered to listen to me.

3. Being free from wrongdoing by observing the precepts

> In order to eliminate the eight parajika,
> The (seventeen) sanghavashesha,
> And the thirty obstructing *nuihsargika-payattika,*[3]
> The assembly is gathered to listen to me.

In the beginning we pay homage to the Three Jewels. The
"dharma" in the Vinaya refers to the regulations in the
Vinaya: the eight parajika, the seventeen sanghavashesha,
and the precepts in the other categories. These came from
the seven Buddhas, as expressed by the following verse.

4. The lineage of the teachings

> Vipashyin, Shikhin, Vishvabhu,
> Krakucchanda, Kanakamuni,
> Kashyapa, and Shakyamuni–
> All these World Honored Ones of great virtue
> Taught this *(Pratimoksha Sutra)* to me.
> I now wish to proclaim it well.
> All you worthy ones listen together.

The first three Buddhas listed here lived in the previous eon,
the Glorious Eon. The next four are the first four Buddhas of

this fortunate eon, the *Bhadra* Eon, in which one thousand Buddhas will appear. These seven Buddhas established precepts so that the Dharma would abide for a long time, thus allowing many sentient beings to benefit from it. These seven Buddhas are mentioned again at the end of the *Pratimoksha Sutra* when their particular precepts are quoted.

5. *The advantages and disadvantages of living and not living in accord with the precepts*

Just as a person whose leg is injured
Is unable to walk,
Similarly those who have broken the precepts
Cannot be born as a god or a human.

Those who wish to be born in the heavens
Or in the human world,
Should always protect all the precepts,
And not violate them in any way.

If the precepts are observed well, many advantages accrue, such as a good rebirth, liberation, and enlightenment. Master Dharmagupta illustrates the importance of the Vinaya through many examples. The first is that precepts are like our feet. Just as our feet carry us forward, ethical discipline is the foundation upon which our Dharma practice can progress. As the first of the Three Higher Trainings, it acts as the basis for the other two: concentration and wisdom. In addition, we need mutually agreed-upon rules in order to live harmoniously with others. Just as we learn the rules of a game in order to play it properly and get along with other players, we learn the precepts of monastic life in order to derive benefit from it and live peacefully with other monastics. Thus, precepts are important not only for our individual liberation, but also for community harmony because they guide our interactions with others and give structure to community life.

6. Warning about dangerous times

Just as a chariot, which enters a treacherous road,
Suddenly breaks its axle and loses its linchpin,
Similarly one who has broken the precepts
Is afraid at the time of death.

Without its axle, a vehicle cannot be held together, let alone move forward. Similarly, if we neglect to keep our precepts, our Dharma practice cannot progress.

7. Words for normal times

Just as when looking in a mirror
The beautiful feel happy,
While the ugly feel sad,
Similarly during the recitation of the Pratimoksha,
Those who keep the precepts feel happy,
While violators feel sad.

8. Summarizing the results of observing or not observing the precepts

Just as when two armies fight together,
The brave advance while the cowardly retreat,
Similarly during the recitation of the Pratimoksha,
The pure are serene,
While the defiled are afraid.

While the brave advance in a battle, we similarly advance to peace and happiness by following the precepts. Just as the cowardly flee when facing danger, should we violate our precepts we subject ourselves to danger and thus fear the results of our negative actions.

9. Encouraging the assembly to observe the precepts

A king is the greatest in the world.
The ocean is the greatest body of water.
The moon is the greatest among stars.

The Buddha is the greatest sage.
Among all the regulations,
The highest is the *Pratimoksha Sutra*.
The *Tathagata* set forth these precepts,
Which are to be recited every half-month.

The second part of the introduction—convening the assembly before the actual recitation of the precepts—contains a series of questions and answers in which the reciter asks questions and the respondent answers on behalf of the assembly.

Sutra Reciter: Is the sangha assembled?
Respondent: The sangha is assembled.

To perform poshadha, a sangha must consist of four or more bhikshunis. If less than four bhikshunis are present, an actual poshadha cannot take place. Nevertheless, two or three bhikshunis can benefit from gathering together and reciting the *Pratimoksha Sutra*. If two bhikshunis live together, the sutra reciter asks, "Has so-and-so come?" If three bhikshunis live nearby each other, she asks by name if the other two have come.

Sutra Reciter: Is it in harmony?
Respondent: It is in harmony.

"In harmony" has different meanings according to the circumstance. Usually it indicates that the sangha members are happy and free from quarrels. But here, "in harmony" refers to physical, verbal, and mental harmony. Physical harmony means that all those qualified to attend poshadha are present. Someone who does not come, and has not excused herself, is not in harmony. Verbal harmony is speaking or remaining silent at the appropriate times during the ritual. Those eligible to speak may express themselves at given times during poshadha. Often, when a question is asked, the bhikshunis respond by being silent, indicating that they agree. A bhikshuni who chats or makes a lot of noise during the ceremony is not in harmony verbally. Mental harmony refers to the motivation. If someone is not able physically to attend the recitation, she can attend mentally. That is, she has the motivation to be there, expresses her willingness to attend, and agrees with the proceedings.

>   Sutra Reciter: Have all those who are not fully
>   ordained left?
>   Respondent: *(After sending them out:)* They have
>   left. *(If there are none:)* There are none.

Only bhikshunis are qualified participants for bhikshuni poshadha. Bhikshus, shramaneras, shramanerikas, or lay-people are not allowed to be present when the bhikshunis recite the *Bhikshuni Pratimoksha Sutra.*

>   Sutra Reciter: Are there any absent bhikshunis who
>   wish to be present and are pure?
>   Respondent: *(If there are any, declare it in accordance
>   with the regulations. If there are none:)* There are
>   none.

Although every qualified bhikshuni is required to attend poshadha, if someone cannot, she is not necessarily in disharmony. In certain situations a bhikshuni may be excused from attending, for example, if she is doing work for the Three Jewels or for the monastery, taking care of the temple, resting due to illness, or caring for a sick bhikshuni. In such a case, she expresses her willingness to attend to another bhikshuni who then reports it to the assembly. A bhikshuni asking to be excused says three things. First, when she reports her inability to attend to another bhikshuni, she states that she is pure during that period, meaning that she has purified any precepts she has transgressed during that period by confessing them to another bhikshuni. Second, she explains the reason why she is not able to attend. Third, she expresses her willingness to accept any resolutions the assembly makes during their meeting. The bhikshuni she told then reports to the assembly, "Bhikshuni So-and-so is doing this-and-that. She asks to be excused, expresses her willingness to attend, and will accept all resolutions the sangha makes at this meeting." This procedure shows that bhikshunis are considerate of each other: they show their support of the community, ask to be excused, and maintain the purity of each other's conduct.

> Sutra Reciter: What is the purpose of this harmonious assembly?
> Respondent: To recite the pratimoksha karma.

This series of questions and answers is recited at every important *sanghakarma*, or official act of the sangha, such as the ceremonies for ordination, beginning and concluding the summer retreat. The answer to the last question varies according to the different situations.

The Buddha gave two types of precepts: one is prohibitive and delineates what the sangha should not do, and the other is prescriptive, describing what it should do. This set of questions and answers falls into the latter category. Thus, neglecting to do it violates the Buddha's guidelines.

> Elder Sisters of the sangha, listen. Today is the fifteenth (fourteenth) of the month, the day when the sangha recites the precepts. If the sangha is ready, let the sangha listen attentively as the precepts are recited in harmony.

> Sutra Reciter: This is the announcement. Will it do?
> Respondent: Yes.

The reciter announces the date and the assembly's forthcoming activity once. In Chinese the period from new moon until full moon is called the "bright moon" because the moon is getting brighter. The full moon occurs on the fifteenth day of the month, and at this time the sangha recites the *Pratimoksha*

Sutra. The "dark moon" is from the sixteenth until the new moon, when the moon wanes. According to the lunar calendar, a month consists of twenty-nine and a half days. In order for poshadha to be on the new and full moons, every other month—i.e. in the odd numbered lunar months—instead of saying "Today is the fifteenth," we say, "Today is the fourteenth day of the dark moon."

> Elder Sisters, I now wish to recite the pratimoksha precepts. All of you, listen attentively and reflect upon them well. Those who have not violated them should remain silent. By your silence, we shall know the Elder Sisters are pure. If you are asked other questions, answer in the same way.

> If any bhikshuni in the assembly, after three inquiries, remembers her transgression, but does not repent, she commits the offense of deliberately lying. The Buddha said that deliberately lying is a hindrance on the path of Dharma. If a bhikshuni remembers her transgression and wishes to seek purity, she should repent. Repentance will bring peace and happiness. Elder Sisters, I have recited the prologue to the *Pratimoksha Sutra.* Now I ask you, Elder Sisters, are you pure in this regard? (This question is repeated three times.) Elder Sisters, since you remain silent, you must be pure in this regard. It is so acknowledged.

The prologue emphasizes the importance of confessing and purifying our wrongdoings. If we recognize our wrongdoings yet conceal them, that concealment is also a wrongdoing. Confession, on the other hand, purifies and frees us from the unpleasant karmic results and psychological burdens arising from those wrongdoings. When we act negatively and conceal it, guilt and fear make us unhappy. When we admit our mistakes and make amends, our heart feels lighter, and we learn from our errors.

"Are you pure in this regard?" is repeated three times to give the bhikshunis a chance to recall any transgressions they may have committed. This question is also found at the end of each category of precepts. If we realize during the recitation of the *Pratimoksha Sutra* that we have violated a precept, we theoretically have to confess at that moment. However, if each bhikshuni raises her hand to confess, the reciter will never be able to finish reciting the *Pratimoksha Sutra!* For this reason, the confession is usually conducted before or occasionally after the recitation of the sutra.

The type of confession required varies according to the category of precept transgressed and the severity of the transgression. Committing a parajika is compared to one's head being cut off, because one no longer qualifies to be a bhikshuni and is expelled from the sangha. Violating a sanghavashesha is similar to being handicapped. For a period of time, one's regular privileges as a bhikshuni are suspended. While giving bhikshuni ordination requires at least ten bhikshunis and ten bhikshus, rehabilitating a bhikshuni who has committed a sanghavashesha requires twenty bhikshunis and twenty bhikshus. Thus, the severity of completely transgressing a precept in one of the first two categories is evident. The third category, naihsargika-payattika, regards our daily supplies such as clothing, bowls, and robes. Because a bhikshuni has these in excess or has obtained them in an inappropriate manner, she must first give the object away to a sangha consisting of at least four bhikshunis in order to purify this transgression. Violations of *pratideshaniya* and prayascittika precepts are purified by revealing the wrongdoing to another bhikshuni. Violation of a shikshakaraniya precept requires only self-examination: we reflect on our wrongdoing and determine not to do it again. The nature of the various offenses and their corresponding confessions will be discussed in more detail in the following chapters.

The Body of the Precepts

At the beginning, the sutra reciter said, "I will now proclaim the regulations (*dharma*) of the Vinaya." The content of the dharma of the Vinaya is the various categories of precepts, which the sutra reciter now recites. The bhikshus' 250 precepts fall into eight categories, while the bhikshunis' 348 precepts fall into seven categories. Although the seven points for quieting disputes contained in the last category are not actual precepts, they are counted as one category of precepts. The eighth category for the bhikshus is the undetermined precepts. Each section of the *Pratimoksha Sutra* that deals with a category of precepts has three parts:

1. The general subject mentioning the category of precepts which follow
2. The explanation in detail, during which each precept in this category is recited
3. Closing questions, at which time the sutra reciter inquires if the bhikshunis are pure regarding the observance of the precepts in that category

The recitation of the *Pratimoksha Sutra* can be thorough, individually reciting each precept from the first to the last. It can also be abbreviated in one of three ways:

1. The most abbreviated. Here the reciter says:

   What follows, the eight defeats (parajika), the seventeen suspensions (sanghavashesha), the thirty lapses with forfeiture (naihsargika-payattika), the 178 simple lapses (prayascittika), the eight requiring confession (pratideshaniya), the many training rules (shikshakaraniya), and the seven methods of ending disputes (*adhikaranashamatadharma*), come in the recitation of the *Pratimoksha Sutra* every half-month, so you have heard them before or will hear them later.

2. The middle abbreviation. Here the reciter reads the eight parajika in full and then says:

> What follows, the seventeen suspensions, the thirty lapses with forfeiture, the 178 simple lapses, the eight requiring confession, the many training rules, and the seven methods of ending disputes come in the recitation of the *Pratimoksha Sutra* every half-month, so you have heard them before or will hear them later.

3. The least abbreviation. The reciter reads the eight parajika and the seventeen sanghavashesha in full and then says:

> What follows, the thirty lapses with forfeiture, the 178 simple lapses, the eight requiring confession, the many training rules, and the seven methods of ending disputes come in the recitation of the *Pratimoksha Sutra* every half-month, so you have heard them before or will hear them later.

The Conclusion

The conclusion includes final words of encouragement to those present and dedication of the positive potential from observing precepts. It has four parts:

1. The closing

> Elder Sisters, I have recited the prologue to the *Pratimoksha Sutra*, the eight defeats (parajika), the seventeen suspensions (sanghavashesha), the thirty lapses with forfeiture (naihsargika-payattika), the 178 simple lapses (prayascittika), the eight requiring confession (pratideshaniya), the many training rules (shikshakaraniya), and the seven methods of ending disputes (adhikaranashamatadharma). These are from the *Pratimoksha Sutra* taught by the Buddha and are to be recited every half-month.

2. The final advice

> If there are any further practices in harmony with these, they should be done.

New situations may arise for which the Buddha did not previously prohibit or prescribe behavior. In these cases, we should reflect on the meaning of his previous advice and act in harmony with the principles emphasized in them.

3. The general discourses given by the seven Buddhas

> Patience is the foremost path.
> There is nothing comparable in the Buddha's
>   teaching.
> If one who has left the household life disturbs
>   others,
> She cannot be called a renunciant.[4]

> That is the precept of Tathagata Vipashyin, the unattached, the fully enlightened one.

> Just as a person with clear eyesight
> Can avoid a treacherous road,
> So a wise person in the world
> Can avoid all unwholesomeness.

> That is the precept of Tathagata Shikhin, the unattached, the fully enlightened one.

> Do not slander or envy others.
> Always maintain the precepts.
> Be content with food and drink.
> Always be happy living in solitude.
> Concentrate the mind and take delight in vigorous
>   effort.

> That is the precept of Tathagata Vishvabhu, the unattached, the fully enlightened one.

Just as a bee feeding on flowers
Does not spoil their color or fragrance,
But just extracts their flavor,
So a bhikshu(ni) entering an inhabited place
Does not interfere with others' affairs
Or notice what they do or do not do,
But is mindful only of her own behavior,
Whether correct or incorrect.

That is the precept of Krakucchanda, the unat-
    tached, the fully enlightened one.

Do not lose control of the mind.
Diligently study the sacred Dharma.
Thus freed of anxiety and sorrow,
Concentrating the mind, one enters nirvana.

That is the precept of Tathagata Kanakamuni, the
    unattached, the fully enlightened one.

Avoid all negativity.
Always practice all virtues.
Purify your own mind.
This is the teaching of all the Buddhas.

That is the precept of Tathagata Kashyapa, the
    unattached, the fully enlightened one.

Guard well your speech,
Purify your mind,
Avoid all negativity of the body—
Purify the actions of all three.
Being able to do all this
Is the path of the great sage.

That is the precept of Tathagata Shakyamuni, the unat-
tached, the fully enlightened one, who taught that for
twelve years to the undefiled sangha. Only after that was
it elaborated. If a bhikshuni takes delight in the Dharma

and the renunciant life, has a sense of shame and remorse, and takes delight in learning the precepts, she should study what is found herein.

During the first twelve years after his enlightenment, the Buddha Shakyamuni taught the undefiled sangha. After that, when some bhikshus and bhikshunis acted inappropriately, he set up the precepts in response to actual events that occurred. The precepts were not laid out in advance, but arose organically as the sangha developed. In this way, the Buddha helped monastics conduct their lives in ways that benefit the individual's spiritual progress, the sangha community, and the society in general.

4. The dedication

1. The advantages of observing the precepts

> A wise person who can keep the precepts
> Can enjoy these three:
> Good reputation, material gain,
> And a birth in heaven after death.

> One should contemplate like this:
> Wise ones diligently keep the precepts.
> Pure precepts give rise to wisdom.
> Thus is the foremost path attained.

By observing precepts, we derive temporal benefit while still in cyclic existence: good reputation, material gain, and rebirth in the celestial realm after death. "Good reputation" means that people will respect and trust us. "Material gain" means people will financially support us so that we can continue our practice. After death, we will not fall into the three unfortunate realms of rebirth and will be reborn in the god realm or as a human being. Thus, observing precepts purely brings peace and happiness in this and future lives.

The ultimate benefit of keeping the precepts is attaining the supreme paths through practicing the Three Higher

Trainings of Ethical Discipline, Concentration, and Wisdom. A proper Dharma practice consists of putting equal focus and effort on each of these three. If we observe the precepts without cultivating wisdom, we could easily confuse cultural customs and traditions with the precepts. Without concentration and wisdom, we cannot completely eliminate our defilements and attain nirvana.

On the other hand, if we ignore ethical discipline and only focus on developing wisdom, our daily conduct may be offensive and destructive, and people will rightfully think that our wisdom is odd. Many problems arise when people do higher Dharma practices but neglect the foundation of ethical conduct, as evidenced by scandals regarding sex, power, and money that have occasionally occurred in the Buddhist community. In sum, because the Three Higher Trainings are interrelated, none should be ignored or neglected. Although this book deals with the Higher Training in Ethical Discipline, the other two higher trainings are extremely important to practice as well.

2. Encouragement to respect the precepts

> The Buddhas of the past, the future,
> As well as the present World Honored One,
> Who are able to transcend all sorrow,
> All respect the precepts.
> This is the Dharma of all the Buddhas.

> Those who seek the path of the Buddha
> Should, for their own sakes,
> Always respect the true Dharma.
> This is the teaching of all the Buddhas.

All the Buddhas of the past, present and future respect the precepts. If we seek the Buddha's path, we too should respect this teaching of the Buddha.

3. The fruits resulting from following the Dharma

> The seven Buddhas, World Honored Ones,
> Cut through all defilements,
> And taught seven Vinaya Sutras
> To free us from all fetters.
> They have already achieved nirvana
> And eliminated all wrong views forever.

> To follow the words of the Great Sage
> And the precepts honored by the worthy ones,
> This is the practice of the disciples
> Who achieve serene nirvana.

Our objects of refuge, the seven Buddhas, taught the precepts to help us eliminate our disturbing attitudes and destructive actions and to attain nirvana. This is the practice that we, the disciples, should follow.

4. Solemnly entrusting the teachings of the pratimoksha

> When the World Honored One achieved nirvana,
> Great compassion arose.
> He gathered the assembly of bhikshus together,
> And this is what he taught:

> "Do not say, after my passing,
> That pure practitioners have no protector.
> Now that I have taught the *Pratimoksha Sutra*,
> And the excellent Vinaya teachings,
> Even though I achieve final nirvana,
> Treat these as the World Honored One.

> "If this sutra remains long in the world,
> Buddhadharma will be widespread,
> And because it becomes widespread,
> Nirvana can be achieved.

"If one cannot keep these precepts
Or observe the *uposhadha*[5] as one should,
It will be like the sinking of the sun,
When the world is shrouded in darkness.

"One should always keep the precepts,
Just as a yak protects its tail,
Always staying together in harmony,
In accordance with the Buddha's words."

Before the Buddha passed into parinirvana, he told his disciples that the precepts were their guide and protector. Following the precepts leads us toward nirvana and prolongs the existence of the Buddhadharma in this world.

5. Final conclusion and dedication

I have recited the *Pratimoksha Sutra*
And the assembly's uposhadha is concluded.
I now dedicate all the merit
Of reciting the *Pratimoksha Sutra*
That all sentient beings may achieve Buddhahood
Together as one."

The purpose of our observing precepts is to help every sentient being to become a Buddha. Here, a difference between the Dharmaguptaka and the Theravada Vinaya is evident. In the Theravada tradition, attaining nirvana is the highest goal; helping all sentient beings to attain Buddhahood is not mentioned. Cherishing the Mahayana tradition, the Chinese adopted the Dharmaguptaka Vinaya, which is more in accord with the practice of bodhichitta. Here, we aim to become fully enlightened Buddhas in order to benefit all beings.

CHAPTER SIX

The Boundaries for Remaining
a Monastic

Observing precepts properly impacts our Dharma practice as well as our continued status as a bhikshuni. Knowing the boundaries within which our conduct must lie in order to remain a monastic enables us to be mindful to stay within them. Thus, we must know which precepts are most important and what constitutes their transgression. Distinguishing natural precepts from preventative precepts is helpful in this regard.

Natural precepts involve deeds that by their nature are unethical, such as killing, stealing, lying, and unwise sexual behavior. All world religions advise against these activities. If someone does these, whether or not she has taken a precept to abandon them, she accumulates negative karma. On the other hand, preventative precepts were established by the Buddha to prevent major transgressions of the natural precepts and to avoid criticism from the public. If actions described in the preventive precepts are done, we may easily become involved in actions that threaten our status as a bhikshuni. In addition, society will disparage the sangha if we do actions proscribed in the preventative precepts. Of course, the expectations society holds for a monastic's conduct vary according to culture, place, and historical period. For example, in India monastics were not allowed to cut wood or grass, but because the situation in China was different, few monastics could avoid doing these activities, and society did not criticize the sangha for doing them. What is considered improper or impolite in one culture may not be in another because cultures have different ways of conducting their affairs.

Among the natural precepts, we find major and minor transgressions. For example, accidentally killing an ant while wiping a table is less severe than the premeditated killing of a human being. Since behaviors range from light to heavy, their karmic results and their effect on our status as a monastic vary as well. For example, intentionally killing a human being is a parajika offense and results in our being expelled from the sangha and losing our ordination. Intentionally killing an animal is a prayascittika offense, which does not jeopardize our ordination and can be confessed to another bhikshuni.

A few years ago, some scholars at a conference in Taiwan said that some people join the sangha and then break their precepts, and in this way questioning their status as monastics. Accusing monastics of breaking precepts should not be done lightly. On the other hand, we monastics must examine whether we carefully follow each precept. Do we know what exactly constitutes breaking a precept? Do we know which transgressions are irreparable and result in loss of our status as a monastic? How do we practice those precepts that are not applicable in our society?

Some of these academic scholars proposed dropping or revising precepts that cannot be followed in modern society. We Buddhists must closely examine the issue of changing the precepts; it existed at the time of the Buddha as well. On his way to Kushinagar after the Buddha's parinirvana, Mahakashyapa and five hundred bhikshus traveling with him encountered many of the Buddha's disciples crying sadly. After the passing of their teacher, they had lost all hope. But a monk named Upananda said, "Why cry? We followed the Buddha to seek liberation. When this old man was alive, he made so many rules—we can't do this, we can't do that. Now he is gone and we are free to do whatever we want. Isn't this our greatest liberation?" Hearing this, Mahakashyapa began to worry, "When the Buddha was alive, his teachings and his disciples were of high quality. This, as well as the Buddha's excellent guidance, enabled the Dharma to flourish. Now our leader has gone, and some disciples no longer want to follow the Vinaya. The Dharma may disappear just like smoke, and future generations may have many incorrect ways of thinking."

To prevent this, Mahakashyapa concluded that the sangha had to compile the Dharma and the Vinaya. At the rains retreat that year, five hundred arhats met in Rajagriha to do this. Ananda was assigned to recite the sutras, while Upali recited the Vinaya. Mahakashyapa would ask Upali, "What is the first parajika? Where was it made? Whose action prompted it? Under what conditions was it made?" In this way Upali described the details of each precept. He classified other advice into categories, which later became the Skandha.

At the beginning of the compilation, Ananda said, "Before his parinirvana, the Buddha said that we can relinquish minor precepts." Mahakashyapa asked, "Did you ask him which are minor precepts?" Ananda replied, "Because I was in such deep sorrow at that time, I did not." A discussion ensued about the criteria of a minor precept. Some arhats said only the parajika were important, and all other precepts were minor. Other arhats objected and said the parajika and sanghavashesha were important and the others minor. Another group of arhats insisted the parajika, sanghavashesha, and naihsargika-payattika were the important precepts and rest were insignificant. Since no agreement could be reached, Mahakashyapa said, "Elders, since different ideas exist and we are not sure which precepts the Buddha regarded as minor, we will not change any of the precepts the Buddha established. In addition, no new precepts will be added."

This decisive statement influenced the course of Vinaya. Thus nowadays, we receive the entire set of precepts, every single one of them, when we ordain. However, we face many situations unique to our own culture and time in history that did not exist in ancient India, so that some precepts no longer seem to be applicable. How should we follow those precepts? How should we handle distracting activities that have arisen as times changed and that the Buddha did not specifically prohibit?

The pratimoksha was not modified when it came to China. Instead, supplementary precepts evolved to cover situations unknown in India. Most temples follow guidelines listed in *The Book of Pure Conduct* by Master Pai-zhang, and some temples have developed additional regulations, written as a code of pure conduct for its inhabitants. These rules vary from place to place and from temple to temple. In addition, previous great masters composed commentaries interpreting the precepts according to Chinese culture.

As bhikshunis, we received all 348 precepts in the *Bhikshuni Pratimoksha Sutra*. We should do our best to observe all of them and pay specific attention to those that cannot be violated or changed under any circumstances. If we transgress any of those, we will no longer be a bhikshuni. To aid us, the renowned Chinese Vinaya master Hong-yi, who kept the Vinaya strictly, reviewed, inspected, and revised Vinaya material written after the Song Dynasty. In doing so, he delineated the minimum standard for keeping the pratimoksha in his book, *Commentary on the Four-part Vinaya of Dharmagupta*. This is as follows:

1. Prohibitive precepts:
  - 4 parajika for bhikshus, 8 parajika for bhikshunis
  - 13 sanghavashesha for bhikshus, 17 for bhikshunis
  - 2 undetermined (for bhikshus only)

2. Prescriptive precepts:
  - Establish the geographical boundary (*sima*) for the monastic community
  - Give precepts, i.e. full ordination (*upasampada*)
  - Confess wrongdoings and seek forgiveness
  - Recite the *Pratimoksha Sutra* (poshadha)
  - Do the summer (rains) retreat (*varsha*)
  - Do the confession ceremony at the end of the summer retreat (*pravarana*)

Abandoning prohibitive precepts is done by individual monastics, while keeping the prescribed precepts is done by the monastic community. To remain a monastic, the individual must not transgress the parajika and sanghavashesha prohibitive precepts. To maintain the continuity of monastic lifestyle, the sangha must perform the prescriptive practices.

Although not required to remain a monastic, adhering to minor rules of conduct and basic manners is important. While actions such as killing animals, telling lies, taking intoxicants, eating at unregulated hours, or engaging in behavior that attracts society's criticism are not as serious as parajika or sanghavashesha offenses, they still warrant our close attention. They act as a protective fence making it more difficult to transgress the major precepts.

Bhikshuni precepts differ from the five lay precepts in that they are much more detailed and explicit. For example, not killing animals is included in the first of the five lay precepts, to avoid killing. But for monastics, not killing animals is a separate precept. Taking animals' lives is a prayascittika, not a parajika offense of killing. Although killing animals creates negative karma, it does not undermine our status as a bhikshuni.

Another example is not taking intoxicants, the fifth of the five lay precepts. For bhikshunis, it is a prayascittika. Taking intoxicants attracts society's criticism, and by reducing our mindfulness, it facilitates transgressing a major precept. Although some precepts, such as this one, are not natural precepts and at first glance do not seem so important because they do not relate to our status as monastics, ignoring them could eventually have a negative impact on our ability to observe the root precepts.

So that we will clearly know the areas regarding which we must be especially conscientious in order to remain monastics, I put the parajika and sanghavashesha precepts into eight categories. The number of the precept and its topic are listed below:

1. Sexual conduct
   * parajika 1 (sexual activity), 5 (bodily contact), 6 (eight transgressions)
   * sanghavashesha 1 (match-making), 7 (four situations of being alone), 8 (accepting food and robes from a lustful man), 9 (encouraging other nuns to accept food and robes from a lustful man)

2. Stealing
   * parajika 2 (stealing something of value)
   * sanghavashesha 4 (suing a layperson)

3. Killing
   * parajika 3 (homicide)

4. Telling lies
   * parajika 4 (lying about spiritual attainments)
   * sanghavashesha 2 (making unfounded accusations), 3 (accusing others with false evidence)

5. Concealing
   * parajika 7 (concealing another bhikshuni's parajika)

6. Refusing to accept admonition
   * sanghavashesha 10 (harming the harmonious sangha and not accepting admonition), 11 (assisting others

to harm the harmonious sangha and not accepting admonition), 12 (corrupting households, accusing the sangha of partiality, and not accepting admonition), 13 (giving bad advice and not accepting admonition), 14 (living intimately with another bhikshuni and not accepting admonition), 15 (encouraging those defiled bhikshunis to continue their behavior, accusing the sangha of partiality, and not accepting admonition), 16 (angrily renouncing the Three Jewels and not accepting admonition), 17 (being fond of arguing, accusing the sangha of partiality, and not accepting admonition)

7. Acting against the sangha's decisions
  * parajika 8 (following a suspended bhikshu)
  * sanghavashesha 6 (performing the karma of rehabilitation outside the boundary)

8. Others
  * sanghavashesha 5 (fully ordaining a thief)

Categories of Offenses

According to the severity of wrongdoing, Vinaya offenses are categorized into five groups:

1. Parajika, the most severe offense in Vinaya, means beheaded, abandoned, or deserted. Committing this offense makes one similar to a person whose head has been cut off and who has no hope of survival, for one is expelled from the sangha. The eight parajika listed in the bhikshuni precepts and the four parajika in the bhikshu precepts comprise this category.

2. Sanghavashesha offenses are less severe than parajika. One committing this offense is like a person badly crippled, who is hanging on by just a thread. She needs to rely on other monastics to complete the manatta repentance and purify this offense. The seventeen sanghavashesha precepts of bhikshunis and the thirteen sanghavashesha precepts of bhikshus belong to this category.

3. Prayascittika means to fall. Those who commit this kind of offense will fall into either a hot or cold hell. The thirty naihsargika-payattika and the 178 prayascittika precepts of bhikshunis and the thirty naihsargika-payattika and ninety prayascittika precepts of bhikshus are in this category.

4. Pratideshaniya means confessing to others. To purify this offense, one has to confess the wrongdoing to another bhikshuni. Eight pratideshaniya precepts exist for bhikshunis and four for bhikshus.

5. *Dushkrita* means verbal or physical wrongdoing. The one hundred shikshakaraniya precepts and seven rules for ending disputes for bhikshus and bhikshunis, plus the two undetermined precepts for bhikshus fall into this category.

Sometimes this list is expanded to include two additional offenses: *sthulatyaya* and wrongdoing in speech. Sthulatyaya means a big hindrance to the virtuous path and often results from an incomplete transgression of a parajika or sangha-vashesha precept. Wrongdoing in speech is a branch of the dushkrita offense mentioned above. When wrongdoing in speech is particularly mentioned, then dushkrita refers to physical wrongdoing.

Please note that such terms as "parajika," "sanghavashesha," and "pratideshaniya" can refer either to a category of precepts or a type of offense, depending on the usage.

When Precepts Are Transgressed

Abiding by the precepts strengthens our Dharma practice, enriches our mind with positive potential, brings good future rebirths, and leads to liberation. Violating the precepts causes deterioration to our practice and causes us to experience unhappy results. By respecting our precepts, our mindfulness, introspection, alertness, and conscientiousness increase, and thus it is easier to develop concentration, wisdom, and compassion and to achieve the higher paths.

Because most sangha members are ordinary beings with defilements, they transgress precepts. What is the result of such transgressions? For a parajika, the *Bhikshuni Pratimoksha Sutra* says, "If a bhikshuni has committed any of these eight parajika, she is no longer allowed to live with the other bhikshunis. She will be what she was before (i.e. a layperson). A bhikshuni who commits a parajika may not stay in the order." If a bhikshuni commits any of the parajika, she can no longer live with the bhikshuni sangha, nor can she consider herself a bhikshuni. By her actions, she has distanced herself from the sangha and is expelled from the order. She may no longer participate in any decision-making of the sangha; she may not receive people's offerings to the sangha; she may not take disciples; she may not give ordination to others; and she may not take an important position in the monastery. These are the immediate results of violating a parajika. The karmic repercussions in future lives are in addition to these.

The second circumstance precipitating complete expulsion from the order is someone's not being fit to be a member. For example, someone joins the sangha with the corrupt motivation to destroy the Dharma by "stealing the Dharma," that is by learning the Dharma with a motivation to strengthen one's own incorrect beliefs. Such a person might adopt some Buddhist beliefs into her own system so that her teaching appears similar to the Buddhadharma, and in this way, she gains support and respect from the public. However, her purpose is satisfy her egoistic ambitions and sustain her incorrect views. Another case of someone unfit to be a sangha member is a person with one or more of the thirteen major hindrances preventing ordination. If such a person ordains without revealing her hindrance and it is discovered later, she should be expelled.

Shramaneras and shramanerikas are expelled if they transgress one of their four root precepts: to abandon killing, stealing, sexual contact, and lying. They may also be expelled if they refuse to give up certain wrong views—such as the wrong view that sexual desire is not a hindrance to the path—after being admonished by a bhikshu or bhikshuni.

Regarding the consequences of transgressing a sangha-vashesha precept, the *Bhikshuni Pratimoksha Sutra* says, "If a bhikshuni commits any one of these (sanghavashesha) offenses, she must perform manatta among both (the bhikshu and bhikshuni) sanghas for a half month. Once the manatta has been performed, rehabilitation (abbhana) must be done. The bhikshuni is to be rehabilitated before both sanghas consisting of forty people. If there is even one person less than forty and the rehabilitation rite is performed, that bhikshuni cannot be rehabilitated, and the bhikshunis are at fault. This is the procedure."

Sanghavashesha means impaired, disabled, and relying on the assembly to survive. Although one is still a bhikshuni, her status is in danger, and she must rely on the sangha to take immediate action and save her endangered monastic life. To purify a sanghavashesha, a bhikshuni must take three steps. First she completes the practice of *parivasa*, or probation. She confesses to the bhikshuni sangha, stating which sanghavashesha she transgressed and how long she concealed it. Then she lives apart from the community to contemplate her misdeed. However, since a bhikshuni is not allowed to live alone, she remains close to the sangha. The length of her parivasa is the same as the number of days she concealed her sanghavashesha offense before confessing it. During the period, the thirty-five privileges of a bhikshuni, such as expressing her views in meetings, receiving offerings given to the sangha, or accepting service from junior monastics, are suspended. If a bhikshuni confesses a sangha-vashesha offense before the dawn of the day after committing it, she has not concealed it, and there is no period of parivasa.

Second, after the parivasa period, the bhikshuni performs manatta, or penance, for a half-month.[1] "Manatta" means to crush one's pride and humble one's ego. During this period, to show her willingness to alter her mistaken ways, this bhikshuni offers service to the sangha, for example, by preparing seats for the bhikshus or bhikshunis returning from alms round, preparing water for washing their feet, and so on. She must tell the assembly her whereabouts at all times, and if she goes to town, she must leave late and return early. If the assembly is satisfied with her performance of manatta, it will gladly remove her from it. For this reason, manatta is also called "decision of the assembly." In addition, the term means "comfort in the mind" because both the guilty nun as well as the bhikshuni sangha are comforted because a heavy transgression is being purified and uprooted.

The third step is to perform abbhana or rehabilitation, which releases the bhikshuni from the discipline related to her sanghavashesha offense. The abbhana rite must be performed in the presence of a monastic assembly. For bhikshus, the assembly must consist of twenty bhikshus, and for bhikshunis, the assembly must be composed of at least twenty bhikshus and twenty bhikshunis. The rite is invalid if the number is even one less. Although the guilty bhikshuni goes to the bhikshu sangha for rehabilitation, she does not confess the wrongdoing to them, for that is done to the bhikshuni sangha. After the rehabilitation rite, she may resume her former status in the bhikshuni sangha.

The Vinaya mentions three types of expulsion:

1. Complete expulsion. This results from committing a parajika or being unfit to be a member, as mentioned above. This individual loses her status as a bhikshuni and can no longer perform the sangha's karma (activities and practices), such as poshadha. A shramanerika may also be expelled for not giving up wrong views after admonition.

2. Expulsion resulting from breaking up a harmonious sangha, for example, as Devadatta did. Although this person does not lose her bhikshuni status, she cannot live with the sangha for the rest of her life.

3. Temporary expulsion. This can arise in three situations: if
the offender

* Refuses to admit her wrongdoing (actions such as corrupting households, engaging in negative deeds, and
so forth)
* Refuses to accept others' admonition
* Refuses to repent or give up her wrong views (for
example, holding that sexual desire is not a hindrance
on the path to liberation)

To settle this dispute, the sangha has the offender live
separately so that she can think over her attitude and actions. She still retains the identity of a bhikshuni, but is
not allowed to interact with the assembly or to join in activities, such as poshadha. When her attitude about her
offense changes, and with sincere remorse, she completely
confesses and repents her inappropriate actions, the
sangha agrees to dissolve its previous decision. At that
time, she may again live with the community and take
part in its activities and group practices.

Giving Up the Vow

Examining the method for giving back the vow enhances
our understanding of the primary elements necessary to remain a sangha member. Giving up the vow means to relinquish the precepts one has previously received. There are
four situations in which this may occur:

1. Voluntarily giving back the vow:
* Sudden and total renunciation. One returns the
bhikshuni, shramanerika, and upasika precepts, is no
longer a Buddhist, and becomes a member of the public straightaway.
* Gradual renunciation. One returns the bhikshuni precepts but keeps the shramanerika precepts, or one
returns the bhikshuni and shramanerika precepts, but
keeps the upasika precepts.

2. Natural termination. For example, at the time of death the vow naturally is relinquished; on the dawn of the following morning, the one-day vow naturally ends.

3. Becoming a hermaphrodite

4. Cutting the root of virtue. One commits a parajika and is expelled from the sangha.

The reasons the Buddha allowed monastics to voluntary give back their precepts are:

1. To help that person avoid committing a parajika. If a monastic is in danger of committing a parajika, giving back one's vow and returning to lay life before doing the prohibited action is better than transgressing a parajika. In that way, one kept the precepts purely during the time one had them.

2. To enable people to enter and leave the sangha without hindrances. No one is forced to remain a monastic against his or her will. After ordination, if one finds oneself unwilling or unfit to be a monastic, he or she may give back the vow and return to lay life.

3. To avoid the person being held in contempt by others. If a person returns to lay life without breaking the precepts, he or she will not attract criticism or condemnation for committing a parajika.

Different levels of giving back the vows exist. Some people only give back the bhikshu/bhikshuni vow and remain a novice with the shramanera/shramanerika vow. Some give back the shramanera/shramanerika vow too, remaining lay followers of the Buddha with the upasaka/upasika vow. Some give back the upasaka/upasika vow, and some people decide not to be a Buddhist any more. When relinquishing one's precepts, a person must clarify which vow(s) he or she intends to give back.[2]

The procedure for voluntarily relinquishing the vow is as follows: one states one's wish in the presence of a bhikshu, bhikshuni, or any person who can understand the meaning of one's words. If someone wants to give up all her vows, including her refuge in the Three Jewels, she says, "I renounce the Buddha, the Dharma, the Sangha, the preceptor, the *acharya*, and the training. I renounce ethical discipline, Vinaya, *shikshapada* (precepts of training), and accept the life of a layperson." The renunciation takes effect as soon as the statement is finished. If someone only wants to give up her bhikshuni vow, she says, "I give up the bhikshuni vow and keep the shramanerika and lay vows."

If a monk gives back his bhikshu vow without having committed a parajika, returns to lay life, and later wishes to be a monastic, he must receive ordination once again. He may become a bhikshu up to seven times in this life, and his monastic age starts from the time of the most recent ordination. For example, prior to 1949 some Chinese monks gave back their vow and joined the army during the time of political upheaval. Later they came to Taiwan and after being discharged from the army, wanted to become monks again. They were ordained anew and, as new monks, sat at the end of the line. The time they were monastics in mainland China did not count as part of their ordination age. Although they may have been senior in terms of practice or knowledge, they were now junior in terms of length of ordination.

According to the Dharmagupta Vinaya, a woman may be ordained as a bhikshuni only once in this lifetime. Regardless of whether she has violated a parajika, once a bhikshuni gives back her vow, she cannot become a bhikshuni again in this life. I do not know the reason why this difference exists for women and men. It could be because the sangha relies on the leadership of the bhikshus. In any case, because bhikshunis are responsible for teaching the minor members of the sangha and taking care of sangha affairs, their maintaining the purity of their ethical behavior is essential. This strictness motivates us to keep our intention clear and firm and our conduct proper.

I was told that in the Mulasarvastivadin Vinaya followed in the Tibetan community, a woman may become a shramanerika up to three times if she has given up the shramanerika vow without having completely transgressed a root precept. Similarly, in the Chinese tradition, a woman who has not violated any of the root precepts may be ordained more than once. However, such a situation rarely occurs. Shramanerika precepts are not as strict as bhikshuni precepts.

The second case of relinquishing the vow is called natural termination, indicating that the time of keeping the vow has naturally expired. This occurs at death. One's pratimoksha ordination does not continue from one lifetime to the next. In each lifetime, one has to receive it anew. Another example of termination by nature occurs with the eight precepts that laypeople take for one day. When the time period for which one has taken the vow has expired—in this case one day—the vow is lost automatically.

Third, if a person becomes a hermaphrodite, the vow is lost. This usually occurs in the case of one who joined the sangha at a young age, when the sexual organs were not fully developed. Later on, the person develops a second sexual organ, making it difficult to determine whether the person has the bhikshu or bhikshuni precepts or should stay with the bhikshu or bhikshuni sangha. Similar situations happen in athletics as well. Over twenty years ago, Ms. Yao, who competed in the women's division of the Asian Sport Games, developed more male characteristics, until her participation in the athletic competitions was no longer permitted.

Fourth, the vow is lost if a person completely transgresses a parajika precept. By committing this offense, the person has shown that he or she no longer has the willingness to be a monastic. This person may not be ordained as a monastic again in this life. Committing a parajika is different from experiencing difficulty in keeping the bhikshu/bhikshuni vow and giving it back without having violated a parajika. In the latter way, the purity of the sangha and of the individual is still maintained. Only a person who is still pure in observing the precepts has the right to renounce their vow(s). Someone who has committed a parajika lacks this right, and instead the sangha expels him or her. Examining the above cases, we see that one's ordination may be terminated because of voluntary, involuntary, or natural reasons.

Ethical discipline is the foundation upon which we build the rest of our Dharma practice, and the Higher Training of Ethical Discipline involves receiving and observing the various levels of ordination. Therefore, to ensure optimum conditions for developing concentration, wisdom, and bodhichitta, we should be attentive to remain within the boundaries of our vows.

CHAPTER SEVEN

Working with Attachment:
Root Precepts Regarding
Sexual Contact

One of the three poisonous attitudes preventing liberation is clinging attachment. As human beings in the desire realm, the two principal desires we have are sexual desire and desire for food and enjoyments. Sexual desire—lustful attachment between two people—is in general our strongest attachment. To help us subdue our attachment to this, the Buddha established a number of parajika and sangha-vashesha precepts concerning sexual contact or actions that could make us interested in sexual contact. Because craving for the physical and emotional pleasure of sexual relations is the most common cause for monastics losing or giving up their vow, we will look at this topic first.

> Parajika 1: If a bhikshuni engages in sexual activities, even with an animal, she commits a parajika and is expelled from the order.

One does not have to be a monastic to practice the Dharma. Laypeople can have sexual relations and a family and also learn and practice Dharma. The Buddha cautioned laypeople against sexual misconduct, but he prohibited any sexual activity for monastics. Why? Monastic training is intense and its objective is higher. To actualize the Higher Trainings in Concentration and Wisdom leading to liberation and enlightenment, a full-time commitment to the Dharma is necessary, and this requires giving up distractions and attachments. Of course, we still need to eat to stay alive, but giving up romantic emotional relationships and sexual desire will not threaten our lives. The precept regarding sexual conduct comes first because sexual desire can have a strong impact on our practice. Also, placing it first illustrates our firm determination and willingness to practice the Dharma, as our chief attachment is the first thing we need to give up as monastics.

If a woman wishes to join the sangha, I ask her if she can be celibate for the rest of her life. Can she live without an intimate relationship? Will she feel comfortable without the emotional support provided by a husband and family? Can she be peaceful without sexual relations? If so, she may continue her spiritual journey as a monastic.

Some women wonder if they can still become monastics if they had boyfriends or were married in the past. What they did before does not matter. As long as they are determined to become monastics and observe the precepts in the future, I see no problem. However, if they find difficulty observing these precepts, remaining as a lay practitioner is better. They should not feel guilty or somehow inferior because of this. Being honest about our needs and abilities is more effective and comfortable than forcing ourselves into a life style that is not suited for us and being tormented by conflicting emotions.

The first precept prohibits sexual involvement with human beings, animals, or others. Three principal incidents triggered this precept. During the rains retreat twelve years after

the Buddha's enlightenment, people suffered a terrible famine, and the monastics were not able to collect enough alms.
One monk from a wealthy family went back to his home-
town, where he was certain to receive food. His mother was
overjoyed to see her son and repeatedly asked him to disrobe and remain with the family. Preferring to remain a monk,
he refused. Finally his mother pleaded, "If you won't disrobe, at least give me a grandson, so he can inherit the family property." To fulfill his mother's wish, the monk had sex
with his former wife, who later gave birth to a son. However, after he returned to live with the sangha, the monk was
upset and unhappy about what he had done. Hearing about
this, the Buddha asked, "Why does a monastic still engage
in sexual activities?" and set up the first precept prohibiting
sexual activity.

The second incident involved another bhikshu who did
not observe the precept. Every once in a while, he would
sneak back to his home and have sex with his former wife.
When the Buddha came to know of this, he said, "If you want
to be a monk, you must maintain pure ethical discipline. If
you do not want to be a monk or are unable to follow the
precepts, you should disrobe. Then you can do whatever laypeople do." Thus the Buddha allowed monastics to give back
their precepts.

The third incident involved a bhikshu who lived in the
forest. When another bhikshu visited him, he noticed that
the monkeys around his friend's hut behaved strangely.
Puzzled, he hid and observed them. Returning from alms
round, the monk ate and gave the leftovers to the monkeys,
after which he had sex with a female monkey. Shocked, the
friend related this incident to the Buddha, who asked this
monk, "Why do you have sex with animals?" He replied,
"You only said we couldn't have sex with women. Nothing
was said about animals." Because of this, the Buddha revised this precept, adding that monastics cannot have sexual
relations with animals.

In total, sixteen incidents concerning this precept, each with a unique feature, were recorded in the Vinaya Pitaka. The phrase "even with" in the first parajika implies the existence of other situations and broadens the scope of what is prohibited by this precept. The object of sexual engagement for monks includes a woman and a female animal, as well as a female non-human, a eunuch, a hermaphrodite, another man, an insane person, a corpse, or even with himself. Intercourse with or without a cover in either of the parties can take place at any of three places: the mouth, anus, or vagina. Any of these constitutes a parajika offense, resulting in loss of one's status as a monastic. Applied to bhikshunis, this precept refers to sexual engagement with men, male animals, or a male corpse.

The Vinaya contains a detailed discussion of the behavior constituting a parajika. Four conditions are necessary for a complete parajika:

1. The place where the sexual contact occurs is the mouth, anus, or vagina, whether or not a condom was used
2. The motivation is sexual desire
3. The movement or act is performed
4. Intercourse, with entry even the depth of a hair, occurs. In the case of a bhikshuni consenting to intercourse, her experiencing pleasure is not necessary for a parajika to occur. Simply contact with the male's organ, even if its entry is the depth of a hair, is sufficient as the fourth condition.

For rape to be a parajika offense, the conditions differ:

1. The place is one of the three places: mouth, anus, or vagina
2. The person is forced
3. Intercourse takes place
4. The person has a sense of enjoyment

At first glance, we see a woman who is raped as the victim. However, if she experiences enjoyment for even a moment during the rape, it constitutes sexual activity and is a parajika violation. Although she did not initially have the motivation to engage in sexual relations and even if she finds the rape predominantly disgusting, if she experiences pleasure for even a moment, her mind has changed. For this reason it is considered a parajika, and she no longer qualifies as a bhikshuni.

At first glance, this may seem unfair, but the strictness of the precept makes a bhikshuni very conscientious. It helps prevent situations which sometimes occur in which a woman semi-voluntarily receives a man's unwanted advances while half-heartedly protesting his actions. Thus, threatened by rape, a bhikshuni must wholeheartedly reject a man's advances. If the rape occurs, she must control herself so that she experiences no sense of enjoyment. Some masters advise that she bites her tongue so hard that the pain overpowers the sensation of sexual contact. If no enjoyment is felt during the rape, she remains a full-fledged bhikshuni.

Thus, the first precept concerns not only a bhikshuni's physical and verbal activities, but also her motivation and emotional reaction. These determine whether a transgression has been committed, and if so, its degree of gravity.

If a bhikshuni experiences pleasure during a rape, yet still wants to be a monastic, she can be a "learner of parajika." This refers to a person who, with no intention to conceal the action for even a moment, immediately expresses sincere remorse upon the commitment of a parajika and requests to remain in the community as a monastic to learn parajika precepts. If the sangha unanimously grants the request, the person can remain in the community as a learner of parajika, even though he or she no longer qualifies to be an actual bhikshu or bhikshuni. Among monastics, learners of parajika come after bhikshus or bhikshunis, but before shramaneras or shramanerikas. Learners of parajika must follow additional rules. For example, they may not give full ordination, take shramaneras or shramanerikas as disciples, teach Vinaya, and so forth. For more detail regarding this, please refer to chapter 16 of this book and to the Vinaya Pitaka.

One time, an arhat-nun was sleeping when she felt a man forcing himself on her. Using her superhuman powers to fly in the sky, she went to see the Buddha. After prostrating to him, she reported this incident. The Buddha asked "What was your state of mind at the time of the rape?" "It was like being burned by hot iron. There was no joy," she replied. The Buddha said, "You did not violate a parajika." She asked whether she had violated the rule prohibiting a bhikshuni from sleeping alone, and the Buddha replied that sleeping alone was not an offense for those who had liberated themselves from samsara.

Another similar incident happened to this bhikshuni while she was sleeping. Since her sleep was so deep, she did not notice a man intruding into her room. Nor did she notice the rape that took place while she was sleeping. However, upon awaking, she saw the mess around her and suspected a rape. She asked the Buddha, who said that due to her realizations, no offense was committed, but that bhikshunis should not sleep with the door unlocked.

In a similar situation, an extremely beautiful bhikshuni attained arhatship. Before she joined the sangha, many men chased after her, and even after she was ordained, groups of men followed her around. One evening, after a long Dharma discourse, she returned to her room exhausted. She fell sleep without noticing that a man was hiding under her bed. In the middle of the night he crept out and raped her. She felt no pleasure and thus a parajika was not committed. Nevertheless, because of this incident, the Buddha required bhikshunis to make sure a man is not in the room and to lock the door before going to sleep or bathing to prevent being in a vulnerable situation.

Physical contact without intercourse between a bhikshuni and a man, when both parties are lustful and other conditions are met, is a parajika offense as expressed in parajika 5 and 6.

Parajika 5: If a bhikshuni with lustful mind has physical contact with a man with lustful mind in the area between the

armpits and the knees, be it touching, holding, stroking, pulling, pushing, rubbing up or down, lifting, lowering, grasping, or pressing, this bhikshuni commits a parajika and is
expelled from the order.

This precept concerns physical contact, short of intercourse,
with a man. The triggering incident involves a bhikshuni who
was in love with a man before she joined the sangha. One
day, her former boyfriend invited the entire sangha to his
house for a meal. Not seeing this bhikshuni there, he ran
back to the temple to look for her after the sangha had begun to eat. He found her lying on her bed, approached her,
and embraced her. With lustful minds, they engaged in the
actions mentioned in this precept—touching, holding, stroking, pulling, pushing, rubbing up or down, lifting, lowering,
grasping, and pressing each other in the area from the armpits to the knees—although they stopped short of intercourse.
A shramanerika nearby observed this scene and later told other
bhikshunis about it. The bhikshunis informed the bhikshus,
who reported it to the Buddha. Accordingly, the Buddha set
up this precept. Six conditions are necessary for its violation:

1. The other person is a male.
2. The bhikshuni perceives him as a male.
3. Both parties are affected by sexual desire.
4. The body parts where they have contact are sensitive areas,
   i.e. between the armpits and the knees. This precept differs
   from the first precept in that to transgress the first precept,
   contact of the sexual organs must occur. Here, the area of
   physical contact is much larger. In the Mulasarvastivada
   Vinaya the area is even wider, extending from the hairline
   downwards, including the face and lips.
5. Both parties have performed all these behaviors. They hug
   each other, caress each other, and so forth. Only intercourse
   is missing.
6. Both parties have a sense of enjoyment.

Two points in this precept are important: first, both parties are dominated by sexual desire; second, the bhikshuni has a sense of enjoyment from the contact. A bhikshuni definitely should not touch a lustful man with desire in her mind. However, how do we handle the physical contact that often occurs between people of the opposite sex in modern society? For example, we may accidentally brush against someone while passing him on the street. When traveling by bus or plane, we may have physical contact with a man seated next to us. We may accidentally fall down and be helped up by a man. Or we may help or be helped by a man in cases of flood, fire, war, or attack by an animal or person. Even at crowded Dharma teachings or rituals, we may find ourselves in physical contact with a man. Although this contact is not intentional and does not constitute a parajika, we still have to be mindful. If we are not, frequent physical contact with men could create a problem in our spiritual practice.

In Western countries, acquaintances shake hands, hug each other, kiss each other, and touch their cheeks together. I do not know how those of you living in the West should behave to prevent this kind of physical contact. This is not the custom in Eastern countries, so nuns there do not face these difficulties. If a nun in Asia even shook hands with a man, the laypeople would be shocked.

To prevent unnecessary physical contact, we should wear our robes properly. Low-cut blouses or see-through cloth are inappropriate. Although we may dress in a relaxed way in our rooms, we should always be properly dressed in our robes when greeting laypeople or monks. Unless a dangerous or unusual situation requires it, monastics should wear their robes, never lay clothes, in town.

In addition, guests, be they male or female, should be seen in the reception room of the temple, monastery, or Dharma center, not in our bedroom. Bringing visitors into the bhikshunis' living quarters will disturb our roommates. Since both laypeople and monastics attend activities at temples and

Dharma centers, we need to designate areas open to the public and those restricted to the bhikshunis. If both monks and nuns live at a temple or center, their living quarters should be far apart, and they should not enter each other's living areas. When constructing a temple, we should pay attention to the function and design of various spaces to facilitate the monastics there keeping their precepts.

Several points related to physical contact, which is the focus of this precept, can be raised here. If a bhikshuni frequently touches or caresses others, including children, or is touched or caressed by them, an imaginary feeling or longing for physical contact could easily arise. Although no sexual activity has occurred, such longing could eventually undermine a bhikshuni's spiritual practice. Even bhikshunis hugging each other, hitting each other playfully, or putting their arms on each other's shoulders could become problematic. Therefore, bhikshunis should avoid contacting each other in this way. Some masters of the past did not consider physical contact when joking around as misconduct, but Vinaya Master Ling-chih said it is not proper behavior for monastics and results in a dushkrita offense.

> Parajika 6: Suppose a bhikshuni with lustful mind knows a man has a lustful mind, yet allows him to hold her hand, grasp her clothes, and lead her into a secluded place, where they stand together, talk together, walk together, lean on each other, and make an appointment to meet (to make love). If a bhikshuni engages in these eight transgressions, she commits a parajika and is expelled from the order.

The same two individuals involved in the fifth parajika also triggered this one. Since their love for each other was not over, they made a date and went out together. They held hands; the man grasped her garment; they went to a secluded place where they talked to each other, walked together, and leaned on each other. When this bhikshuni's actions came to the attention of the Buddha, he created this precept.

"Grasping her clothes" refers to her clothing, purse, hat, or other belongings. A secluded place is one in which no one can see or hear them. If they ask others to leave the place, it becomes a secluded place. Each of the eight parts of this transgression easily leads to the next one, and at the end, they make a date to meet again with the idea to do the actions described in either the first or the fifth parajika. For that reason, the eighth part of this transgression is crucial. Although they have not had sexual intercourse, the situation is getting closer and closer to that.

Five conditions must be present for this parajika to occur:

1. The other person is a male
2. The bhikshuni perceives him as a male
3. Both parties are affected by sexual desire
4. She has no remorse for having done the first seven activities
5. The eighth activity occurs

All five conditions must be present and all eight activities must be performed for a parajika to occur. If only the first four conditions are present and only the eighth activity is not performed, a parajika has not been committed. Nevertheless, each of the first seven activities results in a sthulatyaya offense, that is, a grave offense resulting from an incomplete act of parajika or sanghavashesha. If these eight activities occur between two females, the result is a dushkrita, that is, a wrongdoing committed either physically or verbally. If the bhikshuni and the man have desirous minds but take no action, or if they do similar actions without desire, no violation occurs.

In daily life, these eight activities are not uncommon, so we must be attentive to our motivation and mindful in each situation. Especially in monasteries and Dharma centers where men and women work together, care regarding this precept is essential. Sometimes we hear of a teaching or ritual that will take place in a private room. We should employ our wisdom to distinguish a real teaching or ritual from an excuse to be near someone. In a similar vein, bhikshunis should not accept a ride on a motorcycle or scooter with a man for the sake of convenience. Both parties being more aware of their motivation and behavior could prevent many unfortunate cases of abuse.

Some nuns told me that once in a while they feel the need for some physical comfort and contact with another person. I recommended that they look inside, "What is this need? Is it for sexual contact? Is it for emotional support and intimacy?" They need to use the Dharma to calm these attachments and remind themselves that real happiness and satisfaction comes from practicing the path and attaining enlightenment.

Following sexual desire will have a negative impact on monastics' practice. The Vinaya Pitaka relates the story of a bhikshu who meditated on the ugliness of the body to free himself from desire for physical contact. Having meditated on this for a while, he believed himself free from sexual desire. However, one day he saw a beautiful woman and was instantly attracted to her. When she offered him food, he had the strong urge to embrace her. But when she smiled, he saw her teeth, and this made him remember the ugliness of all the various parts and organs of the body. At that moment, the bhikshu regained his mindfulness and successfully let go of his sexual desire. Continuing to practice, he later attained arhatship.

Bhikshus have four parajika: to abandon sexual intercourse, killing a human being, stealing, and lying about spiritual attainments. Bhikshunis have four additional parajika, and two of these relate to sexual conduct. For bhikshunis this behavior is very serious. In the three parajika regarding sexual conduct, the first is sexual intercourse, the second physical contact, and the third the eight activities. The first is the most severe, while the second and third, by expanding the line of defense, prevent the first one from happening. Frequent physical contact often leads to attachment, and when strong attachment undermines the basis for spiritual practice, a bhikshuni will depart from her original intention of attaining liberation. Some people say that bhikshunis having more parajika than bhikshus is unfair, but I believe we are better protected from spiritual obstacles because of them. We will pay more attention to preventative measures.

Two cases exist in which the action described in a parajika is committed but a parajika offense does not occur. One is if the person is insane, has no idea of what is happening, and therefore cannot be held responsible for her behavior. The second is when the action was done before the Buddha established a precept prohibiting it.

If a bhikshuni violates any one of the parajika, she loses her bhikshuni vow. Some people mistakenly believe that she has to violate all eight parajika before she is no longer a monastic, but this is incorrect.

To be a monastic, we need to be mature, mentally stable, clear about our motivation and goals in life, and firm in our determination. If someone is not yet clear about her motivation and commitment, I recommend that she remain a layperson and practice Dharma in that way. In recent years many people have been enthusiastic about becoming monastics, and many temples have accepted them without sufficient screening and preparation. Further down the road, many of these people have problems observing the precepts. This situation has a detrimental affect not only on the individual's practice, but also on the Buddhist community as a whole.

To observe precepts, we need to be knowledgeable about the details of the precepts and aware of our physical and psychological circumstances. In secular school, teachers instruct the students in liberal arts and the sciences, but few teach us how to examine and understand our changing body and mind. To help us better understand ourselves, the Buddha taught the four mindfulnesses—of body, feelings, mind, and phenomena. Mindfulness of the body makes us aware of its parts—the skeleton, organs, and so forth—and their impurity. Visiting a morgue or cemetery causes us to reflect on the nature of the body and reduces sexual desire and mental and physical restlessness, thus facilitating Dharma practice. Prostrating to the Three Jewels, reciting sutras, and doing service work to benefit others are also helpful if the mind is disturbed by sexual desire

The categories of parajika, sanghavashesha, and so forth apply only to bhikshus and bhikshunis. A shramanerika does not have these precepts because she is not fully ordained. Shramanerikas observe ten precepts—often expanded into thirty-six—and these are used to determine their offenses. Shramanerika precepts are considered a similitude of bhikshuni precepts. A shramanerika who has sexual intercourse thus has not committed a parajika offense. However, she has transgressed a shramanerika precept and is no longer a nun.

Bhikshunis, not bhikshus, have the responsibility to watch over and guide shramanerikas and see that they observe the ten precepts properly. Many women's issues are difficult for bhikshus to handle, so bhikshunis must be in charge and responsible for the purity of the bhikshuni sangha and the shramanerikas. Bhikshus only see shramanerikas during teachings and rituals. Because they do not live with the shramanerikas, bhikshus are not in a position to give the detailed personal guidance required in a nun's training. Bhikshunis, on the other hand, are well suited to do this. Shramanerikas, in turn, should rely upon and respect bhikshunis. In this way, they will receive good training, become excellent bhikshunis themselves one day, and uphold the purity of the sangha.

CHAPTER EIGHT

The Sticky Nature of Attachment: More Precepts Concerning Sexual and Physical Conduct

Three precepts in the parajika category concern sexual interactions, as do several precepts in other categories. Studying these not only deepens our understanding of this topic but also clarifies the differences between categories of precepts. For example, if a bhikshuni initiates sexual intercourse with a man, a parajika is created by even a moment of contact. In other categories, the criteria for offenses differ. Most of the precepts in this chapter do not speak of direct sexual contact, and therefore we may wonder why they are included in this category. They act like a fence protecting the root precepts. They protect bhikshunis from being in situations where sexual desire could arise and later be acted upon, thus endangering their parajika precepts. The activities prohibited in these precepts deal with several principal themes.

Matchmaking

> Sanghavashesha 1: If a bhikshuni acts as a go-between, carrying messages from a man to a woman or from a woman to a man, and by doing so helps to realize their marriage or liaison, even of a short duration, this bhikshuni commits a sanghavashesha if she does not refrain from her misconduct upon the first admonition.

While the first, fifth, and sixth parajika concern a bhikshuni having a sexual relationship with a man, the first sanghavashesha deals with a bhikshuni helping or encouraging other people to have sexual contact. Although marriage is accepted and popular in the world, this precept indicates the extent to which bhikshunis should be involved in it.

The incident triggering this precept involved a bhikshu who was a high government official, knowledgeable about laws and customs, before he joined the sangha. Because people trusted him, even after he was ordained, many came to him for advice, especially regarding marriage. They asked him to determine the suitability of two parties for each other. If the marriage turned out well, people praised him and gave him offerings. However, when the marriage turned out bad, they blamed this bhikshu for their misfortune, criticized the sangha in general, and refused to support monastics.

What percentage of marriages turn out well? Since the majority of marriages are not happy, the sangha members are likely to be criticized if they arrange them. In addition, monastics who are serious about their practice and careful in their behavior do not want to get involved in these affairs, nor do they want other monastics in the monastery to be distracted by them. Arranging marriages can take a lot of time. I do not know the customs in Western countries, but in Chinese society, marriage involves not only two individuals, but also their families and thus can be complex.

Six conditions must be present for this sanghavashesha to be committed:

1. The message involves people of the opposite sex
2. They must be human beings and the bhikshuni must perceive them as such
3. The message is about marriage or liaison
4. The bhikshuni assumes the message is about love affairs
5. The message being transmitted is clear and understandable
6. The bhikshuni carries the message from one party to the other and brings back the response

If a monastic delivers messages back and forth from a man to a woman and vice-versa, he or she violates this precept, whether or not the two parties get married. Their sexual liaison outside of marriage also constitutes a violation. Although their sexual relationship may be temporary, a bhikshuni carrying messages leading to it commits a sanghavashesha.

If a bhikshuni is asked to carry messages, letters, or pictures back and forth between a man and a woman who are single, she should inquire about their nature. Although she may not clearly know that the message is romantic, she errs if she does not ask about the nature of the message before carrying it.

If we extend the implications of this precept, questions arise: Can a bhikshuni perform a wedding ceremony? Is there a difference between performing the wedding and acting as the matchmaker who arranges it? The Buddhist community in Taiwan heatedly debates this. Some say that the two parties already know each other, decide to get married, and come to the temple to take their vow in front of the Buddha. Thus, they say, a monastic is simply witnessing their vow by performing the ceremony.

Some monastics say that to flourish, Buddhism must be involved in the needs of the people, especially at crucial times such as birth, marriage, illness, death, and so forth. In Asia, most people show their faith in the Dharma by calling monastics to say prayers after a family member dies. However, if monastics only care for people after they die and not during their life, society will lose its faith. For example, in several Asian countries some people worship Jesus when they are alive and chant Buddhist mantras when they are dying. People assume that seeing a Buddhist monastic at someone's home indicates that someone died there. Wise action on the part of monastics is needed to correct this erroneous stereotype.

Personally, I do not like bhikshunis to perform marriage ceremonies. I prefer that lay Buddhists who are good practitioners do this. They are in a better position to advise the new couple on methods to establish a harmonious sexual relationship, raise children, and balance their business activities and their spiritual practice.

The abbess of a temple should attend, but should not perform, the wedding of couples who have their marriage ceremony at her temple. Performing the wedding ceremony comes close to bringing about their liaison by introducing them—the action prohibited by this precept. However, if the two people know each other and decide to marry, they are welcome to say their marriage vow before the Buddha at a temple. This benefits them, and monastics may be present at that time. Monastics can also advise them on proper conduct, such as communicating effectively with each other, maintaining trust, and treating each other with kindness and patience.

As monastics of course we must express our concern for people during all the major events of their lives. However, in my opinion, not performing weddings does not mean we do not care about them. We can show our support for Buddhist families in other ways, such as by providing guidance in their lives, relationships, and Dharma practice. We can help them deal with anger and cultivate peacefulness and contentment. If we neglect laypeople's needs, they will naturally go to other religions for help. Their seeking advice and guidance from Buddhist monastics to solve family problems or work dilemmas indicates their trust in us, and we must respond and help them.

In ancient times, most marriages were arranged, and even today many parents in India arrange the marriage of their children. The classified section of newspapers in all major Indian cities contain ads placed by parents seeking appropriate marriage partners for their children! Of course, in the West, nowadays children decide for themselves. Nevertheless, if a bhikshuni has a family before she joins the sangha, she should not act as a matchmaker for her children. If a bhikshuni gives advice to a pregnant woman concerning who the baby should marry in the future, the bhikshuni does not commit a sanghavashesha because she only gave advice and the marriage was not completed. However, she does create an offense.

Acting as a matchmaker differs from helping people establish a happy family. For example, if a couple has a bad argument and the woman leaves the house and seeks help at the temple, a bhikshuni should help her calm down and then discuss with her how to communicate with her husband. The bhikshuni may encourage her to return home, and if the woman does, the bhikshuni does not commit a sanghavashesha because the family already existed; she is simply trying to reconcile the couple and bring harmony to the family. Of course, if it is not safe for the woman to return home, the bhikshuni should not recommend that she do so.

Although sangha members do not want to become overly involved in laypeople's problems, helping them is certainly appropriate. Even the Buddha helped laypeople to increase their wealth, improve their status in the world, and create a happy family. For example, in the *Sigalovada Sutra* the Buddha explained the qualities of a good employer, employee, husband, wife, teacher, student, and so on.

A bhikshuni who advises people who raise horses to breed their horse with another horse to continue the excellent breed, violates this precept. Vinaya Master Hong-yi compiled views on this from various sources. According to the *Mahasangha Vinaya*, advising others on mating horses to produce a good breed is a sthulatyaya offense, while advising them how to mate other animals is a dushkrita offense. However, according to the book of Buddhist discipline, *Pi-Nai-Ye*, a sangha-vashesha is committed, regardless whether horses or other animals are concerned.

Accepting Offerings from a Desirous Man

> Sanghavashesha 8: If a bhikshuni with lustful mind knows a man has lustful mind, but still accepts food or other things from him, she commits a sanghavashesha if she does not refrain from her misconduct upon the first admonition.

During a severe famine in the Buddha's time, the monastics did not receive sufficient alms to sustain themselves and many times returned empty-handed from the village. Meanwhile, one very beautiful bhikshuni remained well-nourished. Other bhikshunis were puzzled and asked her, "Why are other monastics thin and you are well-fed and healthy?" She explained that every day she went to a businessman's home for alms and received fine food from him.

One day when she went to his house, he offered her food and then grabbed her hand, saying, "Come with me. Five hundred golden coins are needed to purchase a wife and I have spent that much on you. Now you are my wife." The bhikshuni screamed, attracting a crowd. One person confronted the man, "How dare you grab this bhikshuni?" He said, "I spent five hundred golden coins on her. She is mine." The people asked her, "Did you know that this man offered you food because he was attracted to you and wanted you to be his wife?" "Yes," she replied. "If you knew his intention, why then did you scream?" they retorted. Later many pure bhikshunis who practiced diligently heard of this incident and were ashamed of a bhikshuni behaving like this. As a result, the Buddha set up this precept.

Here, both the bhikshuni and the man are influenced by sexual desire. If she knows of his selfish intention and still accepts offerings from him, she violates this precept. This story reveals a lot about ancient Indian customs: sometimes men would purchase a wife; other times they would grab a woman as their wife. Although this is not the situation in our countries now, we must nevertheless be attentive to the motivation of a male benefactor as well as to our own motivation.

Five conditions are necessary for this sanghavashesha to be committed:

1. The other person is a man
2. The bhikshuni perceives the subject as a man
3. The offering, be it food or clothes, is meant as a means of seduction
4. The bhikshuni is aware of the donor's motivation
5. She receives and uses the offering

The offering he gives her may be staple food such as rice or noodles, permitted food such as vegetables or fruit, or other offerings such as clothing, jewels, or money. If both people are aware of the other's lustful feelings and she receives and consumes his offering, she commits a sanghavashesha. However, if both parties have a lustful mind but the bhikshuni does not accept the man's offering, she does not commit a sanghavashesha. Nor does she if her motivation is pure, yet she receives and consumes the man's offering without recognizing his desirous intention. If both parties are pure in their attitude, no transgression is committed.

If a bhikshuni knows a man is attracted to her, she must be careful and not continue the relationship. She should not go to his house any more. Other bhikshunis can go there instead to ask him for support for the sangha. Using skillful means to alter the relationship, we can prevent ourselves or another bhikshuni from committing an offense. Changing or discontinuing the relationship also prevents the man from creating negative karma.

Sanghavashesha 9: If a bhikshuni tells another bhikshuni, "Elder Sister, what does it have to do with you if he has a lustful mind or not? As long as you yourself have no lustful thought, you may accept food from him without guilt," that bhikshuni commits a sanghavashesha if she does not refrain from her misconduct upon the first admonition.

After the Buddha established sanghavashesha 8, the bhikshuni no longer went to that man for alms. However, since a famine still existed, the bhikshunis had difficulty obtaining enough food. Another bhikshuni, a friend of the first one, encouraged her to go again to that man's house, saying, "Obtaining food is the first priority. You don't need to be concerned whether or not the man has a desirous attitude. If your motivation is fine and he gives you the food at the proper time, you may accept it. Then, bring the food back here and share it with the community."

This kind of reasoning sounds good—it sounds like the Dharma—but is actually misleading. The second bhikshuni knows both the donor and the first bhikshuni have lustful minds, but she still encourages her to go to him for alms because she wants a share of the food. Having a selfish motivation, she does not care if the first bhikshuni observes the precepts. Nor does she help her friend to practice correctly. In fact, she actually leads her astray.

How long can the sangha sustain itself from this kind of support? These precepts indicate that the Buddha wanted us to live with right livelihood, according to the noble eight-fold path. Monastics should obtain food, clothes, and other daily supplies in the correct manner. In that way, we can continue our spiritual practice and maintain the purity of the sangha.

If the first bhikshuni follows this misdirected advice and accepts food from a lustful man, she commits sanghavashesha 8, and the second bhikshuni commits sanghavashesha 9. If the first bhikshuni does not follow the advice, she does not commit a sanghavashesha. However, if the second bhikshuni's words and meaning are clear, she generates one sanghavashesha for each statement of wrong advice she gives.

The above two precepts illustrate an important point: problems can arise if a bhikshuni receives offerings just from one layperson or if a layperson makes offerings exclusively to one bhikshuni. When receiving offerings from laypeople—be they men or women—monastics should accept them in the name of the community. In that way, the offerings go to the community instead of to an individual. Even if the relationship between a bhikshuni and a layperson is close, the bhikshuni should transfer the relationship to the community. We should not grasp things for ourselves. For example, a king wanted to give his bamboo garden to the Buddha. The Buddha recommended that he give it to the sangha community instead and said, "Because I am a member of the sangha, your supporting the sangha is supporting me."

Earlier I told the story of the Buddha restraining one bhikshu from using his superhuman powers during a famine to take his fellow sangha to places where they could receive food. Here too, the Buddha shows his care for ordinary practitioners: everyone should sustain herself the same way the other nuns do, rather than obtain requisites by making herself special or by violating the precepts. When other sangha members endure famine, it is not right for one bhikshuni to use her beauty for her own advantage, and with a desirous mind receive offerings from a lustful man. As bhikshunis, we must cultivate contentment. When others eat porridge, so do we. If others can endure little food, so can we. We should not obtain support in a wrong way, but follow the intention of the precepts and live like everyone else.

The first nine of the seventeen sanghavashesha speak of a bhikshuni not refraining from her misconduct after the first admonition, while the last eight speak of her not refraining after the third admonition. If a bhikshuni does the action proscribed in sanghavashesha 8 or 9, other bhikshunis should admonish her, explaining that this behavior is not in accordance with the Dharma and she should refrain from doing it. If the negligent bhikshuni changes her behavior after being advised in private by another bhikshuni, no offense is created. If she refuses to accept admonition in private, the assembly of bhikshunis holds a meeting during which one bhikshuni raises the issue and confronts the guilty bhikshuni. If the negligent bhikshuni expresses her regret before the virtuous bhikshuni has finished her admonition, she does not commit a sanghavashesha, although she does commit a lighter offense. However, if she maintains her position without heeding the admonition, then as soon as the virtuous bhikshuni has finished speaking, the negligent bhikshuni commits a sanghavashesha offense.

If a bhikshuni does an action proscribed in the last eight sanghavashesha, another bhikshuni should first admonish her privately. If the negligent bhikshuni refuses to accept admonition in private, the assembly holds a meeting, raises this issue, and admonishes her. If she regrets her behavior before the third admonition is completed, she does not commit a sanghavashesha. If not, she commits a sanghavashesha. If she shows her regret during the first or second admonition, she commits a sthulatyaya offense, which is not as serious.

Being Alone in Dangerous Situations

> Sanghavashesha 7: If a bhikshuni crosses water alone, enters a village alone, sleeps alone, or walks alone behind others (out of their sight and hearing), she commits sanghavashesha if she does not refrain from her misconduct upon the first admonition.

These four situations of being alone—when crossing water, entering a village, sleeping, or walking—are especially serious for bhikshunis. Each one results in a sanghavashesha. The purpose behind this precept is for a bhikshuni to avoid danger, embarrassment, or harassment.

Crossing water alone refers to walking or swimming across a body of water, not taking a boat or plane across. During the Buddha's time, one bhikshuni crossed water by herself.

Her soaking wet clothes clung to her body, and when she got to the other bank, a group of spectators harassed her. To be bothered by ill-intentioned people when one is already wet and miserable is similar to sexual harassment. To help bhikshunis avoid this situation, the Buddha said they should not cross water alone.

The primary focus of this precept is to avoid danger, either from dangerous waters or ill-intentioned people. If two bhikshunis are wading across water together, but one goes ahead leaving the other behind, she commits a sanghavashesha. If they start crossing the water together, but become separated by strong current or by another person's interference, they do not commit a sanghavashesha. Thus, to determine if a transgression has occurred, we must examine not only the external circumstances, but also the bhikshuni's determination to protect her precepts. In Taiwan, some areas are beset by floods during heavy rains. Nuns should avoid going out during such times when travel is dangerous.

Four conditions must be complete for this sanghavashesha to occur:

1. The body of water is wide, such as a lake or river
2. The bhikshuni is crossing it alone
3. Her reasons for making that trip are insufficient
4. She arrives at the other side, thus completing the action of crossing water

A bhikshuni who uses superhuman powers to cross water does not violate the precept not to cross water alone. However, she does violate the precept not to show off her superhuman powers because the Buddha prohibited his disciples from revealing their superhuman powers.

The second part of the precept involves entering a village alone. One bhikshuni who had many disciples once went to a village alone. Because women did not usually travel alone— in ancient as well as modern India— people began to gossip, saying that the bhikshuni must be going to see a man. As a result, the Buddha set up this precept. Bhikshunis should be with at least one companion whenever they enter a village. As they walk, they should be within hearing distance of each other.

Women are more susceptible to harassment than men. Recently, our society has discussed at length methods women can use to protect themselves and avoid such unpleasant situations. Several of the bhikshuni precepts were created for this very reason. The Buddha did not permit nuns to wander from place to place or to sleep in the forest or under trees, although monks were allowed to do this. While in ancient times, bhikshunis crossed fields and in modern times we transverse cities, in either case, bhikshunis should not travel alone but go with a companion and be within arms' reach of each other.

In the West, few nuns' communities exist and so a bhikshuni may not always be able to go out with a companion. In addition, women have jobs, and society accepts them going out alone. The focus of this precept is safety, to prevent bhikshunis from encountering dangerous situations. If no companion is available, a bhikshuni may go out alone at safe times and in safe places. However, she should avoid traveling alone late at night or in unsafe areas.

The third part of the precept is not to sleep alone. In the Buddha's time, many bhikshunis were sexually violated or were badly criticized by the public for sleeping alone. To protect them, the Buddha set up this precept. Bhikshunis should sleep within an arm's reach of each other, so that they can help each other if need be. However, they should not share a bed, a blanket, or a pillow. Bhikshunis should avoid living in an apartment or a mountain hut alone. Also, they should lock their doors when sleeping or bathing.

Although this precept is specifically about sleeping alone, I would like to consider the broader topic of bhikshunis having their own rooms in the monastery. I have seen cases where each bhikshuni has her own room, and some bhikshunis, with the help of their parents, furnish theirs like a luxury apartment with many modern conveniences. They can sleep, eat, wash, entertain, and make phone calls in their room without ever interacting with their fellow practitioners. As convenient as it is to have everything at their fingertips, this situation is not beneficial for spiritual practice. Because we human beings naturally tend to cherish ourselves, we need to interact with others to advance our practice. Daily activities such as washing, eating, and studying are occasions for these interactions. As commonplace as they may seem, they are closely related to our practice. If we have our own comfortable room where we can do whatever we like without having to relate with others, our attachment and stubbornness remain unchallenged. In that case, how can we progress spiritually?

When constructing a temple, we should designate areas for specific purposes. For example, bedrooms are for resting. We should not receive guests or eat there. Except for the elderly and the ill, whose bathrooms should be nearby, everyone else should have to leave her bedroom to wash. Bhikshunis should eat together with the community, unless they are ill or doing special work for the monastery. If a nun has her own stove, refrigerator, and sink in her room, she may either isolate herself from the community or turn her room into a social place for her friends. Then the monastery is no longer a place for spiritual practice. We should not ignore such details, because they affect the atmosphere of the monastery.

The fourth part of this precept concerns walking alone, outside of another bhikshuni's hearing distance. One day, a bhikshuni started out walking with a group of bhikshunis, but since she did not want to be with them, she purposely lagged behind. When someone asked her why, she said, "I'm waiting for someone." This aroused the laypeople's suspicions, and they criticized her. Thus, the Buddha made this precept.

Whereas Asian nuns live in communities, the majority of Western nuns live by themselves. I do not know how they can observe this precept. I hope you discuss among yourselves how to create a safe environment and how to protect yourselves from danger, harassment, and undeserved criticism.

Homosexuality

> Sanghavashesha 14: Suppose some bhikshunis live intimately together and engage in negative deeds together. Their bad reputation spreads about and they cover up for each other. A (virtuous) bhikshuni should admonish them saying, "Elder Sisters, do not associate intimately with each other and engage in negative deeds together such that your bad reputation spreads around and you cover up for each other. If you stop associating intimately with each other, you will benefit by the Buddhadharma and abide in peace and happiness." If the bhikshuni persists in her misconduct and refuses to repent when admonished by the (virtuous) bhikshuni, the (virtuous) bhikshuni should admonish her three times. If she gives up her misconduct on the third admonition, good. If she does not, she commits a sanghavashesha requiring repentance upon the third admonition.

Homosexual intercourse for both bhikshus and bhikshunis is a parajika offense. For bhikshunis, intimate sexual contact without intercourse with a lustful woman is a sanghavashesha offense.

> Prayascittika 90: If two healthy bhikshunis lie together on one bed, they commit a prayascittika.

> Prayascittika 91: If bhikshunis lie together on one mattress and share the same quilt, they commit a prayascittika unless it is exceptional times.

Situations that could lead to sexual contact between bhikshunis should be avoided. Although bhikshunis should not sleep alone, neither should they sleep together on one bed or cover themselves with one blanket or share a pillow. While practicing Dharma, we need friends and should take care of each other. However, being too close is not wise.

> Prayascittika 74: If bhikshunis pat each other's (sexual organs), they commit a prayascittika.

Interaction among bhikshunis should be positive and helpful, and sharing sexual pleasure distracts them from the path. In addition, two bhikshunis developing a special relationship of attachment affects the entire community. We need to find a balance between being isolated and being too close to others. A bhikshuni needs companions with whom she can practice the Dharma, but she should not become physically intimate with them, because that will cause her to forget that her purpose is to practice the Dharma.

Masturbation

> Prayascittika 71: If a bhikshuni shaves the hair of three places (pubic area and two armpits), she commits a prayascittika.

At the time of the Buddha, a bhikshuni sat in a way that revealed part of her body. Some laywomen saw and thought that she shaved her pubic area. To make sure this was the case, they invited her to bathe with them. At first she refused, but the laywomen pressured her. When they undressed in the bathing house, they confirmed that the bhikshuni had shaved her pubic and underarm hair. Out of curiosity, they asked her why she did that, to which she replied, "It is my habit. I did it before I became a nun too." Puzzled, the laywomen said, "We shave the hair of the three places either to attract our husbands or boyfriends or to have some sexual pleasure. As a nun, why do you do this?" As a result, the Buddha made this precept.

Some exceptions to this precept exist. If an ill bhikshuni needs an operation requiring the shaving of this hair, no transgression is committed. In this case, shaving the hair is not done for sexual satisfaction or to look good for her partner.

> Prayascittika 72: When a bhikshuni cleans her vagina with water, she should not use more than the first finger joints of two fingers. If she exceeds that (by using more fingers or going deeper), she commits a prayascittika.

Here the bhikshuni not only cleans herself but begins to masturbate.

> Prayascittika 73: If a bhikshuni makes a male organ with glue (and uses it for masturbation), she commits a prayascittika.

The reason for this is clear.

The same action done by bhikshus and by bhikshunis may be different types of offenses. For example, homosexual contact for bhikshus is more likely to be a parajika because penetration is easy. For bhikshunis, intense homosexual contact is more likely to be a sanghavashesha and lighter homosexual contact is a prayascittika. However, for bhikshunis, sexual activities, such as petting and so forth, with a man is a parajika, while for bhikshus, such contact with a woman is a sanghavashesha. For bhikshus, masturbation is a sanghavashesha; for bhikshunis it is a prayascittika.

Intoxicants

> Prayascittika 36: If a bhikshuni drinks alcoholic liquor, she commits a prayascittika.

Although this precept is not in the category of sexual conduct, it relates to the desire for pleasure and thus its root is similar to the desire for sexual pleasure. At Buddha's time a bhikshu diligent in his practice sought a place to stay the night when he was traveling. A householder told him, "We don't have a spare room, but an empty house is available. However, because a poisonous dragon lives there, it is haunted and dangerous." The bhikshu went there, and at night, when the poisonous dragon came out and tried to harm him, he remained focused and meditated on compassion. Because his mind was not disturbed, his compassion tamed the dragon, who ceased trying to harm him.

The next day the bhikshu emerged from the house with the poisonous dragon in his alms bowl. Everyone marveled at his ability, and he immediately gained a great reputation. Even the king was impressed and thought, "If this person has such power, his teacher, the Buddha, must be spectacular." Suddenly the bhikshu, the Buddha, and the entire sangha were famous in the land.

To thank the bhikshu, the king invited him to the palace and told him to partake of whatever he liked. Being fond of liquor, the bhikshu drank a lot. On his way home, he vomited, passed out, and lay in his own vomit at the side of the road. Attracted to the vomit, crows encircled him. At that time, the Buddha walked by with his attendant, Ananda, to whom he sadly commented, "Due to his ability to control a poisonous dragon, this disciple became famous. However, now he can't even control his own body or prevent crows from pecking at him." Because of this incident, the Buddha established the precept that monastics may not take intoxicants.

When people consume alcohol, take recreational drugs, or smoke cigarettes, their purpose is to get satisfaction. However, the pleasure they experience is fleeting. It disappears quickly, and the pain of craving and dissatisfaction returns. This thirst for satisfaction from drinking, drugging, and smoking is similar to the desire for sexual satisfaction. We have to look inside ourselves and examine, "What is it within me that is troubling me and driving me to search for satisfaction from external objects and people?"

Our minds are under the influence of the three poisons: ignorance, anger, and attachment. We are attached to the things we like and get angry upon encountering things we dislike. At first we think the cause of our attachment or anger is the external object or person, but in fact, these emotional reactions come from within us; they are rooted in ignorance.

In our search for happiness, we often act destructively because we do not understand that the cause of suffering and the cause of happiness exist inside ourselves. For example, a person may search for love, but not being aware of how her mind and emotions function, she grasps at food for satisfaction whenever she feels restless. On the one hand, she frets about gaining weight, on the other, she continues to eat and then spends a lot of money to lose weight. Not looking inside herself, she does not see that her problem is rooted in ignorance.

To continue our spiritual practice, we must try to understand how our emotions arise and function. For example, when we search for love, we should examine, "What is this thirst inside me?" We can't deny that we experience happiness from being loved, but how long does that happiness last? It changes so quickly that feeling completely satisfied is impossible. When we seek satisfaction from our senses, we will never reach an end to that search. Understanding this helps subdue our mind.

Although the study of Vinaya ostensibly seems to involve learning monastic precepts, to live in the precepts successfully and happily, we have to pay attention to our mind. The precepts help us understand the cause of our behavior; they show us how our mind works and how to subdue it. The more we understand how our disturbing attitudes arise and how to counteract them, the easier it will be to observe the precepts. Then we will be firmly planted on the path to liberation and enlightenment.

Bathing

> Prayascittika 101: If a bhikshuni bathes naked in a river, a spring, a stream, or a pond, she commits a prayascittika.

While sanghavashesha 7 prohibits crossing water alone, here taking a bath in an uncovered place such as a river, spring, or pond, is contraindicated. In ancient times, people bathed outdoors, not in a bathroom. However, if a bhikshuni bathes nude in an open place, she will attract unwanted attention which could lead to harassment or provoke criticism from laypeople. Bhikshunis should take care not to expose their bodies freely or carelessly.

In this regard, I noticed that nuns in the Tibetan tradition wear sleeveless shirts, which reveal part of their body. Although this is the accepted dress for nuns in that tradition, strictly speaking, sleeveless shirts are for monks only. In the Vinaya, nuns' clothes were designed differently so that our underarms, shoulders, and breasts are well covered.

Prayascittika 37: If a bhikshuni plays in water, she commits a prayascittika.

This precept was set up due to a bhikshu's inappropriate behavior, but it applies to bhikshunis as well. Are bhikshunis allowed to go swimming? In the Chinese tradition, they are not. Several years ago, some Western men were ordained in Taiwan. Afterwards, they asked to go swimming because the weather was so hot, and someone took them to Yangming Mountain to swim. Perhaps this person made an exception because the monks were Western, but generally, if monastics go swimming in Taiwan, they are criticized for violating this precept.

I asked Catholic nuns in the United States if they are allowed to swim. Most of them replied no. Some Catholic orders have changed their dress regulation and now wear lay clothes, not the habit. Many of these nuns go swimming, but in a pool open only to Catholic nuns, not in a public pool or at a public beach. For Buddhist nuns, swimming in our robes would be difficult. Do you think it is proper for a bhikshuni to put on a bathing suit that exposes her figure and lie in the sun with laymen nearby? Although there is no precept which specifically prohibits bhikshunis from swimming, I believe that it is better not to. Swimming may be good exercise and help us to be healthy, but there are other ways to accomplish the same goal without running the risk of attracting men's attention.

Massage

Prayascittika 150: If a bhikshuni applies perfume on her body, she commits a prayascittika.

Prayascittika 151: If a bhikshuni applies sesame paste on her body, she commits a prayascittika.

Prayascittika 152: If a bhikshuni has a bhikshuni rub her body, she commits a prayascittika.

Prayascittika 153: If a bhikshuni has a shikshamana rub her body, she commits a prayascittika.

Prayascittika 154: If a bhikshuni has a shramanerika rub her body, she commits a prayascittika.

Prayascittika 155: If a bhikshuni has a laywoman rub her body, she commits a prayascittika.

The above six precepts prohibit a bhikshuni who is motivated by attachment to pleasure to ask various individuals to apply scents to her body or to massage her body. If, due to illness, a bhikshuni needs a massage for treatment, no transgression is created. But a bhikshuni should not have a massage simply for enjoyment or other entertaining purposes.

Some precepts prohibit bhikshunis from decorating their body with ornaments and garlands. In addition, when going outside the bhikshunis' private quarters in the monastery, we should wear our robes properly. This prevents drawing unwanted attention to our body or becoming vain, and thus prevents hindrances in our practice. While we should keep our body healthy and clean, we should not fuss about it, and instead use it as a vehicle to practice the Dharma and to benefit others.

Relations with Men

Prayascittika 4: If a bhikshuni sleeps overnight in the same room with a man, she commits a prayascittika.

This precept was discussed previously, related to an incident concerning a bhikshu. However, another incident concerning

a bhikshuni also occurred. At the Buddha's time, a bhikshuni's sister died, and she went to her family's house to
pray for her sister. Because night had fallen by the time the
prayers were completed, she could not go back to the monastery alone and stayed in her sister's house. Thinking she
wanted to return to lay life, her brother-in-law asked her to
marry him. The bhikshuni expressed her determination to
be a nun, yet her brother-in-law argued all night long trying
to talk her out of it. When dawn came, she immediately ran
back to the monastery and reported the incident to the Buddha. To protect bhikshunis from uncomfortable situations
like this, he established the precept that a bhikshuni should
not stay overnight in the same room with a man.

> Prayascittika 147: If a bhikshuni develops an abscess or any
> kind of boil and lets a man open it and bandage it without
> informing the assembly or other bhikshunis, she commits a
> prayascittika.

During the Buddha's time, a bhikshu suffered from hemor-
rhoids that required surgery. The doctor performed the op
eration in front of the monastery without giving the bhikshu
any anesthetic. Needless to say, the bhikshu screamed during the operation. In addition, the doctor invited passersby
to take a look. When the Buddha returned to the monastery,
the doctor called him over saying, "Look what a terrible illness your disciple has!" But the Buddha responded by cen-
suring the doctor for his behavior.

Abscesses and boils refer to any problem with our skin or
muscles. There are two parts to this precept: one is letting a
man open the wound and bandage it; the other is not in
forming the assembly or other bhikshunis of this. All of us
will inevitably fall ill. When we go to the doctor, we should
inform the assembly and go with a female companion, be it
a bhikshuni, shramanerika, or laywoman who can offer assistance in case of need. This protects us from harassment
and makes us more attentive not to let sexual attraction arise
if a male doctor touches our body.

Prayascittika 9: If a bhikshuni teaches more than five or six sentences of Dharma to a man, unless a knowledgeable woman is present, she commits a prayascittika.

Prayascittika 30: If a bhikshuni sits alone with a man in an open place, she commits a prayascittika.

Prayascittika 80: If a bhikshuni enters a village and stands and talks with a man in a screened place, she commits a prayascittika.

Prayascittika 81: If a bhikshuni enters a secluded place with a man, she commits a prayascittika.

Prayascittika 82: If a bhikshuni enters a village and in a street or a lane, sends her companions away and stands whispering with a man in a secluded place, she commits a prayascittika.

Prayascittika 86: If a bhikshuni enters a dark room together with a man, she commits a prayascittika.

The above precepts have a similar purpose: to protect a bhikshuni from becoming too friendly with a man. By doing so, they prevent possible hindrances to our spiritual practice and help us maintain our original motivation to attain liberation and enlightenment. They also prevent others from having the opportunity to make false accusations about our purity. For example, in recent years some Dharma teachers have been accused of sexual improprieties with their students. If these teachers had never been alone or had not been too friendly with those students, such accusations—be they true or false—would not have been made.

Prayascittika 33: If a bhikshuni goes to see a military parade, unless it is for an allowable reason, she commits a prayascittika.

Prayascittika 34: A bhikshuni may stay for two or three nights in a military camp, if it is for an allowable reason. If she stays beyond that, she commits a prayascittika.

Military sites include military bases, stations, training camps, parades, or battlegrounds. An offense is not committed if a monastic passes by a place without knowing that a military site is located there or that two parties are at war there. The *Four-part Vinaya* describes the three primary purposes of these two precepts:

1. To respect the nobility of the Buddhadharma
2. To avoid criticism, such as others thinking one is a spy or prostitute
3. To eliminate various non-virtuous actions, such as developing interest in weaponry and military matters, and to increase virtuous actions.

Visiting Laypeople

Prayascittika 65: If a bhikshuni enters the door of the palace of an anointed *Kshatriya* king before the king has come out and the treasure has been hidden, she commits a prayascittika.

Kshatriya is the ruling and warrior caste of ancient India, and an anointed king is one who has been enthroned. "The treasure being hidden" means this person is not dressed properly, while "the door of the palace" refers to the threshold of the inner palace. Entering into this area is like entering his home.

In the Buddha's time, a certain queen enthusiastically supported the sangha. Before she became queen, she was a garden maid named Huang Tou worked for a Brahmin. Standing in the garden one day she thought, "When will my role as a maid finish?" That day the Buddha passed the Brahmin's house and Huang Tou respectfully offered him a bowl of plain rice. Witnessing his peacefulness, she said with sincerity, "'This insignificant offering is too coarse for the Buddha, but it is the best I can offer." The Buddha asked if she had any wishes, to which she responded, "Being a maid is terrible. I wonder if it is possible to terminate this fate." "Your sincerity will soon bring you out of this misery," the Buddha said to her. Delighted to have made an offering to the Buddha, Huang Tou returned to the garden, happily thinking about the Buddha's words.

In the garden she saw a young man sleeping under a tree. Puzzled why this tired young man was there, she offered him some water when he awoke. The young man was taken by her kindness and good nature and asked her to come home with him. He was the king, and after paying for Huang Tou, he took her to the palace where they were married. Huang Tou later received the five precepts and encouraged the king to do so as well. Appreciative of the Buddha, she asked the king to permit bhikshus and bhikshunis to enter the palace without prior notice. She promised to support them unconditionally, and from that time on, the monastics freely entered and departed from the palace.

One day a certain bhikshu went into the palace while the king and queen were sleeping. Upon hearing his arrival, the queen got up quickly, and accidentally her dress fell off. After the bhikshu left, the king asked her if the bhikshu had seen what happened, and she told him that she regarded monastics as brothers and sisters and was not concerned. However, the bhikshu jokingly told people about what he had seen in the palace, and his speech invoked much criticism. As a result the Buddha established this precept.

> Prayascittika 28: If a bhikshuni impudently stays in a donor's house where there are valuables, she commits a prayascittika.

> Prayascittika 29: If a bhikshuni sits in a screened area in a donor's house where there are valuables, she commits a prayascittika.

These two precepts came into existence when a bhikshu, going to his friend's house for food, remained there a long time with no intention of leaving. He sat in a secluded place and talked with the hostess. Interrupting the family's life, he also put himself in a vulnerable position.

The expression "donor's house" in Chinese literally means "nutriment place" or "place of sustenance." The Vinaya speaks of four types of nutriments or sustenance: physical food, contact, volition, and consciousness. Here, the food spoken of is that of sensual contact because men and women living as householders long for sensual contact with each other. They also seek "valuables," i.e. material possessions of value. Thus, a bhikshuni should avoid staying in laypeople's homes longer than necessary, for if she does, she could be adversely influenced by their interest in sensual pleasures or wealth.

Monastics should be considerate of laypeople and avoid dropping in unexpectedly or overstaying their welcome. Of the many devoted laypeople who sincerely support the sangha, some work closely with monastics. As a result, the interactions between them become more personal and informal, and a bhikshuni may start to visit them any time she wants or enter their home as if it was her own house. Such behavior is improper for monastics. We should not go into laypeople's homes freely, but go only when necessary. For example, if the temple sends us, we can visit a family, but we should call first and set up a convenient time. When the purpose of our visit is fulfilled, we should leave, and not hang out in laypeople's homes without a purpose. The family members who appreciate the Dharma may appreciate our visit, but other family members who do not have faith in the Dharma may feel disturbed. We must be sensitive to others' needs.

Entertainment

Prayascittika 79: If a bhikshuni goes to see entertainment, she commits a prayascittika.

Bhikshunis should not go to places of entertainment, for example, to theaters, concerts, or movies. Nor should they watch soap operas and general entertainment on television. However, for educational reasons, we may go to the cinema or watch television. We have to evaluate our motivation as well as the educational quality of the program before seeing it. As monastics, we have renounced worldly activities and adopted a spiritual life style. Since the time we have for Dharma practice is already insufficient, why waste time on watching entertainment with an attitude seeking distraction or amusement? Doesn't this run counter to our initial intention for ordination? Movies, television programs, and advertisements are designed to instigate people's attachment and aversion, precisely the attitudes that we are trying to counter in our spiritual practice. Thus, for monastics, entertainment devoid of any good purpose creates hindrances to our Dharma practice and impedes us from actualizing our aspiration for liberation.

CHAPTER NINE

Taking What Has Not Been Freely Given: Precepts Regarding Stealing

Parajika 2: Suppose a bhikshuni, with the intention of taking what is not given, takes something in an inhabited place or a deserted area, and is arrested by the king or a high official of the king, or tied up, executed, or deported (with these words): "You are a thief, you are a fool, you are ignorant." If a bhikshuni takes what is not given in this manner, she commits a parajika and is expelled from the order.

The precept concerning stealing brings up some complex issues such a bhikshuni's means of procuring financial support and her relationship to the law of the land. The triggering incident involves a bhikshu who one day returned from alms round to find his hut demolished and the hay and wood from which it was constructed carried away by neighbors for firewood. A potter before ordination, he then made clay bricks and built a house for himself. Because the bricks were red, the house could be seen from far away, and one day as the Buddha passed nearby, he asked what it was. The bhikshus told him, and he said that bhikshus should not live in that type of house because it is unhealthy and ordered it torn down. Disappointed, the monk followed the Buddha's order and once again found himself homeless.

This time, to build a house conducive for good health, the monk decided to use wood. Going to a friend who was guarding the king's forest, he said, "The king promised that bhikshus could have wood." Because they had known each other for a long time, his friend believed him and permitted him to cut wood. With it, he built a house for himself. One day while a high minister was patrolling the city, he discovered the damage done to the king's forest. The guard told him what had occurred, but the minister, doubting that the king would consent to cutting of trees in his forest, asked the king. The king confirmed that he had not given permission, so the high minister arrested the guard. The guard asked the bhikshu to testify on his behalf, and the bhikshu said, "Your Majesty, during your inauguration ceremony you told the populace that monastics and Brahmins were free to take water, grass, and wood in the land." The king replied, "Yes, I did say this, but the meaning is that they may take unowned grass and wood. I didn't say that they could take property belonging to others."

This crime warranted a death sentence according to the law of the land, but because the king was a devout Buddhist, he did not want to sentence a bhikshu to death. Instead, he scolded, "You are thief. You are a fool. You are ignorant," and set the bhikshu free. Unhappy with this, the king's ministers said, "Holding anyone exempt from the law will create chaos in the country, and we will be unable to govern." Similarly, the citizens were angry and criticized the sangha for being an assembly of thieves. From that time on, they no longer welcomed bhikshus to their villages or wanted to learn the Dharma. Hearing about the uproar, the Buddha asked the bhikshu, "Did you do this?" and received confirmation that he had. Then the Buddha asked another bhikshu who had been a high government official before ordination, "According to the law of this land, what degree of stealing is punishable by death?" He replied, "The law states that if a person steals five units of currency or its equivalent, he will be executed." The Buddha then established the precept that if a bhikshu or bhikshuni takes something worth five units of currency or more without it being given, he or she commits a parajika.

Six conditions must be fulfilled to commit this parajika:

1. Someone legally owns the object
2. Although the actual owner may not be known, the bhikshuni clearly knows that someone owns this object
3. The bhikshuni has the intention to steal or to possess this object
4. The stolen object is precious
5. The bhikshuni takes action to possess the object
6. The object has been moved and the action completed. For example, if a person transfers money from one bank account to another, although the money may still be in the same bank, it has been moved. In the case of stealing a house, the title, not the house, has been moved.

The fourth condition, the value of the object, needs further clarification. The object stolen is not a pen or a packet of tissue, but a valuable object. How do we determine what is valuable? What is the modern equivalent of five units of ancient Indian currency? How should we account for inflation?

Instead of trying to fix a particular amount, another way to determine an object's value is to examine the law of the land. Since the Buddha had wanted to know what amount is punishable by death according to the law of that land, we can ask the same question regarding the law of the country in which the theft occurred. If a bhikshuni steals an object worth that amount or more, she commits a parajika. What constitutes a parajika would differ according to the country in which it occurred. For example, in a country where the citizens have abolished the death sentence for stealing, a bhikshuni could not commit a parajika for stealing. In other countries, people may be severely punished for stealing a small item, and there the parajika of stealing could be committed more easily. From this precept, we see that the sangha's precepts are related to the law of the land.

What does ownership mean? Owned objects are of three kinds:

1. Those owned by human beings
2. Those owned by animals and non-human beings
3. Those owned by the Three Jewels or by the sangha community

Stealing objects belonging to human beings is covered in detail by the law of that country, and since the customs of each place impact who owns an object and the legality of ownership, I will not discuss this in detail. For example, if we are in a land where water is more valuable than oil, if a bhikshuni steals water, she will be punishable by law. However, in another country where water is plentiful, taking it without asking will not be punishable at all.

In many countries, religious people or religious organizations enjoy tax-exempt status. We must be careful not to abuse this. For example, wanting help to reduce his taxes, a layperson may ask a bhikshuni to use the temple's tax-exempt status in an illegal manner. If she complies, she commits a transgression. Similarly, we may think that since many people will use a temple, no fault occurs if we occupy another's land and construct a temple or a Dharma center on it. This is incorrect. If we think that because a certain large sum of money is for a monastery or a Dharma center, we can bring it into a country without declaring it if required by law, we are at fault. Also, we violate people's rights if we publish Buddhist books without asking permission from the party holding the copyright. In other words, we should not think that because the work we are doing is for the Three Jewels, we can break the law.

Many cows wander the streets of India. Although they are not legally owned by one individual, we cannot catch them and raise them as our own. Someone may have set those cows free, but the Indian law protects the cows, and we cannot regard them as unowned.

An object owned by non-human beings could be owned by animals, ghosts, spirits, or gods. For example, in Asia we often see small temples along the roadside or cairns in a field or on a mountain. If those temples are cared for by human beings, they own the offerings in them. However, if there is no caretaker, we should regard the offerings as unowned and take them. Before taking any offering left at a temple or cairn, we should ask permission from the ghost or god. Objects which are owned by animals include the food accumulated by mice and the prey killed by tigers. After they have finished eating, however, we can take the remains.

Vandalizing others' property is not considered stealing, because by definition stealing is to take something not freely given to us. Vandalizing, on the other hand, involves destroying someone's property. The vandal must negotiate with the owner and determine the extent to which he or she will compensate the cost of the damage.

Objects Belonging to the Three Jewels

Objects belonging to the Three Jewels include stable materials, such as land and buildings, as well as consumable objects, such as food, clothing, and other daily supplies. Within these, some objects belong to the Buddha, some to the Dharma, and some to the Sangha. Objects belonging to the Buddha include statues, pictures, robes and ornaments adorning statues, banners, altar furniture, various ritual implements, and the offerings on an altar. The lights, incense, fruit, and so forth were offered to the Buddha; they were not meant as offerings for us, so we may not take something from

the altar as we desire. Objects belonging to the Dharma include scriptures, bookshelves, book covers, and ornaments
for the texts. Objects belonging to the Sangha include monasteries, fields, gardens, robes, bowls, food, and so forth. Each
object is managed differently, depending on if it belongs to
the Buddha, Dharma, or Sangha, and a temple assigns particular monastics to oversee this.

In the Buddha's time, the objects belonging to the Buddha
consisted of the offerings people gave to Shakyamuni Buddha, and he decided how to manage and distribute these.
Often the Buddha would designate that the ownership of
these materials be transferred to the sangha. Now the Buddha has entered parinirvana. At temples, people still offer
jewelry, statues, and so forth to the Buddha, but he is not
present to decide upon their management. What do we do?
Certain objects, including food, facilities, and food, are generally used by the sangha community. However, if a precious
object such as a diamond necklace or a brocade robe is offered to the Buddha, the sangha must be careful how it is
used because taking a valuable object transgresses a parajika. In this situation, the assembly must decide by consensus how the object is to be managed; a majority vote is not
sufficient. It may decide to keep the diamond necklace in a
safe or to change it into currency. If the assembly decides to
sell it, the money can be used for the Buddha only. Objects
belonging to the Buddha or Dharma may not be used for
other purposes unless the sangha agrees, and even then, their
use is extremely restricted.

Two types of objects belong to the Sangha: public and private. Private objects are consumable items used by one monastic, such as robes, bowls, and food. Public objects belong
to all monastics and include buildings and land. The monastics living at that monastery at any particular time cannot
consider public items as theirs alone and freely dispose of
them, because they are to be shared by all present and future
monastics. Treating the land and buildings of a monastery

like our personal property or putting it up for sale with this attitude creates a grave transgression.

This concept of ownership is different from our ordinary one. Since public objects belong to the present and the future monastics, the number of individuals sharing in its ownership is countless. Taking a public object as one's own means harming not only each of the present sangha members, but also all of the future ones. To purify this karma, one has to confess to each sangha member individually and request forgiveness, and this would take eons to complete. Therefore, misusing sangha property is considered a grave transgression.

I have not found any specific guidelines regarding selling an old monastery so that the sangha can move to a new one. Nor have I seen guidelines for selling property donated to the sangha in an unsuitable location in order to purchase property in a conducive environment for a monastery. Nevertheless, a few points mentioned in the bhikshuni precepts and related commentaries are worth considering in this regard:

1. Do not mix up the usage of these objects, i.e. things donated to the Buddha remain for the Buddha, things donated to the Dharma are used for the Dharma, and so forth.

2. The sangha community must come to a complete consensus to change how this property is used. For example, to remodel a Buddha's statue, to build a new place for the Buddhist scriptures, or to improve the living conditions of the sangha, the sangha needs to reach a complete consensus.

3. The donor's intention should be considered and respected.

As members of the sangha, we must be aware of the demarcation between two individuals in the community, between an individual and the community, and between the community and the Three Jewels so we will not violate the precept of stealing. For example, the members of a monastery have an agreement that they can use the bedrooms, bathroom, library books, common areas, water, food, and drinks freely.

Doing so is not stealing. However, if we take things that have not been designated for free use, we run the risk of stealing from the sangha, a heavy negative karma. Similarly, we do not have the right to take things from the storeroom, sell them, and keep the money for ourselves. Nor may we take the monastery's property with us when we leave.

The person who makes an offering is the one who decides who is to receive it: the residents, the guest monastics, or everyone. In the cases where no specification is made, a consumable offering made on Buddhist holidays that is easily dividable—for example, robes, food, or money—should be distributed to residents and guest monastics alike before or during lunch, the main meal for monastics. All monastics present before noon are called "present monastics," and each one should receive an equal share of the consumable offerings made to the sangha. According to Vinaya, residents of a monastery cannot wait until evening, after the guest monastics have departed, to distribute offerings. If a layperson designates an offering to be only for specific monastics who are present, his or her request should be respected. For example, a computer offered for the monastery office is not shared between resident and guest monastics.

When food is placed on the table, all present monastics may take whatever amount they wish. However, once food has been removed from the table and put in the storage room, we may not go there and take it. Doing so is an act of stealing. Nor may we take an offering before or after the regulated hours when it is put out for the entire community. Vinaya specifies that a community should make provisions for monastics in poor health who require a special diet or more meals. For example, food may be placed in designated areas where it can be freely taken by all monastics at any time.

The precept of stealing is associated with the economic life of a community. Monastics need material and financial support, and we have to know how to obtain this correctly.

Carelessness in this regard could lead to accidental violations of the precept to abandon stealing. Although committing a theft that warrants the death sentence is difficult,
engaging in wrongdoings when handling the sangha's
money or managing its financial affairs is much easier. The
bhikshunis selected to manage property belonging to the
Three Jewels are responsible for carrying out the assembly's
decision regarding their use. Some sutras describe the hor-
rible karmic results that evolve from mishandling objects
belonging to the Three Jewels.

Laypeople often bring food to the temple to offer to the
Buddha. When putting this offering on the shrine, a layperson may say to the monastic caring for the temple, "You can
use this later, after it has been offered." His intention is for
the sangha as a whole—not just that individual—to use it.
The caretaker of the shrine should not get confused and think
that it is for her personal use. Rather, as the one doing that
job, she represents the community and has the responsibility to remove the food and distribute it to everyone.

The donor decides how his or her offering is to be used.
When the nuns of our temple are not clear to whom an offered object belongs to—the Buddha, Dharma, or Sangha—
I, as the abbess, say to the donor, "You have offered this object,
and the community would like to use it in this way," and
explain our plan. If the donor agrees, we do that. If the donor does not agree, we must honor his or her wish. In this
way, we respect the donor's intention. Thus, careful bookkeeping in monasteries is essential. We must know the donor, the amount or item given, and the way the donor would
like it to be used. Then, if questions arise regarding the use
of an object, we can easily contact the original donor and ask
him or her.

In our temple, we use money offered to the Buddha to
make Buddha statues, build the meditation hall and the
shrine, and decorate the shrine. To plan and execute their
construction or purchase involves administrative expenses—

computers, stationery, and telephone—and this taken from
the money offered to the Buddha. However, our general computer usage, stationery, telephone, and so on are paid for
from general offerings to the temple. The nuns overseeing
the special projects are not paid for their work, but they are
listed among the donors.

Money put in the temple's donation box by devotees is
used for the sangha's food and supplies, but money donated to the Buddha is not used in this way. We cannot use
funds donated to the Buddha to build housing for the
sangha, although we can use it to build a meditation hall
and classrooms.

The question arises: Can we also use money offered to the
Buddha to pay the rent for a Dharma center? Here, we need
to distinguish between building a hall and renting one, and
between things belonging to the Buddha and things used by
the Buddhist community. A hall that we construct is offered
to the Buddha, and the Buddha will be there for generations
to come. However, a rented site is for the benefit and use of
the people who attend events there. It does not belong to the
Buddha. Although a Buddha statue may be there, the primary purpose of renting the facility is for those currently
using it to have a place to hold their activities. Therefore, the
people who use the rented place should cover the rent; it
should not be taken from offerings made to the Buddha. A
temple, no matter how inactive it may be, will still have a
Buddha statue, and people will come to pay their respects to
the Buddha. The facility will continue to benefit people in
however subtle a way. This situation differs from a rented
Dharma center, where, if no meaningful activities occur,
people will not continue to pay the rent. Thus, although funds
offered to the Buddha may be used to construct a temple,
they should not be used to rent a facility.

In the West, laypeople bring fruit and flowers to the temple
or Dharma center to offer to the Buddha, but most of them do
not consider that the sangha needs support as well. Similarly,

years ago in Taiwan people donated money to make Buddha statues and other things related to the Buddha, but they did not realize the value of sangha and the benefit they received from monastics and did not know they needed support. To change the situation, monastics openly asked laypeople to expand their generosity to include the Buddha *and* the sangha. Sometimes we asked the donors for their permission to use their offering to the Buddha, saying, "The Buddha's fundamental concern is to sustain the Dharma, and monastics who study and practice well will be able to do this. They will benefit lay followers and society as a whole. Therefore, may we use part of the money you offered to fulfill the Buddha's wishes by educating and strengthening the sangha?"

A donor may offer a valuable object to the Buddha, not knowing that the Dharma center or monastery is in dire need of money to pay the rent. In this case, we may talk to the donor, explain the situation, and request his or her permission to use the offering for the rent. This is one way to legally transfer the usage of objects belonging to the Buddha to another purpose. A second way is for the assembly to agree by consensus on the new usage. However, the range of usage to which the money may be transferred is limited. For example, the assembly cannot agree to use money offered to the Buddha to buy food or make clothes. In times of severe need, monastics may borrow money from the Buddha's fund to purchase daily supplies. This must be repaid when sufficient funds are obtained. Accurate financial records and account books are essential to avoid accidental misuse of funds. These guidelines are not designed to unnecessarily restrict practitioners, but to make us conscientious. Their side effect is to make us creative when fund raising for the sangha.

People who come to our temple in Taiwan wishing to make an offering often have not yet made a firm decision concerning its specific use. At this time, the nuns present a list of choices for them. Among these, one will be to let the temple, i.e. the nuns, decide on its best usage. If the person agrees to this, we put the money into whatever project needs it; or if there is no urgent need, we may save it for future projects. When the person selects another, more specific choice, we use their donation as they direct. If a person comes to the temple with a gold necklace and has already decided to offer it to the Buddha, we will not influence him to change his mind. However, if he consults us before making a purchase, we may suggest other ways of offering to the Buddha: for example, he could donate it towards the construction of the temple or a Buddha statue or to support Buddhist education.

When asking people to support the construction of a temple, we show them the plans. This includes a shrine room for the Buddha statue where people may also pray or meditate. Other facilities, such as rest rooms, living quarters for monastics, and guest rooms for laypeople may also be included. The plan's details are clear so people will know what result to expect.

Sometimes people clean out their garage and give the items they no longer use to a temple. In general accepting people's offerings is a compassionate act and enables them to accumulate positive potential. However, when these people become more knowledgeable and are receptive, they should be taught to make pure offerings, not simply to give away things they do not want. Some temples in Taiwan require donors to call in advance to make sure the items to be donated are really needed.

The Vinaya is strict about how the sangha's possessions are used. Some additional principles to keep in mind are:

1. A monastery may give its excess supplies and food to other monastics or monasteries.

2. An individual sangha member should not give away the sangha's possessions to laypeople, unless it is one's own share.

3. The sangha may give food and clothing to laypeople engaged in building a stupa, temple, living quarters or providing a

special service for the sangha community as a token of gratitude and to compensate their efforts.

4. Neither an individual monastic nor a community should give offerings away to laypeople in order to win their favor or in hopes of receiving a larger gift in return.

5. Food remaining after the sangha's midday meal may be given to beggars, mendicants from other religions, and so on, although a monastic may not give it with his or her own hands. She may ask another person to do that, or the food may be placed somewhere where the other people may take it. The bodhisattva vow puts a slightly different slant on the issue of giving sangha property to laypeople. For example, many monasteries in mainland China offered food to the lay community in times of war and famine. In the recent prosperous years in Taiwan, some monasteries cannot consume all the food offered to them and give it to laypeople or to charities to avoid its being wasted. Doing this with a pure, altruistic intention is in keeping with the bodhisattva vow.

Why must we be so careful regarding the use of sangha property? First, it was offered by devotees with sincere faith in the Three Jewels. Second, it belongs to a community of people, not to one individual. If an individual takes sangha property and gives it to her family and friends, she is disrespecting both the donor's genuine faith and kindness and the virtue of the sangha community.

A bhikshuni must be careful before she accepts offerings of questionable origin, that is, something she suspects the donor got by means of wrong livelihood. For example, she should not accept an object that she knows to be stolen. If she suspects it is stolen but is not sure, she should ask about its origins before accepting it. However, if nothing seems suspicious, she is not at fault if she accepts it although it may have been stolen. Similarly, a bhikshuni should not accept money that she knows came from selling drugs.

Law Suits

> Sanghavashesha 4: If a bhikshuni, during the day or at night, goes before a government official to file a suit against a layman, his son, his servant, or his guest, even for the time of a thought, for a fingers' snap, or for a single moment, this bhikshuni commits a sanghavashesha if she does not refrain from her misconduct upon the first admonition.

Once, a layman built a small house for a bhikshuni. Some time later, she went to another place, leaving the house and field deserted. After the donor passed away, his son did not want the place to remain unattended and began to cultivate the land. When the bhikshuni returned, she wanted the house back, but the son claimed that he had the right to work the land because she had abandoned it long ago. Frustrated, the bhikshuni filed a lawsuit against the donor's son. After hearing the case, the judge decided in favor of the bhikshuni. To punish the son, the court confiscated his property and all of his savings. Some virtuous bhikshus heard this news and felt that it was improper for a bhikshuni to cause such tragedy to a layperson. They reported the situation to the Buddha, who established this precept.

Another incident involved a king's wife who offered a house to a bhikshuni. After living there for a while, the bhikshuni left, and the queen gave the house to a practitioner of another religion. Later, the bhikshuni returned to the house, and finding the other practitioner living there, said, "This is mine, not yours. Leave!" The practitioner refused to leave, so the bhikshuni pushed her out of the house. Angry, the practitioner went to court and filed suit against the bhikshuni. When the time of the hearing arrived, the bhikshuni refused to go for fear of violating the precept. When this news reached the Buddha, he said that monastics must go if they are called to testify in court. Thus, a bhikshuni should not initiate a lawsuit against someone. However, if she is sued or called to testify, she must go to court and explain.

Sometimes legal disputes over ownership and other issues may arise between monastics and laypeople. In this case, a bhikshuni may ask her parents or other laypeople knowledgeable in the law to provide advice, or she may appoint a representative to negotiate and resolve the dispute. The Buddha required monastics to have more tolerance and compassion to handle problems in this world. With kindness and patience, we can take care of ourselves, do what is fair, and negotiate a solution. A temple or monastery is a religious place and our focus is to practice Dharma. However the people living on the premises have the responsibility to protect the property of the monastic community and preserve it for future generations. Since our primary purpose is to practice and to spread the Dharma, we should not treat such a problem only as a financial dispute.

CHAPTER TEN

The Remaining Root Precepts: Abandoning Killing, Lying, Concealing Others' Transgressions, and Going against the Sangha's Decisions

It is necessary to observe the parajika precepts as purely as possible in order to remain a bhikshuni and to experience the purificatory effects that the precepts have upon our mindstream. Thus far we have discussed the three parajika concerning sexual contact and the one dealing with taking what has not been freely given (stealing). In this chapter, the remaining parajika will be discussed, those dealing with killing, lying, concealing others' transgressions, and going against the sangha's decision.

Killing

Parajika 3: If a bhikshuni kills a human being with her own hands, gives a knife to someone (for that purpose), admires death, praises death, or exhorts death, (saying reproachfully to someone, "What is the use of living such a wretched life? It is better for you to die than to live)," that bhikshuni commits a parajika and is expelled from the order.

In order to eliminate attachment to the body and to sexual pleasure, many bhikshus at the Buddha's time meditated on the ugliness of the body. Practicing diligently, they came to feel their body was a disgusting nuisance and wanted to be free of it. One bhikshu said to another, "Please help me by killing me. After I am dead, you can have my robes, bowl, and all my belongings." Thinking he was helping his friend, the other bhikshu killed him. Subsequently, other bhikshus asked this bhikshu for his help to die. Complying, he killed many other bhikshus. When the Buddha heard of this, he was appalled and established this precept against killing human beings. Five conditions must be fulfilled to commit this parajika:

1. The object is a human being
2. The perception is clear that the object is a human being
3. One intends to kill that person
4. Means are employed to kill that person
5. The action is completed and the other person dies

In the original incident, the bhikshu used a knife to kill, but other weapons could be used as well. Some people use words, not weapons, to kill, saying, for example, "Your life is so wretched. Surely you would be happier if you died." In this way they encourage death, praise death, or urge a person to die either by his own or another's hand. All three means—killing a human being oneself, telling someone else to kill, or encouraging someone to die or to commit suicide—constitute a parajika.

In this story, a bhikshu thought that abandoning his body by dying was the path to liberation. Is this correct? We must know how to accurately evaluate our progress on the path. Giving up our body is not necessarily a sign of progress. Rather, the waning of our defilements and an increased sense of internal peace indicate that our Dharma practice is going well. The increase of attachment, pride, anger, jealousy, or ignorance is a sign that we are not putting the teachings into practice properly.

Today people discuss whether monastics should engage in euthanasia as a means to help someone who is in extreme pain. The bhikshu in the story killed others because they requested him to do so. If a person who is sick or in great pain asks our help to die, should we comply? Is it compassionate to urge or hasten someone's death? His illness and pain result from previously committed destructive actions. Because that karma was not purified, he has to experience its results. Although dying ends the suffering of this life, no guarantee exists that the next life will be better. So, does euthanasia solve the problem?

The Vinaya relates in detail many incidents pertaining to killing, so that we will know clearly the boundaries constituting a parajika offense. For example, some women who were pregnant due to extra-marital affairs approached the bhikshunis for help in terminating their pregnancies. Some bhikshunis chanted mantras and used various medicines to cause the women to abort. This is an act of killing that falls under this parajika.

If a group of five bhikshunis ask another bhikshuni to kill a human being and she does so, all six bhikshunis commit a parajika and are expelled from the order. A monastic who kills a human being is held responsible not only by the law of the land, but also by the sangha. In fact, the sangha has to take action first and resolve the case before the government sentences the person. This is true if a monastic is involved in any other criminal act, such as stealing. Even after the sangha or the government resolves the case, the karma remains with that person, and unless she purifies it, she will experience its results, most likely in a future life.

Some bhikshus during the Buddha's time climbed onto the monastery roof to repair it. By accident a tool dropped, hit a passer-by, and killed him. This is not a parajika for the bhikshus because they lacked any intention to kill. Once a monk was helping a sick sangha member use the rest room and bathe. The sick monastic died at this time, but because the care-giver neither had the intention to kill him nor took action to do so, he did not commit a parajika. If, while insane, a bhikshuni kills someone, she does not create a parajika. After she has received treatment and has recovered her sanity, the sangha should take action and resolve the case.

Although monastic precepts primarily regulate physical and verbal behavior, to determine whether an offense has been created, and if so, how severe it was, we must examine a person's motivation before and during the action. Thinking that the pratimoksha precepts concern only external behavior is incorrect, for our physical and verbal actions are motivated by our mind. Thus, taming our mind by observing the precepts purely enables us to advance in our Dharma practice and to develop the Higher Trainings in Concentration and Wisdom.

> Prayascittika 46: If a bhikshuni deliberately kills an animal, she commits a prayascittika.

> Prayascittika 47: If a bhikshuni drinks water, knowing that there are insects in it, she commits a prayascittika.

Killing an animal or insect is less severe than killing a human being. Nevertheless, a wrongdoing is committed. The action is a prayascittika offense and can be repented. In the bodhisattva vow followed in the Chinese tradition, a root precept prohibits intentionally killing any sentient being: humans, animals, and so forth. If a bhikshuni who has taken the bodhisattva vow kills an animal, she still retains her monastic status, but she violates a root bodhisattva precept. The offense of killing an animal differs in the pratimoksha and the bodhisattva precepts.

In general the view of animals differs in the pratimoksha and bodhisattva practices. In the bodhisattva practice, we see all sentient beings as equal. However, the pratimoksha vow accords more with the common view of society that the life of a human being is more important than that of an animal. In general, common people view animals in one of two ways: either as property or as pets. As property, people use animals to do work or they raise animals for their skin and meat. As pets, animals are objects of affection and entertainment. Although the skin, fur, and meat belong to the animal itself, most animals also belong to an owner. How the owner regards that animal is an important factor in determining what kind of offense is committed by killing or stealing it. Whether we personally see animal life as equal to human life or not, we know that animals suffer considerably. Thus we should try to avoid creating the karmic causes to be born as an animal and try to have compassion for those who are.

Let's investigate the interface between killing and stealing. If someone wears animal skin or eats meat, is she stealing from an animal? When we use eggs, milk, or honey, are we engaged in stealing objects belonging to animals? If we take something from another human being who is unable to express his or her wishes, are we stealing? We need to think about these topics.

According to the Dharmaguptaka Vinaya, stealing is taking an object belonging to another being, while killing is taking life. If someone kills a deer, that being's life is taken away without permission, but that is not stealing an object belonging to the deer; it is killing. In addition, although the animal is a living being, it is also a possession belonging to a human being. The way the owner of the deer regards it influences the types of offense committed. If the owner regards the deer as property and killing it deprives him of his livelihood, the offense is different than if he regards it as a pet and grieves its loss emotionally.

Lying about Spiritual Attainments

Parajika 4: Suppose a bhikshuni, who is actually ignorant, praises herself, saying, "I have achieved superhuman faculties,"

"I have penetrated the sages' wisdom and the supreme Dharma," "I know this. I perceive that." Later on, in order to be cleared of guilt, she says, whether questioned or of her own accord, "Elder Sisters, I really do not know or perceive what I said I did." Because she praised herself with the intention to deceive, not out of pride in her superior attainments, this bhikshuni commits a parajika and is expelled from the order.

Prayascittika 8: If a bhikshuni talks about her superhuman faculties to someone who is not fully ordained, saying, "I know this. I perceive that," she commits a prayascittika, even if what she says is true.

These two precepts deal with talking about superhuman faculties, such as clairvoyance, single-pointed concentration, and the realization of emptiness. The difference between them is that in prayascittika 8, the bhikshuni actually has higher spiritual attainments and commits a prayascittika by telling others. The bhikshuni in parajika 4, however, has not attained superhuman faculties and is intentionally lying.

Parajika 4 was established due to the following incident: during one summer retreat, the Buddha and five hundred bhikshus planned to spend the summer retreat in Vaishali. At that time, people were suffering from severe famine, and food to support the sangha was scarce. The Buddha told the monastics that since supporting the sangha would cause the laypeople great hardship, they should divide into small groups and go to different places for the summer retreat. At the conclusion of the three-month retreat, the monks gathered together to see the Buddha. Having become very thin during those three months, some bhikshus wore ragged robes and looked quite unhealthy. But other bhikshus looked bright, healthy, and well fed. When the Buddha inquired about their summer retreat, the thin bhikshus said, "We couldn't find enough food," while the healthy bhikshus said, "We had a clever approach to get food. We told the lay community that one bhikshu was a stream-enterer, another was a once-returner, a third was a non-returner, and the fourth was an arhat. The lay community was so impressed by the number of liberated saints in the sangha that they saved their limited resources and donated them to us." The Buddha chastised them, "Foolish monks! How could you lie and sell the Dharma to get food and robes? Your dishonesty is damaging." He then established this precept.

Nan San Hsing Shih Chau, a commentary on the Four-part Vinaya, states that nine conditions should be present to commit the parajika of telling a great lie:

1. The object of the conversation, i.e. the listener, is a human being
2. The bhikshuni perceives the listener as a human being
3. The contents of her speech are false
4. She knows that the contents are false
5. She has the motivation to deceive the other person
6. She talks about superhuman accomplishments
7. She expresses that she has achieved the superhuman level
8. Her words are clear
9. The listener understands what she says

Deliberately lying about spiritual accomplishments for personal gain is called a great lie and is much more severe than telling other kinds of lies, speaking divisively, criticizing, or swearing. The reason lying about spiritual attainments is serious enough to warrant expulsion from the order is that it confuses people who have faith in the Buddha's teachings by leading them to think someone is a holy being when she is not. Liberated beings and enlightened ones are the hope of the world, and seeing them as leaders, people respect them and seek their advice. If a monastic tells great lies and deceives people due to his or her bad motivation, she crushes people's hope, pollutes their faith, and destroys their optimism when they later discover her real qualities.

Sometimes people may ask you if you have attained higher spiritual levels. What will you answer? We do not necessarily need to speak in order to lie. We can lie through our body language and gestures. For example, we could use a particular gesture that means yoga, indicating that we are approaching higher spiritual levels. Or we could simply smile, giving the impression that we have great realizations.

In some situations, it may seem someone has transgressed this precept when she has not. For example, some monastics practiced diligently and attained a high level of *samadhi*. Because of their concentration, their defilements did not manifest, and they mistook this state for liberation. Later their defilements manifested again, and they realized they were not yet arhats. Concerned that they had told a great lie by mentioning their accomplishment to others, they told the Buddha, who advised them to practice harder. Following his advice, they later attained higher levels on the path. In this case, they did not commit a parajika. Their motivation was not to deceive others; they mistakenly overestimated their spiritual progress. Upon discovering their error, they remedied it and did not seek personal benefit from it.

Another example is a person who practices the Dharma and actually attains higher levels of accomplishment. To verify her attainment, she explains her experiences to her teacher or to a realized practitioner who will determine if her attainment is valid. Her intention in telling her accomplishments is not to show off or to deceive others, but simply to verify her progress. Thus, she does not create a transgression.

A person may be born with any of the first five clairvoyant powers. If she tells others that she has had this clairvoyant power since birth but has not attained enlightenment, the ultimate elimination of defilements, she is not lying and has not committed a parajika.

This precept prevents a bhikshuni from confusing ultimate spiritual goals with her polluted, worldly motivation for a good livelihood. Due to attachment that seeks material possessions or a good reputation, we must not use Buddhism as a means to gain food or daily supplies. Some people say that telling others one's spiritual level is skillful means to help them generate faith in the Dharma. However, in my observation, using this approach to attract people to the Dharma is not wise. It creates more problems, confusion, and false expectations down the road. Remaining humble is best.

Concealing Others' Transgressions

Parajika 7: Suppose a bhikshuni, knowing that another bhikshuni has committed a parajika and concealed it, does not tell it to others or report it to the sangha. Later, after that bhikshuni has died or been publicly exposed, or has abandoned the path or joined a non-Buddhist group, if she says, "I knew that she had previously committed such a transgression," this bhikshuni commits a parajika and is expelled from the order because she concealed the other's serious offense.

In this case a bhikshuni commits a parajika and tries to conceal it. Nevertheless, another bhikshuni, knowing of her transgression, says nothing. Why is concealing another's wrongdoing so serious? The bhikshuni who committed a parajika was not able to purify the transgression by revealing her fault and applying the antidotes. Had her wrongdoing had been exposed, she could have purified the negativity and advanced her practice. But, because the second bhikshuni concealed her transgression, the first bhikshuni lost the opportunity to practice the Dharma while there was the chance. Although the precept mentions the first bhikshuni dying, joining a non-Buddhist group and so on, even if she is still alive and lives with the Buddhist sangha, if another bhikshuni conceals her parajika, even for a day, the latter commits this parajika. The *Commentary to the Bhikshuni Pratimoksha* mentions six conditions that need to be present for a complete transgression of this precept:

1. The one whose fault is being concealed is a bhikshuni
2. She has committed a serious transgression, namely, a parajika

3. The second bhikshuni knows about the first bhikshuni's transgression
4. The second bhikshuni has the intention to conceal it
5. The second bhikshuni does not reveal it
6. The dawn of the next day occurs

Going against the Sangha's Decisions

Parajika 8: Suppose a bhikshuni continues to obey a bhikshu whom she knows has been suspended by a karma of the assembly in accordance with the Dharma, the Vinaya, and the Buddha's teaching and has not yet been absolved because of his refusal to obey and confess. The other bhikshunis say to her, "Elder Sister, that bhikshu has been suspended by a karma of the assembly in accordance with the Dharma, the Vinaya, and the Buddha's teaching and has not yet been absolved because of his refusal to obey and confess. You should not obey him." If she persists in her misconduct when being thus admonished by the bhikshunis, the bhikshunis should admonish her twice or even three times to desist. If she desists upon the third admonition, good. If she does not, that bhikshuni commits a parajika and is expelled from the order, because of following a bhikshu convicted in a karma.

During the Buddha's time, a brother and sister joined the sangha. The brother was very bad-tempered and caused so much trouble in the bhikshu sangha that after admonishing him several times, the bhikshus suspended him and prohibited him from living with the bhikshu sangha. Still, he refused to repent. After wandering around for a while, he went to his sister, a bhikshuni, who prepared good food and served him well. The bhikshuni sangha, however, saw the danger to her practice if she continued to associate closely with him. They cautioned her, "That bhikshu engaged in misconduct, and refusing to repent, was suspended by the bhikshu sangha. You should not support him or follow his instructions." Nevertheless, this bhikshuni defended her behavior, saying, "First, according to the Buddha's instruction, a bhikshuni should respect and pay obeisance to bhikshus. Second, the Buddha said that we should support and help our relatives. He is my brother; therefore I should take care of him." Although the bhikshu sangha had made its decision to suspend him according to the Dharma, the Vinaya, and the Buddha's teaching, this bhikshuni refused to accept their decision and continued to support this bhikshu and follow his instructions even when admonished by other bhikshunis. Upon hearing of the situation, the Buddha established this precept.

According to *Shih Feng Lu Su*, a commentary on the Four-part Vinaya, six conditions need to be present for a violation of the precept of going against the sangha's decision to occur:

1. The bhikshu was disciplined by the bhikshu's sangha
2. The bhikshuni knows that the accused bhikshu refused to discontinue his misconduct and to repent
3. She obeys this bhikshu
4. The bhikshuni sangha admonishes her according to the Dharma and the Vinaya
5. She refuses to follow the bhikshuni sangha's advice
6. The proper karma (one announcement followed by three proclamations) has been completed

This precept emphasizes that a bhikshuni should obey and follow the decisions of the bhikshu sangha. Not doing so brings severe results for bhikshunis. If a bhikshuni disobeys the bhikshus' decision and refuses three times to accept admonition from the bhikshuni sangha, she commits this parajika. However, these days bhikshunis may not always know if a particular bhikshu has been censured in a meeting of the bhikshu sangha according to the Dharma, the Vinaya, and the Buddha's teaching. We need to be mindful of whose instructions we follow. We must know how to protect ourselves when in the presence of an expelled or mentally defiled bhikshu.

The Vinaya describes certain situations in which bhikshunis should not follow bhikshus. For example, if a bhikshu is very bad-tempered and unduly criticizes or strikes bhikshunis, bhikshunis should not follow his instructions. Seeing the misconduct of a bhikshu, the bhikshuni sangha can make a decision to not respect, support, or live near that bhikshu until he changes his behavior and requests to be forgiven by the bhikshuni sangha. The bhikshunis can make this decision without the bhikshu being present. Later, if he changes and requests to be forgiven, the bhikshunis should meet and revise their decision.

This precept also emphasizes that a bhikshuni should neither be blind to others' misdeeds nor depend too much on personal relationships. We should use our intelligence to distinguish right from wrong so that we do not foolishly strengthen the power of imprudent bhikshus. While bhikshunis should respect bhikshus in general, both bhikshus and bhikshunis are responsible for maintaining the purity of the sangha.

General Advice Regarding Parajika

Some parajika can be committed by instructing others to perform the action; others must be committed directly by oneself. For example, if a bhikshuni instructs someone to kill a human being and that person does, the bhikshuni commits a parajika. If the one who did the killing was also a bhikshuni, they both commit a parajika. Should a bhikshuni tell another bhikshuni to steal something of value and the latter complies, they both commit parajika. However, to commit the parajika of sexual intercourse, bodily contact, or the eight actions with men, a bhikshuni must engage in the action herself. If one bhikshuni tells another to engage in sexual acts and the second bhikshuni does, the latter receives a parajika, not the former. However, the former does commit a lesser offense.

To summarize, a bhikshuni may commit parajika 2 (stealing) or 3 (killing) either by doing the action herself or instructing another to do so for her. However, the offense committed by instructing another to do the actions in parajika 1 (sexual intercourse), 5 (bodily contact with a man), 6 (eight actions with men), 7 (concealing another bhikshuni's parajika), and 8 (going against the sangha's decision) is less heavy than doing the action herself. She must do these actions herself to commit a full parajika offense. If a bhikshuni lies about her spiritual attainments, she commits a parajika, but if she directs others to do so, the gravity of the offense varies according to the specific situation.

The parajika are most important precepts of which to be mindful and refrain from committing. Many of the precepts in the other categories are like concentric fences protecting these root precepts. By observing the minor precepts, the major ones will definitely be protected. However, even though the major precepts are still intact when a minor precept is transgressed, they are in jeopardy. For this reason, we should avoid becoming too loose in our attitude, thinking, "This is a minor precept. It is not so important if I transgress it." Reflecting on the ways in which various precepts complement and relate to each other increases our mindfulness, strengthens our practice, and helps us to keep our precepts purely.

CHAPTER ELEVEN

Looking at Our Stubborn and Rebellious Side: Precepts about Refusing to Accept Admonition

Many sanghavashesha precepts concern refusing to accept admonition for various misdeeds we have done. These precepts point out not only inappropriate behavior to avoid but also the importance of accepting the admonition of other bhikshunis. The bhikshuni pratimoksha contains many more precepts regarding the refusal to listen to admonition than the bhikshu pratimoksha does, because women tend to be more influenced by personal feelings than men, and this can impede their discriminating general principles from individual situations. When this discernment is lacking, people take comments not meant as criticism as personal assaults upon their character and thus do not want to listen to others' advice.

> Sanghavashesha 2: If a bhikshuni, out of anger or resentment, slanders someone with an unfounded accusation of committing a parajika with the hope of spoiling her pure conduct and later on, whether questioned or not, admits, "My accusation was unfounded. I made the accusation out of hatred,"

this bhikshuni commits a sanghavashesha if she does not refrain from her misconduct upon the first admonition.

Sanghavashesha 3: Suppose a bhikshuni out of anger or resentment cites irrelevant information and slanders a bhikshuni with an unfounded accusation of committing a parajika in the hopes of spoiling her pure conduct, and later on, whether questioned or not, it becomes known that the bhikshuni made the accusation out of anger and resentment and cited irrelevant information. That bhikshuni commits a sanghavashesha if she does not refrain from her misconduct upon the first admonition.

A bhikshu who lived at Buddha's time had a very bad temper. Because rooms at the monastery were assigned in order of ordination, he sometimes got a room that was not so nice. Furious about this, he went to his sister who was a bhikshuni, and together they plotted revenge upon Bhikshu Dravyamallaputra, the monastery manager in charge of assigning rooms: the bhikshuni would say that Dravyamallaputra had sexually violated her. When the Buddha heard about this, he said their behavior was not right and asked some virtuous bhikshus and bhikshunis to advise them in the presence of the sangha. Still, they refused to accept admonition. Thus the Buddha established this precept.

Someone in a position of responsibility in the sangha has to be fair. Nevertheless, due to individual characters, resentment and discontent may occur. In such situations, the sangha should gather and settle the issue. In the above case, the Buddha asked Dravyamallaputra to be present in the assembly and asked him, "Have you done this?" Based on his response and that of the bhikshu making the accusation, the entire assembly settled the dispute. When dealing with such situations, the assembly has to distinguish two separate issues. One is the accused person's behavior: in this case, did he commit sexual misconduct or not? The second is whether he implemented his duty properly. If he is found innocent of the false accusation but guilty of not properly doing his job, he should be instructed how to do his job better, and the one making the false accusation should be admonished by a virtuous monastic in order to maintain the purity of the sangha. A monastic persisting in making such false accusations commits a sanghavashesha.

> Sanghavashesha 14: Suppose some bhikshunis live intimately together and engage in negative deeds together, they become notorious, their notoriety spreads about, and together they cover up for each other. A (virtuous) bhikshuni should admonish them, saying, "Elder Sisters, you should not be so close and engage in negative deeds together, becoming notorious, such that your notoriety spreads about. If you stop associating intimately together, you will benefit by the Buddhadharma and abide in peace and happiness." If those bhikshunis persist when admonished by this bhikshuni, the bhikshuni should admonish them up to three times. If they give up their misconduct by the third admonition, good. If they do not, they commit a sanghavashesha requiring repentance upon the third admonition.

This precept involved two bhikshunis who intimately associated with each other; they became too close physically, verbally, and emotionally. In addition, they concealed each other's transgressions. The bhikshuni sangha gave them advice, admonished them, and encouraged them to live apart. Because they stubbornly refused to listen to sagacious advice, they committed a sanghavashesha.

> Sanghavashesha 15: If, when the bhikshunis are admonished by the bhikshuni sangha, another bhikshuni gives them (bad) advice, saying, "You should live together and not separately. I have seen other bhikshunis live together and engage in negative deeds together, becoming notorious such that their bad reputation spread about, and they concealed each other's transgressions. It is out of anger that the sangha tells you to live separately." The (virtuous) bhikshuni should admonish this bhikshuni saying, "Elder Sister, do not give (bad) advice to those bhikshunis by saying, 'Do not live separately. I have

seen other bhikshunis live together and engage in negative deeds together. Their bad reputation spread about, and they concealed each other's transgressions. It is out of anger that the sangha tells you to live separately.' Now these two bhikshunis are the only ones living together, engaging in negative deeds together, becoming notorious such that their bad reputation spreads about, and concealing each other's transgressions. There are no others like them. If they live separately, they will benefit by the Buddhadharma and live in peace and happiness." If that bhikshuni persists in her misconduct and refuses to repent when being admonished by this bhikshuni, this bhikshuni should admonish her up to three times. If she gives up her misconduct by the third admonition, good. If she does not, she commits a sanghavashesha requiring repentance upon the third admonition.

Here one bhikshuni or several bhikshunis give bad advice to the bhikshunis who are living intimately together by saying, "Pay no attention to those bhikshunis' advice. I have seen other bhikshunis do negative deeds like this, and no one censures them. The sangha is acting unfairly in disciplining you." This precept regulates the bhikshuni who gives bad advice.

> Sanghavashesha 12: Suppose a bhikshuni, living in a city or village, corrupts the inhabitants' households and engages in negative deeds. Her negative deeds are seen and heard about, and so is her corrupting of households. The (virtuous) bhikshunis admonish her, saying, "Elder Sister, you corrupted households and engaged in negative deeds. Your negative deeds were seen and heard about; so was your corrupting of households. Elder Sister, since you corrupted households and engaged in negative deeds, you should now leave this village and not stay here any longer." If that bhikshuni answers, "Elder Sisters, partiality, hatred, fear, and ignorance exist in (the assembly of) bhikshunis. Some bhikshunis are just as guilty as I am, yet I am expelled, while they are not," the (virtuous) bhikshunis should say, "Elder Sister, do not say, 'Partiality,

hatred, fear, and ignorance exist among the bhikshunis. Some bhikshunis are just as guilty as I am, yet I am expelled, while they are not.' Why? Because (this assembly of) bhikshunis is free from partiality, hatred, fear, and ignorance; and (there is no reason for you to say) 'Some bhikshunis are just as guilty as I am, yet I am expelled, while they are not.' Elder Sister, you corrupted households and engaged in negative deeds. Your negative deeds were seen and heard about, so was your corrupting of households." If this bhikshuni persists in her misconduct and refuses to repent when being admonished by the (virtuous) bhikshunis, the (virtuous) bhikshunis should admonish her up to three times. If the bhikshuni gives up her misconduct upon the third admonition, good. If she does not, she commits a sanghavashesha requiring repentance upon the third admonition.

This precept regards a bhikshuni who corrupts laypeople's households and engages in negative deeds. For example, she receives her daily supplies in an incorrect manner, by engaging in business, buying and selling things, or entertaining laypeople in order to receive support from them. Sometimes behavior that is seemingly kind is done with a selfish motivation and is therefore considered corrupting laypeople's households. Examples include giving the sangha's possessions to laypeople to win their favor, giving gifts to prospective new donors to encourage them to give a gift in return, praising people with the motivation to get something from them, and asking those in positions of power to help one's friends and benefactors. When laypeople eventually see the real reason behind such behavior, they lose faith in the Dharma and the sangha. Doing negative deeds includes flirting with men, singing or dancing to entertain others, and making flower garlands and other little gifts to give to laypeople.

To help this bhikshuni stop her destructive behavior, the bhikshuni sangha decided that she should temporarily leave the village and not live there. However, the guilty bhikshuni refused to accept the sangha's decision and instead criticized the sangha, saying the bhikshunis were motivated by partiality, anger, fear, and ignorance. Although the bhikshuni sangha advised the guilty bhikshuni because she was corrupting households and engaging in negative deeds, the main point of this precept is that the bhikshuni refused to accept admonition.

The *Shih Feng Lu Su* (commentary on the Four-part Vinaya) states that monastics may live in a village for two purposes. The first is to receive the food and clothing their bodies require so that they can engage in spiritual practice without physical difficulties. The second is to enable the laypeople to increase their merit by receiving teachings and guidance from monastics and by supporting them. Since the bhikshuni involved in this precept is not practicing the Dharma, her conduct benefits neither the lay community nor herself. If anything, her behavior harms herself and others because she gives the public a bad impression of the Three Jewels. Thus to protect her and the laypeople, the sangha tells her to leave the village for a while.

Sanghavashesha 10: Suppose a bhikshuni desires to harm the harmonious sangha, diligently uses expedient means to do so, accepts methods to destroy the sangha, and refuses to desist. Another bhikshuni should admonish her, saying, "Elder Sister, do not destroy the assembly. Do not use expedient means to destroy the harmonious sangha, nor accept methods to destroy the sangha without desisting. Elder Sister, you should be in harmony with the sangha. By being in harmony with the sangha, you will be happy and not argumentative. You will study with others under the same teacher and mix well with them like milk and water. Thus you will benefit by the Buddhadharma and abide in peace and happiness." If that bhikshuni persists in her misconduct and refuses to repent when being admonished by this (virtuous) bhikshuni, this bhikshuni should keep admonishing her even up to the third time, so that she may repent of her misconduct. If she repents upon the third admonition, good. If she does not, she commits a sanghavashesha which requires repentance upon the third admonition.

Sanghavashesha 11: Suppose a bhikshuni, joining with one, two, three, or even innumerable bhikshunis, says to the (virtuous) bhikshuni, "Elder Sister, do not admonish this bhikshuni. This bhikshuni speaks according to the Dharma and the Vinaya. We delight in what she says. We agree with what she says." The (virtuous) bhikshuni replies, "Elder Sister, do not say, 'This bhikshuni speaks according to the Dharma and the Vinaya. We delight in what she says. We agree with what she says.' Why? Because what this bhikshuni says is contrary to the Dharma and the Vinaya. Elder Sister, do not destroy the harmonious assembly. You should wish to have a harmonious sangha. Elder Sister, being in harmony with the sangha, you will be happy and not argumentative. You will study with others under the same teacher and mix well with them like milk and water. Thus you will benefit by the Buddhadharma and abide in peace and happiness." If this bhikshuni persists in her misconduct and refuses to repent when being admonished by the (virtuous) bhikshuni, the (virtuous) bhikshuni should admonish her up to three times, so that she may repent of her misconduct. If she repents upon the third admonition, good. If she does not, she commits a sanghavashesha which requires repentance upon the third admonition.

Ruining a harmonious sangha means dividing or dissolving a group of monastics who follow the same precepts, perform the same karma, practice the Dharma, and live together. This may be done in two ways: one is to introduce different practices, as Devadatta did in the story that follows. The other is to perform various karma with four or more selected members within the boundary of a group of monastics living together.

Devadatta, the Buddha's cousin and disciple, triggered the two precepts above. Wanting to become leader of the sangha, he asked the Buddha to turn the leadership over to him. The Buddha replied, "I am one member of the sangha, not a leader.

I only teach and share what I have learned with the sangha members." Trying another tack, Devadatta then claimed himself to be as enlightened as the Buddha. He set up five precepts and influenced his fellow monks to become a separate group and call themselves a sangha. The five precepts he created were much stricter than the Buddha's:

1. Do not take meat and be strict vegetarians
2. Eat only food collected on alms, and do not accept invitations to eat at a layperson's home
3. Live only in the forest, not in or near a village
4. Dress in robes made from discarded rags, and do not accept offered robes
5. Do not sleep under a roof, sleep only under trees

Devadatta thus propagated his own version of the Three Jewels: he was the enlightened being; his teachings seemed similar to the Buddhadharma but were actually the opposite; and he organized a group of monks to perform some formal actions (karma) within the Buddha's sangha. The wise, senior bhikshus were able to distinguish right from wrong, but the beginners and those who lacked discriminating wisdom were confused and did not know which Three Jewels to accept— those propagated by the Buddha or by Devadatta. In this way, Devadatta's actions ruined the harmony of the sangha. To settle the issue, the assembly censured his behavior and admonished him, as described in sanghavashesha 10.

Sanghavashesha 11 concerns monastics who follow a false leader and promote incorrect teachings. The sangha must gather together and ask those adhering to wrong views to explain the teachings they follow. The sangha should help this group realize that their views are incorrect and thus restore harmony to the sangha. If the monastics in this group refuse to accept admonition three times, they each transgress a sanghavashesha.

As seen by the above precepts, many situations exist in which a monastic may refuse to accept admonition for his or her misconduct. The sangha must first give advice to the person acting incorrectly. For example, the bhikshuni described in sanghavashesha 16 often said, "I renounce the Buddha, the Dharma, and the Sangha." The sangha should ask this individual if she is serious about what she said. If she is, then upon the completion of her stating, "I renounce the Buddha, Dharma, and Sangha," she has, in fact, given back her monastic vow. However, if she said such things without that intention, the sangha should help her clarify her intention and her speech. Thus, we can see that the sangha cares about this individual and wants her to succeed in her Dharma practice. For this reason, the sangha advises her again and again, asking her to change her conduct. Only after she has refused to accept admonition three times, has she transgressed a sanghavashesha.

These precepts illustrate the importance of our motivation. Motivation lies at the heart of the decision to become a monastic and the ability to remain one. Because comparatively only a small number of people will renounce worldly activities and devote themselves to monastic life, the sangha as a community has to protect and help each individual grow. Ignoring or concealing each other's transgressions benefits neither the community nor the individual. As a monastic community, we have the responsibility to purify the sangha and to employ various methods to maintain the purity of its members.

Giving Admonition

The nuns in our monastery in Taiwan are divided into classes, according to when they joined the sangha. Each class has a bhikshuni who supervises it and acts as a counselor. This bhikshuni cares for the bhikshunis or shramanerikas under her, looking out for potential problems and guiding others in dealing with them effectively. When someone is having difficulties, we give her advice early on and if necessary, admonition, in order to prevent her creating a sanghavashesha later.

If a situation eventually reaches an impasse, the nun is admonished in the presence of the community. The three admonitions are done one after the other, with a pause between each so that the individual can respond if she wishes. If, at the conclusion of the number of required admonitions, she has not agreed to cease her harmful behavior, she commits a sanghavashesha.

The assembly should pay attention to the person's motivation and her mental state while she was acting harmfully, as well as while she is being admonished. Major decisions should not be made hastily. For example, several years ago, a talented and gifted bhikshuni in our monastery suffered from a terrible illness for a long time. After some years, she became impatient with her situation and said to me as well as to her parents and some other bhikshunis that she wanted to disrobe and return home. To respect her rights, I called the assembly together and invited her parents to be present. In the presence of all these people, I asked her to clarify her intention. She insisted that she wanted to give back her vow and return home. I asked her three times, and each time she affirmed her decision.

We all knew that the illness affected her ability to think clearly, so we decided to view this meeting as one event and to ask her again about her intention in a meeting a month later. By the second meeting, her mind had changed and she said to the assembly, "I would like to remain a monastic. My initial motivation for joining the sangha is stronger now. The nuns in the monastery have been very kind and patient with me, and I appreciate them very much." Then she explained that she had wanted to give back her vow and return home because she was embarrassed to have the nuns take care of her and did not want to inconvenience them. Naturally, we were happy that she wanted to remain a bhikshuni. Our decision to give her this extra time to consider her decision was wise.

This concludes the topic regarding boundaries for remaining a monastic, which commenced with chapter six. As this topic is important, we should learn and reflect on it well. Nevertheless, because we are sentient beings with disturbing attitudes, we will make mistakes. By knowing these boundaries, we can minimize our errors, and by knowing the way to purify our wrongdoings, we can stop the negative impact and restore our precepts.

CHAPTER TWELVE

Right Livelihood

How do the times in which we live affect our practice? What differences exist between monastics during the Buddha's time and those in the modern world? Both had to be concerned with obtaining resources for living, including finances, food, lodging, transportation, medicine, and clothing. When I meditated under the Bodhi Tree, I had a hat, shawl, small blanket, and cushion to protect me from the cold. Still, I felt chilly. I wondered, "How did the Buddha survive? Did he have all these things? If so, how he did he carry them all? Nowadays it seems practitioners need a car to carry all their things! How do I continue to teach the simple life the Vinaya advocated?"

Obtaining and using resources in the correct manner is a very real issue for practitioners; it concerns our daily life. Since we must travel to study or teach the Dharma, having a car is useful. But if we have a car, we need car insurance as well as money for maintenance, taxes, and gasoline. In addition, we need health insurance, savings for old age, and people to look after us when we are old or ill. How can we arrange all these and still have time to practice the Dharma?

In our monastery, for example, we also follow many guidelines—called common rules—set up by the bhikshunis who live there. One of these regards money because obtaining resources for living is one of the first issues a monastic encounters. To practice the Dharma, we must sustain our body. The following story illustrates the proper attitude towards caring for our body and material needs.

Once a king asked a bhikshu, "Do *samana* (renounced religious practitioners) spend much time and energy taking care of their body?"

"No, they do not pay much attention to their body."

"If that is the case," queried the king, "why do they rest, sleep, eat, and go on alms round?"

The bhikshu answered, "King, when you are wounded in battle, what do you do?"

"I apply medicine to the wound and cover it with a bandage so that it will heal."

"Does taking care of your wound indicate you like your wound?" asked the bhikshu.

"I pay attention to and care for my wound not because I like it, but to protect it so that it will heal quickly," responded the king.

"Monastics regard their body like a deep wound. If we don't take care of it, it will create trouble and interfere with our spiritual practice. Thus we care for our body by eating, sleeping, and sheltering it properly to minimize the trouble it will cause. Doing so enables us to practice the Dharma, and through that we will be able to free ourselves from cyclic existence as well as benefit others by sharing the Dharma with them," said the bhikshu.

Thus we need to take care of our health and our daily survival—food, clothing, lodging, medicine, and so forth—in order to facilitate our practice and engage in works that benefit others. This motivation is crucial, for if we take care of ourselves simply to be comfortable now, we contradict our motivation for joining the sangha. While we need living resources, we should obtain these properly and not unduly emphasize them. The precepts concerning living resources describe the way the Buddha wanted us to obtain and distribute our supplies in order to create a beneficial monastic life style. From the issues that have arisen over these, the relationships among individuals, between the individual and the monastic community, and between the sangha and society become evident.

Prayascittika 70: If a bhikshuni eats garlic, she commits a prayascittika.

This precept is a good example of the necessity of knowing the incident behind each precept to understand its purpose and the effect it is meant to have on our life. If we only analyze the language of a precept, we may miss its point.

Bhikshuni Sthulananda practiced walking meditation every day next to a garlic field. The owner of the field saw her, and out of respect offered her five garlic bulbs each day. After some time, he said to her, "I would like to offer garlic to all the bhikshunis." One day Sthulananda took the bhikshuni sangha to the garlic field. The owner had gone to the market, so Sthulananda said to one of his workers that the bhikshunis had come to receive their offering. Although the worker said that he could not authorize her take the garlic, she insisted that the master had offered it to the bhikshunis and led them into the field to pick it. Each bhikshuni took five garlic bulbs for herself, five for her teacher, five for her friends, five for today, and five for tomorrow. At the end, all the garlic in the field had been picked. When the owner returned, he was shocked and said, "I never intended this. I only promised to offer garlic to the bhikshunis, not to their friends, teachers, and relatives!" When the Buddha learned of this, he set up the precept that bhikshunis should not eat garlic.

Was the Buddha's intention to prohibit the consumption of garlic or to regulate bhikshunis when they received offerings from laypeople? The Buddha not only guided monastics in how to conduct themselves to continue their spiritual practice, but also was concerned about the sustenance of the laypeople and the greater society. He did not want the sangha to take advantage of or become a burden to the public. The point of this precept is not that bhikshunis should not eat garlic, but that they should not be greedy.

Naihsargika-payattika precepts—or lapses with forfeiture—deal with issues regarding robes, alms bowls, mattresses, blankets, money, and so forth. Possessing certain items in excess hinders a monastic's path. To remedy this, the offending bhikshuni must relinquish the excess material and confess her misdeed to the assembly. Doing this eradicates the negativity of a naihsargika-payattika offense.

Transgressions of both the naihsargika-payattika and the prayascittika precepts create a prayascittika offense, although transgressing a naihsargika-payattika precept is heavier than transgressing a prayascittika precept. The former is remedied as described above, while the latter is purified by confessing to another bhikshuni.

The thirty naihsargika-payattika precepts can be categorized into groups according to the article they concern:

1. Money or jewelry: precepts 9-11
2. Transferring usage of food, money, robes, and so forth: precepts 18, 20-23
3. Robes: precepts 1-8, 13-15, 17, 26-30
4. Food and medicine: precepts 12, 16, 24, 25
5. Miscellaneous: precept 19

Many of the prayascittika and shikshakaraniya precepts deal with these articles as well. The most important of these will be explained briefly in this and the following chapters.

Precepts Concerning Money and Business

Money, as well as food, clothing, and so forth, is also a resource for living. In our society, money is the medium of exchange for the other resources for living. As monastics, what should be our relationship to money?

> Naihsargika-payattika 9: If a bhikshuni personally accepts gold, silver, or money, tells someone to accept it for her, or accepts it orally, she commits a lapse with forfeiture.

Before joining the sangha, one bhikshu had many friends, and after becoming a monk, he had many supporters. One day a big festival occurred in the neighborhood. A layman and his wife had a large piece of pork and agreed to save part of it for this bhikshu. Evening came and still they had not seen the bhikshu to offer the pork to him. The family's son came home and was hungry. His mother gave him money to buy food at the market, but he said, "It is too late to buy food. I'll eat this piece of pork, and tomorrow you can purchase another piece for the bhikshu." The next day when the bhikshu came to the house, the woman told him the story and said, "Please wait. I will go to the market and buy some pork for you." He replied, "You don't need to bother. Give me the money, and I'll take care of it." With the money she gave him, the bhikshu bought many different things at the market. People saw this and criticized, "How can a bhikshu carry money and go to the market to buy things?"

> Naihsargika-payattika 10: If a bhikshuni buys or sells valuable things, she commits a lapse with forfeiture.

Another day, the same bhikshu, with the intention to earn money by buying and selling, took money to the marketplace. He bought jewelry, which he then sold for a profit. You can imagine what people said when they saw a monk wheeling and dealing like this!

> Naihsargika-payattika 11: If a bhikshuni engages in business activities of any kind, she commits a lapse with forfeiture.

The same bhikshu was involved in this incident as well. One day Shariputra went to collect alms in a village. As he was walking by with his bowl, a storekeeper said to him, "Why do you come here with only your bowl?" Shariputra replied,

"Monastics receive our meals by people offering food to us in our alms bowl." The shopkeeper said, "Another bhikshu often comes to my store. He brings ginger and barters it for food. You, too, need to give me money or other goods, and then I will give you food. If you don't, I will not give you food." Thus Shariputra returned home hungry that day, with no food to eat.

Because that particular bhikshu engaged in various business transactions, the Buddha set up these precepts regarding how monastics should deal with money. At the time of his death, that bhikshu had property worth 300,000 ounces of gold. What was to be done with this huge fortune he had accumulated? The king said that the bhikshu's property should go to the government. His family said it belonged to them. The sangha said that since the bhikshu had lived with them, his property should go to the sangha. To evaluate the situation, we must know: Did the monk's fortune come from his family, or did he use his status as a monk to accumulate it? Did he receive the money by doing business or as offerings? What was his motivation?

We must be clear about the origin of the offerings we receive. Our obligations vary depending on whether people offer to us because we are a monastic or because we are their friend or relative. If we are not clear about this, we may confuse the two, and our subsequent behavior could damage the image of the sangha. For example, when people with respect and faith offer to us as a sangha member, we must dedicate and pray for their well being. We are responsible for keeping our precepts well in order to merit their kindness and offerings. Otherwise, if we are flippant and do not follow our precepts, yet expect others to support us because we wear robes, we create heavy negative karma.

According to naihsargika-payattika 9, 10, and 11, bhikshunis should not engage in business, bartering, buying and selling goods, holding, or saving money. If a bhikshuni possesses money, she should give it to the sangha and confess. By this, she purifies her offense.

How, then, do we handle monastics' individual needs that require money? In community life, the individual has no personal property aside from her thirteen garments. Although individual monastics are not allowed to possess money, the monastic community is permitted to have monetary resources. If the money is first offered to the assembly, the assembly can later assign it to an individual to use for her personal needs. Thus we say the community should not be as poor as the individual. The community has to have enough resources to protect, help, and take care of the individual members of the sangha.

Some nuns are not part of a community but live alone. Because of the structure of our society, they feel the need to save money for times when they are ill or aged. The issue is not clear-cut and depends on the person's motivation and attitude.

Monastics during the Buddha's time were prohibited from having personal money. They accepted alms for their meals, made their clothing from discarded cloth or from fabric offered by lay followers. Some years after the Buddha's parinirvana, some monks accepted money. Others disagreed, saying that according to the precepts, this is prohibited. To resolve this and other issues, the Second Council was held at Vaishali. The monks decided that monastics should not accept money as alms. However, even today we face the same issue: how are monastics to obtain their resources for living?

Many of the naihsargika-payattika, or lapses with forfeiture, concern this topic. By understanding well the purpose of those precepts, we apply them to the situations we encounter as best as we can. These precepts were made to protect the mind of the individual monastic as well as to ensure a good relationship between monastics and society. If we do business for our own personal gain, greed and miserliness easily arise. We begin to think of how to get the best deal for ourselves, and this could lead us to cheat and lie. Such attitudes and actions clearly obstruct our spiritual progress. In addition, the laypeople will cease to respect the sangha. If we know more about business and investment than we do about the Dharma, why should the laypeople turn to us for spiritual guidance? Why should they make offerings to the sangha if we use our time primarily to obtain the comforts of this life and not to study and practice Dharma?

In an ideal monastery that is able to take care of the needs of its members, individual monastics do not need private savings. Everyone there is able to keep his or her precepts purely and not worry about daily needs. It takes great courage for a monastery to take that responsibility, because as the number of members grows, so does the amount needed to sustain them. It also necessitates that the individual monastics be less self-oriented and have greater renunciation.

In our monastery in Taiwan, the monastery provides the nuns' daily needs, as well as medical, travel, and educational expenses. Nevertheless, since some nuns may not want to stay at this monastery forever, each month the monastery gives each member a small sum. Those nuns who also work in the temple get an extra amount. This money is transferred directly from the monastery to the nuns' personal accounts, which are managed by a nun appointed by the monastery. Each New Year's Eve, the monastery also gives a monetary offering to each member as a gesture of gratitude. In Chinese custom, this is given in a red envelope directly to the individual. When individuals receive a personal donation, they can decide whether to deposit it in their personal accounts or donate it to other causes. This way each member has some money for emergencies, yet each person is able to keep her precepts purely because she is not literally holding private wealth.

The amount of money allocated for individual use varies from monastery to monastery. In our monastery, the ordination teachers, who had two decades of experience before founding the monastery, made this decision. The other nuns followed without objection. In another monastery in Canada, five percent of the temple's monthly donation is allocated as personal funds for the resident nuns. In a temple established by Taiwanese masters in the United States, a hundred dollars per month is given to the working monastics.

In our monastery, the money offered to individuals is handled by those individuals directly. We do not use the procedure—such as the one prescribed for extra robes—of the individual giving the money to the sangha and confessing, and the sangha returning the money to the individual. However, a nun may do a simple oral confession, saying to another nun in a casual manner, that she received a personal donation of a particular amount. The other nun simply indicates that she heard it. Although the community does not do an official karma for this, most of the nuns do not keep private donations secret.

Each bhikshuni must be conscientious regarding the use of her personal money and avoid spending it on unnecessary objects or sense pleasures. Fortunately, most of the bhikshunis use it to benefit others by offering it to print Dharma books, fund Buddhist education programs, and aid others.

Sometimes a nun needs something that the monastery may not have or she may want to make a personal offering to another monastic or to a charity. In this case, she goes to the nun in charge of the monastic accounts and writes a withdrawal slip. This request is reviewed by a supervisor who knows if the monastery has the item needed. If not, the nun's request is granted and funds from her personal account are used. In this way, the monastery handles the nuns' personal savings.

A monastery also determines if a nun may travel to a special event, such a pilgrimage, conference, or teaching by a revered master. A nun may ask permission directly, or the department in which she works may recommend it. If the event is related to her job in the monastery, permission is generally granted, and in this case, the monastery assumes the related expenses. Even if the event does not relate to her job, as long as her department can handle her work in her absence, the community generally approves. However, as our temple in Taiwan grows busier, leaving to study or do retreat becomes more difficult. The issue is no longer one of finances. For this reason, monasteries must have controlled growth and plan ahead so that their activities do not require more people-power than they have.

Given the structure of our modern society and the fact that people often donate money for the use of individuals, monastics' handling of money seems almost inevitable nowadays. We need to respect the donor's intention, although we can advise them to support the sangha instead of the individual, as the Buddha did when donors wanted to make individual offerings to him.

According to monastic precepts, a lay Buddhist should handle the personal donations for monastics. Unfortunately, in modern times we may not be able to find a capable, supportive, and trustworthy lay person for that job. Thus, one nun or a group of nuns may be assigned to do it. This person is free from wrongdoing because she is taking care of the money for the sangha; she is not handling her own private funds.

Generally speaking, money donated to monastics because they are monastics is treated as the sangha's property when they die. However, money given to them because they are someone's relative or friend is regarded as the property of their family after their demise.

Guarding Others' Valuables

Although monastics are discouraged from personally possessing valuables, situations arise in which they have to protect the valuables of others.

> Prayascittika 66: If a bhikshuni personally holds wealth or precious ornaments or tells someone else to do so, unless it is at a vihara or her residence, she commits a prayascittika. If

she personally keeps wealth or precious ornaments in the vihara or her residence or tells someone else to do so, she should hand it over (when the proper owner) identifies it.

This precept explains an exception in which bhikshunis are allowed to hold wealth and valuables. One day a non-Buddhist layman was in a hurry and carelessly lost a parcel containing a lot of jewelry and money on the road. Some bhikshus happened to pass by, and seeing the parcel, they picked it up and noticed jewelry, money, and other precious things were inside. When the man realized he had lost the parcel, he returned in a hurry. Seeing him, the bhikshus asked if he was looking for a parcel and if this parcel was his. The layman said, "Yes, it's mine," but after opening it, he said to the bhikshus, "I had more gold than is here." Accusing the bhikshus of stealing his gold, he went to court and filed a suit against them. King Prasenajit was a devout Buddhist, and to solve the case, he went to his treasury and took out some gold. He put it into the parcel and asked the layman, "Is this gold yours?" The layman said, "No," and refused to take the parcel back. After investigation, the king found out that the layman was making a false claim. To punish him, the king confiscated the parcel and fined the man.

When the Buddha learned of this event, he told the bhikshus that in the future, when they find a parcel, they should first ask the person who claims it to list all the items in it. If the list is identical with the contents of the parcel, they should return it to the person. If not, they should simply say, "I haven't seen such items." This precept is very practical and we use its advice in similar situations in our temple. Many laypeople come to the temple to worship and join in the ceremonies. Afterwards, they forget their purse or pocketbook which contains money, credit cards, and other valuables, at the temple. To prevent misunderstandings, the nuns ask them to identify their lost possessions before returning them.

Another similar situation happened to some bhikshus who were traveling at the Buddha's time. As night was falling, they asked a goldsmith if they could stay at his house.

Although the man did not have a spare room, he allowed them to stay in his workshop. The bhikshus spent the night there, and the next day, the man asked them, "How did you sleep last night?" The bhikshus said, "We couldn't sleep at all. Your gold, jewelry, and other precious things were all around the workshop. We stayed awake the entire night meditating and watching over your objects." Later the bhikshus reported the incident to the Buddha who said, "If a similar situation arises in the future, to prevent the valuables from accidental loss, they should be collected and put in a safe place." Although he did not specify who should do this, it is better for the monastics to express their concern and the owner to put his possessions in a safe place.

In Shravasti, a wealthy, well-dressed Buddhist lady was going to a festival. En route, she thought, "I'd rather pay a visit to the Buddha than go to the festival," and went to a nearby monastery where the Buddha resided. Once inside, she thought, "I should not visit the Buddha dressed like this. I should take off the jewelry and wear more modest attire before seeing him." She changed clothes under a tree and left her jewelry and expensive garments there while she went to visit the Buddha. After hearing the Buddha's teaching, she was delighted and went straight home, forgetting her jewelry and clothes. When she realized what she had done, she was hesitant to send her servant to claim the things for fear of embarrassing the bhikshus. Meanwhile, a bhikshu in the temple had noticed that she had forgotten her things. Since the Buddha had previously prohibited bhikshus from taking jewelry, he stayed there filled with doubt, not daring to touch her things. Because of this incident, the Buddha modified this precept, indicating that if someone lost his or her jewels in a monastery, a monastic may hold the valuables and keep them in a safe place for the owner to later identify.

These precepts illustrate that monastics can help protect others' jewelry or precious objects when the situation necessitates it. But monastics should not possess precious objects themselves. We should not be greedy or attached to material things, but cultivate contentment with whatever is provided to us.

To learn Vinaya is to let Vinaya guide our practice. Learning the Dharma shapes our view and strengthens our faith. However, actualizing our views and faith in daily life is more complex and involves more than a legalistic attitude towards the precepts. It requires thought, flexibility, and skill.

Transferring Usage

Transferring usage occurs when an offering to one party is given to another or when an offering given for one purpose is used for other.

> Naihsargika-payattika 18: If a bhikshuni knows that an offering is for the sangha, yet begs for and obtains it for herself, she commits a naihsargika-payattika.

This concerns an object intended for the assembly that was diverted to one individual. In this incident, a bhikshu knew a layperson was planning to offer robes to the sangha. He said to the donor, "The assembly has robes already. You could offer them to me instead, as I need them." Thus persuaded, the laypeople gave that bhikshu the robes. Later the Buddha and the assembly accepted this layman's invitation for a meal. Impressed by their conduct, the layman regretted that he had given the robes to the other bhikshu instead of to the sangha. Apologizing to them, he explained that he had really wanted to offer robes to them. Later the Buddha asked that bhikshu, "Why were you so selfish and greedy? This donor's original intention was to offer robes to the sangha, and you diverted them for your own selfish benefit." He then established this precept.

That bhikshu did not commit the offense of stealing because he had the approval of the donor. However, he most definitely was greedy. To remedy his transgression, a bhikshu must give the robes to the sangha and confess his wrongdoing in its presence.

The *Nan San Hsing Shih Chau* commentary on the Four-part Vinaya indicates four conditions for this transgression to occur:

1. The object has been promised to the sangha
2. The bhikshuni understands that this promise exists
3. She transfers the object which was earlier promised to the sangha to herself
4. She obtains the object

The *Nan San Hsing Shih Chau* describes three types of sangha objects:

1. Objects that have been promised to the sangha but have not yet been offered. A bhikshuni violates a naihsargika-payattika by transferring such objects to other usages.
2. Objects such as beds and bedding that are in the process of being made. The purpose for making such objects is to offer them to the sangha, but the donor has not yet made that intention known. A bhikshuni commits a dushkrita offense by transferring such objects to other usages.
3. Objects which have already been offered to the sangha. Transferring these to another usage is a parajika offense for one has stolen the sangha's property.

Naihsargika-payattika 20: If a bhikshuni knows the purpose of a donor's offering to the sangha, but uses it for another purpose, she commits a naihsargika-payattika.

Bhikshuni Anwen was well liked and respected by the laypeople. One day they asked how her practice was going. She replied, "Not so well because the place where I live is very noisy." The laypeople pooled money together and offered it to her so that she could build a better place to practice. Subsequently, Anwen thought, "Constructing a hut is troublesome. I don't want to get involved in such trivial activities." Instead, she decided to use the money to make a garment. After a while, the laypeople again asked her how her practice was going and she again replied that the place was too noisy and she could not practice well. Naturally, the people were puzzled and asked her what had happened to the money they had donated for her new hut. She told them she had used it to make a garment instead. The laypeople were upset because they wanted her, and other monastics after her, to have a quiet hut in which to practice.

This bhikshuni committed the offense of using an offering for a purpose different than that specified by the donor. It differs from naihsargika-payattika 18 because here the person using the offering is the same. However, the purpose for which the offering was to be used was diverted from constructing a building to buying robes. Why is this discouraged? A robe lasts a short time and is generally used by only one person. However, a hut exists longer and can be used by other monastics after this bhikshuni has completed her retreat.

> Naihsargika-payattika 21: If a bhikshuni herself seeks a donation (for a particular bhikshuni), but changes and offers it to the sangha instead and diverts it for another use, she commits a naihsargika-payattika.

This incident also involves Bhikshuni Anwen. She planned to visit another village. When the nuns in that village heard the news, they notified the local people, who then gave money to the nuns so they could get food for Anwen when she arrived. However, Anwen did not arrive on the appointed day. Wondering what to do with the money, the local nuns decided to buy robes for themselves. Many evenings later, Bhikshuni Anwen arrived in the village. When she went on alms round to collect food the next day, the villagers were surprised and asked her; "Don't the local nuns have food?" "No," she responded. Later the townspeople asked the local nuns if they had used their donation to prepare food for Anwen, to which the nuns replied they had not. "Because she did not arrive when she was supposed to, we used the money to get robes for ourselves because it is difficult for bhikshunis to procure garments." The incident provoked the laypeople to criticize the nuns for transferring the donation from Anwen to themselves and for using it for a purpose other than they had intended.

> Naihsargika-payattika 22: If a bhikshuni diverts a donor's offering and uses it for a purpose other than originally intended, she commits a naihsargika-payattika.

> Naihsargika-payattika 23: If a bhikshuni (together with others) seeks a donation and uses it for a purpose other than intended, she commits a naihsargika-payattika.

A group of bhikshunis regularly practiced and recited the *Pratimoksha Sutra* together. Noticing that their meeting place was in poor condition, the lay community offered money to construct a better building where the bhikshunis could learn, meditate, and recite the *Pratimoksha Sutra* together. However, the bhikshunis thought, "We are used to the rain and sun, so continuing to use this building is not a problem. Although a new building would be nice, we need robes more." They then used the money to make garments for themselves.

In all these incidents, the donation was intended for one purpose or person and was later diverted and used for another purpose or person. These incidents also reflect the difficulty the monastics faced in procuring robes at the Buddha's time. Why shouldn't monastics transfer an offering from one purpose or person to another? In the last incident, the offering was used by the same people as it was intended for, so those bhikshunis did not steal anything. However, they were acting selfishly.

The other cases are similar. In naihsargika-payattika 18, the donor intended to offer robes to the entire sangha and out of greed, the bhikshu diverted the offering to himself alone. Although the donor had initially approved, the monk acted out of greed and therefore committed an offense. In naihsargika-payattika 20, the bhikshuni changed the purpose without consulting the donor at all. The laypeople donated money to construct a better residence in which she could practice. Had it had been constructed, other bhikshunis could have used it after her. However, her selfishness prevented this from happening. In naihsargika-payattika 23, the offering was intended to construct a recitation hall for the sangha, an edifice that could be used by the present as well as by future generations of monastics. Instead, that group of bhikshunis transferred the money for their personal usage, making garments for themselves. In their minds, concern for the self was foremost. However, as practitioners, we should train our mind to be concerned with the welfare of others—in this case, the present community and the sangha for generations to come. We will pass away, but the long-term existence of the sangha is of crucial importance. We have the responsibility to pass the Dharma and Vinaya to future generations and to arrange good facilities for them.

This group of precepts applies to individual bhikshunis, as well as to bhikshunis responsible for receiving and managing donations to the sangha. Money donated for an individual bhikshuni or the community to have a specific item should not be used for another purpose. Following these precepts is important, not only to avoid upsetting the donors, but also to curtail our self-centeredness.

Sometimes a donor may give us money for something that we do not need. In this case, we should explain the situation to the donor and ask his or her permission to use the offering for another purpose. We may want to leave it open, saying, "May I decide the best usage of the offering, depending on what I need?" In general, donors are flexible if our reasons make sense to them. Asking permission to change the usage is best done at the time the offering is made, for we may not be able to locate the donor later. If a donor is a good friend and we are fairly certain that she will agree with our decision, we can notify her afterward. If not, we need to get her permission before making any changes.

It may happen that a donor gives us money for a particular item and the amount given is either insufficient or excessive. In this case, at the time the donor makes the offering, we should ask, "If the amount is insufficient, would you be willing to give another offering?" or "If money remains, may I decide how to use it?" We should then follow the donor's wishes. In this way, donors will trust the monastics.

If a layperson gives an individual bhikshuni an offering, she may do with it whatever she wishes. Thus if people offer us items that we cannot use, we can accept it with gratitude and then give it to the monastery, Dharma center, another bhikshuni, or a layperson.

We must pay attention to subtle ways of transferring usage. For example, laypeople make an offering meant for the sangha to the monastery's manager—the person who supervises the community's goods. If, instead of distributing it immediately, the manager holds the offering until the guest monastics have left or until the people she dislikes have moved out, and then distributes it, she has diverted the offering. A manager may think, "I expend more time and effort than others to work for the community, so I deserve a larger share of the offerings." If she acts on this motivation, she transfers usage of the offering. Her action is not the parajika of stealing because she lacks the intention to steal. She simply neglects the donor's intention and twists the usage of the object to fit her own way of thinking. Thus, a manager must be clear for whom an offering was intended, and she must be fair in distributing it to everyone for whom it was intended.

Similarly, if the offering is made to the entire sangha, including generations of sangha to come, it should not be consumed only by the present community. We should use it for things, such as buildings, land, a meditation hall, classrooms, or books, that future generations can enjoy as well.

Sometimes the manager may have to speak with the donor about how to distribute or use the offering. For example, a layperson donates an expensive robe to the entire sangha. Since there is only one robe and many people, each person taking one swatch of cloth would make no sense. The manager should explain to the donor that the community would like to sell the precious cloth, and use the money to purchase other things that can be distributed equally to all of its members.

Establishing Trust

Since monastics represent the Three Jewels, we should act with mindfulness and consideration for others so that lay-people will have confidence in our virtue. Those with official responsibilities in the community, as well as individual bhikshunis, must be fair and honest so the public can trust monastics. When a trusting relationship has been established, the lay community will continue to support the sangha. Through their help, we will be able to study, practice, and teach the Dharma as well as engage in various projects that benefit others.

In some countries, people do not understand Buddhism. Not trusting monastics, they think the sangha live at the expense of laypeople and are parasites on society. Historically speaking, Buddhism has not initially been accepted in many societies where it now flourishes. For example, when the Buddhadharma first came to China, both the common people and the government were suspicious of the new faith and treated monastics poorly.

The support and respect we now receive are due to the efforts of past monastics. This transformation did not happen overnight, nor did it occur effortlessly. Rather, generation after generation of past practitioners devoted their lives to the Dharma. They studied and practiced well; they educated and served the community. Eventually, the public came to understand the Dharma better and to appreciate monastics. The fact that the lay community still supports us although most of us are not yet enlightened is due to the efforts of past practitioners. We are indeed indebted to the kindness of the monastics that came before us.

At the moment, Buddhism is new in the West, and each of you Western monastics is a pioneer in your country. Remembering the joyous effort and courage with which previous monastics endured similar difficulties will give you inspiration to continue your work. By patiently studying, practicing, and teaching the Dharma as they did, you too will be able to spread the Dharma in your countries and benefit many people.

Once I stayed in an area of Hawaii where Buddhism was virtually unknown. Each morning, I would get up early to pray and meditate, and then, carrying my rosary, I would take a walk in the neighborhood. Surprised to see a nun, some people would stare at me. Sometimes I would say hello and stop to chat with people or compliment them on their garden with its beautiful banana and mango trees. A few days later, I found a bag filled with mangoes and bananas on my doorstep. This continued day after day, so I did not have to cook and took bananas as my meal one day and mangoes the next. This gave me confidence that if monastics are humble, pleasant, and honest, laypeople who have not yet met the Dharma will come to appreciate the sangha and the Buddha's teachings.

CHAPTER THIRTEEN

Resources for Monastic Life: Robes

The Four Resources

When he established the sangha, the Buddha instructed the first five bhikshus on the four resources and ways to obtain them:

1. Alms food. From the day a monastic is ordained, he or she should obtain food by collecting alms once a day, in the morning. Exceptions include times when one is ill or elderly and requires extra, when one is invited to a meal, and when people bring food to the monastery, for example, on observance days, such as on the eighth, fifteenth, and thirtieth of the lunar month.

2. Lodging. The Buddha allowed monks to live outdoors under trees, in caves, and in donated houses. However, from the inception of the bhikshuni sangha, he did not permit bhikshunis to live in the forest alone or to sleep under trees for reasons of safety.

3. Ragged robes. Monastics are to take cloth from the garbage dump, abandoned cloth, or shrouds, and sew the pieces together to make their robes. An exception is that

monastics may accept robes offered by laypeople, such as those given at the end of the rains retreat or those given when one's robes have been accidentally destroyed or lost.

4. Medicine. Monastics should take inexpensive, old, or discarded medicine. When ill, they may accept *ghee*, fresh butter, oil, honey, and molasses.

During the bhikshu and bhikshuni ordination ceremonies, candidates are asked if they accept the Buddha's guidelines for obtaining the four resources, and they must express their willingness to do so. Also, they must abandon parajika offenses, including stealing, which is the foremost wrong livelihood.

After establishing the way for monastics to procure the four resources, the Buddha later adapted it as new situations arose. The first change occurred when the parents of one bhikshu invited the Buddha and sangha to their house and offered food to them. At this time the Buddha clarified that monastics may receive food not only by collecting alms, but also by accepting invitations from laypeople. After that many people began to invite monastics to their home to offer food to them. Other lay followers brought food to the vihara and offered it to the monastics there.

Similar changes occurred regarding robes and lodging. Initially monastics were permitted to use only discarded pieces of material which they stitched together. Later some people offered cloth that was much better than that picked up at cemeteries or in the garbage, and the Buddha allowed the monastics to accept it.

The initial advice to live under trees and so forth changed when King Bimbisara donated the Bamboo Garden to the sangha. He built living quarters for the monastics and a large auditorium where teachings were held. The Buddha permitted monastics to stay in the living quarters constructed here.

The Buddha often told sponsors, "Since the sangha bears the responsibility for preserving the Dharma, you create great positive potential by supporting the sangha. Instead of supporting me personally, please help the sangha. Since I am a member of the sangha, I will receive a share of your offering." By being flexible and allowing for change, the Buddha guided the sangha to become an organization whose mission is to sustain and spread the Dharma. We must maintain this purpose and be wise in the means we use to accomplish it.

Robes

A high percentage of the thirty naihsargika-payattika refer to monastic robes. From this we can infer that procuring clothing was difficult during the Buddha's time and that he was concerned it be done properly.

> Naihsargika-payattika 8: Suppose a king, an official, a layman, or a laywoman sends a messenger with money to buy a robe for a bhikshuni. When the messenger arrives at the place where the bhikshuni is, he says to her, "Elder Sister, I have brought money for you to buy a robe. Please accept it." The bhikshuni says to the messenger, "I should not accept this money to buy a robe. If I need a robe, I should accept it purely in the right manner and at the right time." The messenger says to the bhikshuni, "Elder Sister, do you have an assistant?" The bhikshuni who needs a robe answers, "Yes, the sangha caretaker and the upasika are the assistants of the bhikshunis and always assist the bhikshunis with things." After the messenger has gone to the assistant's place and given her the money to buy a robe (for that bhikshuni), he returns to the bhikshuni's place and says, "Elder Sister, I have given the money to buy a robe to the assistant you indicated. Elder Sister, in due time you can go there and get the robe." If the bhikshuni needs a robe, she should go to the assistant's place two or three times and say, "I need a robe." If she goes two or three times to remind the assistant and gets the robe, good. If she does not get it, she may go a fourth, fifth, or sixth time and stand silently before the assistant to remind her. If she goes a fourth, fifth, or sixth time, standing silently before her, and gets the robe, good. If she does not get the robe but seeks

to get it more times than that, and gets it, she commits a naihsargika-payattika. If she fails to get it, she should send someone to the place from which the messenger came and say (to the giver of the money for the robe), "You sent someone to give the money for buying a robe to the bhikshuni, but the bhikshuni did not get it. Go and get the money back lest it be lost. Now is the time."

Whenever a bhikshuni needs an item—be it a robe, alms bowl, needle, and so forth—she should not take a donor's money herself, but ask the donor to give the money to her assistant—an upasika, upasaka, or *sangharama* (someone who provides service to the bhikshunis). Then the bhikshuni tells the assistant what she needs, and the assistant arranges for her to receive the object. In this case, a king, official, layman, or laywoman wants to donate money for a bhikshuni to buy a robe. Being virtuous, this bhikshuni knows the proper procedure to procure a robe, so she tells the messenger that she cannot take the money and he should give it to her assistant. When the bhikshuni needs the robe, she tells her assistant who will have it made for her. If everything goes well, the donor has offered the money for the garment, the bhikshuni has observed the precepts purely, the assistant has provided the needed service, and the bhikshuni has received the robe she needed.

As this precept indicates, this process does not always go smoothly. Here the money was offered for a robe, so the bhikshuni can ask her assistant for a robe only. She may do this up to three times. If she still has not received her robe, she may "ask" another three times by standing silently in front of the assistant to remind her. If, after six efforts, the bhikshuni still has not received the robe and continues to request it, she commits a naihsargika-payattika. What should she do instead? Two options exist: she can write a letter to the donor explaining the situation, or she can go to the donor herself and explain the situation. In either case, she should ask the donor to contact the assistant and reclaim the money.

As monastics, we do not handle money but may ask assistants to do that for us. I know many virtuous monastics that still follow this precept. However, sometimes the laypeople temporarily use the money for other purposes. For example, to earn interest, they buy stock, and in that case the bhikshuni cannot get what she needs quickly or easily. For this reason, our monastery follows a different procedure and assigns bhikshunis to be the administrators and to handle the money for the sangha. The nuns in charge of bookkeeping record the income and the expenditures in detail. When a nun needs an object, she asks the administrator. In this way, a monastic does not hold money for personal usage, but some monastics take care of the money for the entire community. The books are accurate, clear, and open to the community, so everyone knows our income, expenditures, and balance. In that way the members of the sangha can trust each other and live together harmoniously.

Our robes perform three functions:

1. They protect us against weather, cold, and heat
2. They cover our body
3. They are a symbol representing our ordination

The first two are practical concerns that apply to anyone's clothing. They show that the Buddha's main concern when setting up precepts was practicality. The third distinguishes us as monastics and symbolizes our motivation as well as our ultimate goal; the two most obvious signs for people to recognize Buddhist monastics are our shaved head and our robes. Our robes are also an expression of equality. Each member of the sangha wears the same robes, regardless of his or her social status before joining the sangha.

One day the Buddha looked out on the various patches of rice paddies and commented on their beauty. He had the robes of his sangha made in a similar design from various sized pieces of abandoned cloth sewed together. Each patch symbolizes a field of merit, and this merit-field robe is a symbol of

Buddhism. Although the style of the robes varies from one Buddhist tradition to another due to the culture and climate in the places where Buddhism has spread, each Buddhist tradition has garments made of various sized rectangles stitched together. This reminds us not only of the merit field, but also to be humble, as the original Buddhist robes were made of rags and abandoned cloth.

Monastic clothing is different from ordinary clothing. For example, we are not allowed to wear white because that is a color worn by laypeople at the Buddha's time. Nor are we permitted to wear expensive fabrics and ornaments as laypeople do. Our robes should be long enough to cover our knees when we sit, but they should not be so long that they drag on the floor when we walk. The Vinaya allows hooks and belts to be used to hold the robes in place.

Every applicant must have robes and an alms bowl before he or she can be ordained, as this story illustrates. One time two practitioners who did not know each other stayed overnight in a house. One was a Buddhist monk, the other was not. They began to discuss the Dharma, and the former taught the latter the Four Noble Truths and the Eightfold Path throughout the night. The other was very happy and said that he would like to be ordained. The monk sent him out to find a robe and bowl. Unfortunately, since he was in a hurry, he was hit by a cow and died. The monk who taught him that night was the Buddha. Even he had to ask that person to prepare robes and bowl in order to be ordained.

During the time of the Buddha, procuring cloth to make robes was extremely difficult. Many bhikshus lacked sufficient covering for their bodies and had to search continually for abandoned cloth. Sometimes a fight between bhikshus occurred because two of them spotted a piece of abandoned cloth at the same time while walking in a village or field. Often monastics went to the garbage dump or the cemetery to look for abandoned cloth. The Vinaya contains many stories about bhikshus' escapades while trying to find robes.

For example, going to a cemetery in search of cloth, one bhikshu began to unwrap the shroud from a corpse. As he was
doing so, the dead person suddenly woke up. Terrified, the
bhikshu ran away with the dead person chasing him! After a
few steps, the "dead" person collapsed and died once more.
In another incident, a bhikshu walking in a field noticed a
person covered in cloth. Thinking it was a dead body, he
picked up the cloth only to discover it was a shepherd sleeping while looking after his flock. The two began to fight, and
the shepherd nearly beat the bhikshu to death.

Initially the Buddha stipulated that monastics' robes could
be made only from discarded cloth. However, because skir-
mishes arose as noted above, and because monastics were
seen scavenging the streets for cloth, the public's respect for
their spiritual endeavors decreased. Seeing the bhikshus'
poor condition, many devout laypeople wanted to help. Since
monastics could not receive donated cloth, the laypeople pur-
chased cloth and left it on the roadside so a monastic could
pick it up.

Jivaka Komarabhacha, a renown doctor who treated both
the Buddha and the monastics when they were ill, once requested the Buddha to accept an offering of a piece of fine
cloth. In addition, he asked the Buddha to permit monastics
to receive cloth donated by the laypeople. From that time
on, the Buddha allowed this. In general, this donated cloth
was of better quality, and the color of the patches in robes
made from it did not vary as much.

The Buddha said monastics could have two kinds of robes:
those required and those permitted. Required robes are those
that every monastic should have—three for bhikshus and
five for bhikshunis. The three they share in common—the
outer robe which has nine to twenty-five vertical strips, the
upper robe which has seven vertical strips, and the inner
robe which has five vertical strips—are called the "merit-
field robes." Permitted robes are those that a monastic may
or may not have depending on his or her individual needs

and health. Within these two general categories of robes are detailed thirteen garments or cloths (*trayodasa parishkara*) that a monastic may have:

1. *Samghati* (Tibetan: *namjar*) is the outer robe or heavy cloak with lining worn when entering a palace, delivering a Dharma talk, going on alms round in villages, and giving refuge or ordination. Since monastics represent the Three Jewels, they have many opportunities to teach the Dharma when they go for alms. For that reason, they must wear the samghati when entering a village. The samghati is often quite thick and can double as a quilt to be used as a cover when sleeping.

2. *Uttarasangha* (Tibetan: *chogu*) is the upper robe worn when reading sutras, meditating, or attending sangha gatherings.

3. *Antarvasas* (Tibetan: *shamdup*) is the inner robe worn at all times, even when doing manual work. All bhikshus, bhikshunis, and applicants for full ordination must have these three robes.

4. *Nisidana* (Tibetan: *dingwa*) is the sitting cloth put on a bed or cushion, or on the ground before sitting down. Some people set it on the place where they bow.

5. *Nivasana* is an undergarment similar to the underwear we use today. It is one of the five regulated garments for bhikshunis.

6. *Pratinivasana* is an additional undergarment.

7. *Samkakshika* is the shoulder cover that is one of the five garments required for bhikshunis. It is used to cover their breasts, shoulders, and armpits. It is this, not the samghati, that prayascittika 160 stipulates all bhikshunis should wear when entering a village.

8. *Pratisamkakshika* is an additional shoulder cover.

9. *Kayopasanam* is a cloth for the rainy season.

10. *Mukhoposanam* is a cloth, similar to a handkerchief, for wiping the face.

11. *Keshapratigrahana* is a cloth used when shaving the head to keep the hair from dropping onto one's robes.

12. *Kandupraticchadanam* is a cloth used to cover boils or injuries or a bandage used to protect a wound.

13. *Bhaisajyapariskarachivara* is a cloth for covering and treating skin disease. It also is a bandage and may used when changing bandages.

Monastics should wear their garments properly as stated in the first two shikshakaraniya. In addition to the thirteen garments, some additional types of cloth are allowed, such as a bathing cloth, hat, additional garments to protect from cold and heat, and so forth. In ancient India, no shower rooms existed, and even nowadays most families in Indian villages do not have one. Thus, in the Buddha's time, many bhikshus bathed in the rain. However, their being naked outdoors did not please the public, and so the Buddha required them to use a bathing cloth to cover their body while bathing. Nowadays most monasteries have shower rooms that can be locked, so a bathing cloth is seldom used. The Buddha also allowed bhikshunis to have a cloth for menses. Nowadays, however, we use commercial products, not cloth.

Due to individual differences, the articles one needs also vary. The Buddha described four types of individuals and what they need for their physical well-being and spiritual development:

1. Those who are strong and healthy can manage with the three (or five) robes

2. Those whose health is average may possess other daily necessities, but only one of each item

3. Those in poor health may accept extra requisites after having made an assignment[1]

4. Those with extremely poor health may acquire additional requisites such as a mattress, blanket, stick, pillow, and so forth to facilitate their practice

Naihsargika-payattika 6, 7, 13, 14, 29, and 30 speak of the type of cloth that can be used for garments and the method for procuring it.

> Naihsargika-payattika 6: Suppose a layman and his wife prepare money to buy a garment for a bhikshuni and decide to give her a certain sum for that purpose. If, without having been asked to choose, the bhikshuni goes to the layman's house and says, "It would be good, householder, if you prepare such and such an amount to buy a robe for me so that it will be a good one." If the bhikshuni obtains a robe in this way, she commits a naihsargika-payattika.

While accepting alms at a house, one bhikshu overheard a couple's private conversation in which they discussed offering a robe to Bhikshu Upananda. After returning to the monastery, the bhikshu told Upananda of the intended offering. The next day, Upananda went to the donor's house and said, "If you want to offer me a robe, please make it this size with good and durable material to fit my needs. If not, why bother to make the offering?" Hearing this, the intended donors were unhappy and criticized the sangha for being greedy, unappreciative, and shameless.

> Naihsargika-payattika 7: Suppose two lay couples each prepare money to buy a garment for a bhikshuni and decide to give her a certain sum for that purpose. If, without having been asked to choose, the bhikshuni goes to the houses of the two couples and says, "It would be good, householders, if you prepare such and such an amount to buy a robe for me so that it will be a good one." If the bhikshuni obtains a robe in this way, she commits a naihsargika-payattika.

The story concerning this precept is similar to the previous one, except the donors are two couples.

> Naihsargika-payattika 13: If a bhikshuni personally begs for (and procures) yarn and has an unrelated weaver make it into a garment for her, she commits a naihsargika-payattika.

Naihsargika-payattika 14: Suppose a layman and his wife have a weaver make a robe for a bhikshuni. The bhikshuni, without having been asked to choose, goes to the weaver's place and says, "This robe is to be woven for me. Weave it well—wide, long, durable, and close-woven. If it is well done, I will pay you such and such an amount." If the bhikshuni pays him, even as little as (the cost of) a meal and obtains the robe, she commits a naihsargika-payattika.

Naihsargika-payattika 29: If a bhikshuni begs for a heavy garment (for winter), it must not be worth more than four *karisapana* (unit of ancient Indian currency). If it is worth more than that, she commits a naihsargika-payattika.

Naihsargika-payattika 30: If a bhikshuni begs for a light garment (for summer), it must not be worth more than two and a half karisapana. If it is worth more than that, she commits a naihsargika-payattika.

All of these precepts concern being greedy, discontent, and thereby unappreciative of the robes offered to us. A bhikshuni who seeks a better robe—one that is more expensive, nicer color, specially woven or made of better material—is attached to material possessions. Since attachment binds us to cyclic existence, we need to apply our Dharma practice to reduce and eventually eliminate it.

In general, a bhikshuni is allowed to ask laypeople for support if she needs a robe, but if she procures it in one of the above ways, she commits a naihsargika-payattika and must give the robe to the sangha and confess her wrongdoing. Later the sangha returns the robe to her. Although monastics are permitted to have only one inner, upper, and outer robe—the Vinaya considers having more to be excessive—a bhikshuni may keep more than one without violating the precept if she first gives it to the sangha. A nun representing the sangha then gives it back to her, with permission to use it.

All monastics should not be separated overnight from their three or five robes. Robes may be made from linen, cotton, wild silk, wool, hemp, or canvas (any of the above five mixed with jute). A commentary on the Theravada Vinaya lists materials unsuitable for robes: cloth made of hair, horsehair, grass, bark, wood shavings, or antelope hide (and by extension, leather).[2] The Dharmaguptaka Vinaya allows monastics to use hide from smaller animals such as goats for bedding, but hide from larger animals such as lions, tigers, cougars, and so on are prohibited.

Naihsargika-payattika 1, 3, 4, and 5 deal with the proper time for getting or making robes.

> Naihsargika-payattika 1: If a bhikshuni already has the (five) garments and has given away the kathina (i.e. the kathina period has ended), she may keep garments in excess of that for ten days without performing the ritual of pure giving.[3] If she keeps beyond that, she commits a naihsargika-payattika.

> Naihsargika-payattika 3: Suppose a bhikshuni already has the (five) garments and has given away the kathina. If she is offered a piece of cloth outside the regulated time period, she may accept it in case of need and should quickly make it into a robe. If the material is sufficient, good; if not, she may keep it for up to a month, waiting for sufficient cloth to make a robe. If she keeps it beyond that, she commits a naihsargika-payattika.

> Naihsargika-payattika 4: If a bhikshuni begs for clothing from an unrelated layman or laywoman, she commits a naihsargika-payattika except at specific times: namely when her garments have been stolen, lost, burnt, or swept away by water. These are the specified times.

In general, garments should be made after the summer retreat. Those who did not complete a summer retreat begun in the first period—that is, on the sixteenth day of the fourth lunar month—have one month to make their garments. Those who completed the retreat of the first period have five months during which they can make their garments. Some exceptions are listed above. During the Buddha's time, some bhikshus' robes were stolen, swept away by water, burnt, or lost after the kathina period had ended. They returned to the vihara naked, but did not dare go in the gate. Other bhikshus saw and thinking they were naked ascetics (another group of religious practitioners in ancient India), asked why they were there. The naked bhikshus responded, "We are bhikshus, not naked ascetics. However, our robes were lost, and the Buddha said that garments can be made only during the right time. The time is not right now, so we remain naked." Because of this, the Buddha said that in extraordinary situations, monastics may make their robes outside of the proper time.

> Naihsargika-payattika 5: If a bhikshuni's garments have been stolen, lost, burnt, or swept away by water and an unrelated layman or laywoman offers her more robes, she should be content with accepting only what she needs. If she accepts more than that, she commits a naihsargika-payattika.

To help monastics whose garments had been lost, laypeople made many robes for them. Seeing the large pile of robes, some monastics took one after the other. The Buddha prohibited such greedy actions and said that three robes are sufficient for healthy and strong bhikshus to have and five robes are sufficient for healthy and strong bhikshunis to have.

The Four-part Vinaya says that only one layer of cloth is allowed for a new *antarvasa* (inner robe, five-strip robe), one layer for a new uttarasangha (upper robe, seven-strip robe), and two layers for a new samghati (outer robe, nine-strip robe). If the robe is old, two layers are permitted for the antarvasa, two layers for the uttarasangha, and four layers for the samghati. In this way, a monastic can put two old robes together to make one. If the robe is made of abandoned cloth, the number of layers is not restricted.

> Prayascittika 45: When a bhikshuni gets a new garment, she should dye it one of three unattractive colors: (murky) green, black, or brown. If a bhikshuni obtains a new robe but does not dye it one of these three colors, she commits a prayascittika.

Once when a group of bhikshus was travelling, thieves stole their robes. Later when the robes were recovered, the authorities sent word to the bhikshus to come and claim them. However, the bhikshus could not identify their own robes, which provoked the criticism of the laypeople. Therefore, the Buddha stipulated that each new garment should be marked with some dots in the corner so that the owner can identify it. Today many people write their name or iron a label with their name into their clothes to accomplish this purpose. Other items, such as bedding, towels, bags, socks, and shoes need not be dyed, but marking them may be helpful if we live in a community and our laundry is done together.

Precepts regarding giving and lending robes.

> Naihsargika-payattika 15: If a bhikshuni, having given a robe to another bhikshuni, later becomes angry and personally takes it back or tells someone else to take it back, saying, "Return this robe to me. I do not want to give it to you," the other bhikshuni should return the robe. If the bhikshuni accepts it, she commits a naihsargika-payattika.

> Naihsargika-payattika 26: If a bhikshuni promises another bhikshuni a cloth for menses but later refuses to give it to her, she commits a naihsargika-payattika.

During the Buddha's time, one bhikshuni promised to loan another bhikshuni a garment for menses, but later refused to give it. The other bhikshuni faced an embarrassing situation! Thus the Buddha set up this precept.

> Naihsargika-payattika 28: Suppose a bhikshuni trades robes with another bhikshuni. If she later becomes angry and personally takes it back or has someone else do it for her, saying, "Sister, give back my robe. I will not give it to you. Your robe is yours. My robe is mine," she commits a naihsargika-payattika.

If two bhikshunis exchange robes, and latter one of them regrets it and uses force to take her garment back, she commits a naihsargika-payattika. If we borrow a robe from another bhikshuni, we should wash it before returning it. Similarly, we should wash any robes before exchanging them with another bhikshuni.

> Prayascittika 107: If a bhikshuni gives a *shramana* robe to a layperson or a non-Buddhist renunciant, she commits a prayascittika.

Lay Buddhists and practitioners of other religions should not wear monastic robes. Should we see them wearing robes, we have the responsibility to inform them that the robes indicate that one is a Buddhist monastic and that as a layperson, he or she should not wear them. A person who disrobes should change into lay clothes and not continue to wear monastic robes.

> Prayascittika 156: If a bhikshuni wears padding to make her hips look bigger, she commits a prayascittika.

A bhikshuni should not try to reveal her figure, especially her bust or hips. Of course we still have a woman's body, but as nuns, our purpose for wearing clothes is to protect our body, not to look attractive. Wearing lay clothes or trying to show off our figures while wearing robes indicates that our renunciation has waned. Not knowing that we are nuns, men may flirt with us or approach us for a date. In addition, the public loses respect for monastics when monastics dress and act like laypeople.

> Prayascittika 157: If a bhikshuni keeps feminine ornaments, she commits a prayascittika, unless there is occasion for such behavior.

A bhikshuni is permitted to keep female ornaments—necklaces, rings, bracelets, and so forth—in certain situations, for example, if her life is in danger or she faces great difficulty. However, in other situations, a bhikshuni should neither keep nor wear ornaments. As practitioners, our ornaments should be the six *paramita* (six far-reaching attitudes).

Changing the Style of the Robes

The Chinese have changed the style of the robes due to the sensibilities of Chinese culture. For example, having bare arms was considered impolite, so Chinese monastics wore garments with sleeves. Since only the emperor was allowed to wear gold-colored garments, and bright colors did not seem fitting for renunciants in China, the color of the robes was changed to black and gray. In the same way, Chinese monastics have never gone on alms round because Chinese society looked down upon this. Thus, from the beginning, due to the culture in China, the way monastics there obtained their resources for living differed from that in India. I hope one day someone will teach a course about how monastics have conducted themselves historically according to cultural, social, and economic conditions of each country. This would be useful as well as thought-provoking.

The black gown with wide sleeves is worn by Chinese monastics in important ceremonies, for example when we recite prayers, perform the poshadha, and eat together as a community. Underneath it are the clothes we always wear whether we are working, praying, or sleeping. In daily life, when we see others we usually wear a gray outer garment that resembles a long jacket on top of those.

I have not been able to find references that directly deal with the history of robe reform in China. Judging from Master Yin-shun's works, a heated debate about this topic occurred in the Chinese Buddhist community at the end of the nineteenth and beginning of the twentieth century. Although it does not seem that formal meetings were held, many proposals were raised and commented on by contemporary monastic leaders. Minor changes, for example, the length of the robe or the design or the collar, do not require approval by a council. But I believe that when the color of the robe was changed centuries ago, a council made that decision. In general, we should refer to the regulations the Buddha set up and the purpose for them before we consider changing the style of the robes.

Master Yin-shun noted that two guiding principles influenced the Buddha's creation of robes for his sangha. The first was to distinguish them from the laity and the second was practical considerations. These two principles should guide monastics in different times and places if they make any changes in the robes. Regarding the first, monastic robes should be different from lay clothes, although each Buddhist tradition has some leeway to decide the color and design of their robes. Regarding the second, robes should protect and cover the body. The Buddha did not create a new style of clothes for monastics, but simply modified lay clothes to fit the needs of monastics. Similarly, the pants and long-sleeved shirt that Chinese monastics now wear under our other robes were initially clothes worn by the laity many centuries ago. At that time, monastics put a robe on top of these to symbolize their monastic status. Later, when laypeople no longer wore that style dress, it became unique to the monastics. Thus, although alterations were made in the robes in China, they still reflect the primary considerations for monastic dress. Insisting that a particular color or style is the *only* way is to negate the local conditions such as climate and culture and is not in accordance with the Buddha's original intention, comments Master Yin-shun.

Lunch at the Chinese Temple

CHAPTER FOURTEEN

Resources for Monastic Life: Food, Medicine, Lodging, and Travel

Food and Medicine

As monastics, we should obtain our food through right livelihood and eat only food that has been offered to us. During the Buddha's time, monastics relied upon alms to nourish their bodies and sustain their lives. The Buddha also allowed them to accept laypeople's invitations to meals and to accept uncooked food brought to the monastery that laypeople would later prepare.

Going on alms round was a common practice of practitioners of most religions at the Buddha's time. For Buddhists, the purpose is twofold: to eradicate worldly attachment by reducing unnecessary distractions caused by buying and preparing food, thus enabling practitioners to focus more on the spiritual path, and to benefit others by giving them the opportunity to accumulate merit by being generous to religious practitioners who are worthy of respect.

Going for alms enables a bhikshuni to cultivate certain attitudes. For example, she decreases her attachment to delicious food, diminishes her arrogance at being independent, and learns to be compassionate to all people equally. The latter is cultivated because she may not collect alms based on preferences, choosing the rich over the poor or her friends over people she does not like. Rather she walks sequentially past each home, one by one, accepting whatever is offered without commenting, "I don't like this," or "Give me more of that."

To avoid temptation and arousing unnecessary suspicions in others' minds, monastics should avoid collecting alms from houses of entertainment, palaces, and the houses of prostitutes, butchers, and those who sell alcohol. Monastics may not obtain food through improper means such as farming, buying and selling, making astrological forecasts, fortune telling, divination, and flattering the rich or powerful.

By receiving food in the proper manner—that is, the food has been offered by someone—we cut the cause for stealing, eliminate slander about the sangha, reduce our desire, develop contentment, and win the public's respect and trust. In this way, people do not criticize monastics for behavior that seems un-monastic, such as eating frequently and eating food which is not given. In addition, the donors are happy and create positive potential when they are able to be generous. In this way, the Buddha established an interdependent relationship between the sangha and the public. By practicing the Dharma properly, the sangha becomes worthy of offerings, and by making offerings, the laity accumulates positive potential. This also gives laypeople a way to censure unethical, inappropriate, or difficult behavior on the part of the sangha: if a monastic does not keep the precepts, the laypeople will not support him or her by giving food.

Precepts related to food and medicine are numerous and can be found in the *Bhikshuni Pratimoksha Sutra*. They include naihsargika-payattika 16; prayascittika 24-26, 32, 112 and 148; pratideshaniya 1-8; and shikshakaraniya 26-48.

The Vinaya speaks of food and medicine for the four right times:

1. Those for regulated or proper hours, i.e. from dawn to midday.
2. Those for unregulated hours. These may be consumed at times other than the regulated hours when we are ill, traveling, and so forth.
3. Those which may be kept for seven days. These include food or medicine such as ghee, oil, fresh butter, honey, molasses, and so forth which may be consumed within seven days when a bhikshuni is ill.
4. Those for lifetime. These may be taken for the duration of a bhikshuni's life until either the medicine is depleted, the illness is cured, or she dies.

Prayascittika 24: If a bhikshuni eats at improper times, she commits a prayascittika.

Regulated or proper times to eat are from dawn to midday. Dawn refers to the time the sky is light enough to see the lines on the palm of the hand, and midday is the time the sun has risen to its fullest and begins to descend. Five types of solid or staple food—grains, pasta, fried or roasted grains, fish, and meat—and five types of secondary food—roots, stalks, leaves, fruits, flowers, and so forth—may be eaten at this time.

In accordance with the Chinese bodhisattva vow for monastics, all Chinese monks and nuns are vegetarian. Because vegetarian food is digested quickly and vegetarians must take care to have a balanced diet, many monastics take a "medicine meal" in the evening in order to maintain their health.

Due to the geographic, climatic, and social conditions in China and other countries, obtaining food by alms, accepting invitations at homes, and having laypeople cook food donated to the monastery was difficult, and adaptations were made. For example, many monasteries in China were in the mountains, far from villages. Monastics residing in them could not go on alms round due to the distance and the weather. Nor could laypeople easily go to the temple to prepare uncooked food donated to the sangha. However, two principles underlie the precepts regarding food: to abandon attachment to tasty and plentiful food that suits our individual preferences and to abandon ways of procuring food that are unkind or inconvenient for the laypeople. We can still live according to the essence of these precepts when, due to the environment in which we live, we are unable to go on alms round. By doing so the purpose of these precepts—to generate contentment within us no matter what we eat—will be fulfilled.

> Prayascittika 36: If a bhikshuni takes intoxicants, she commits a prayascittika.

This precept was discussed in chapter 8, but it is included in the topic of food and medicine as well. Intoxicants are found in almost all cultures and countries, and so are their bad effects. Clearly, alcoholic beverages, recreational drugs, and abuse of prescription drugs are prohibited by this precept. However, we do not have to take wine or hard liquor to take alcohol. For example, if fruit juice is left out, it will ferment and have the taste of alcohol. Some people say, "I'm drinking juice," but in fact, they have made it into fruit wine.

Because this precept can be controversial, we must distinguish clearly what constitutes a violation. How important is one's motivation? What amount of alcohol constitutes an offense? For example, if a medicine contains alcohol and is taken with the intention of curing an illness, does a monastic violate this precept? A Theravada nun told me they are allowed to take medicine that has been dissolved or preserved in a tiny amount of alcohol. The Dharmaguptaka Vinaya permits alcohol to be taken as medicine only as a last resort to cure a particular illness. Otherwise, not even a drop should be consumed.

Naihsargika-payattika 25: If a bhikshuni keeps too many good utensils, she commits a naihsargika-payattika.

One bhikshu's alms bowl was leaking and needed replacement. Mentioning this to many laypeople, he received a number of bowls because they believed that offering an alms bowl to a monastic created great merit. To prevent such greed, the Buddha set up this precept.

Naihsargika-payattika 24: If a bhikshuni keeps more than one alms bowl she commits a naihsargika-payattika.

During the Buddha's time, one bhikshu possessed many good quality alms bowls that laypeople had offered to him with devotion. One day some people were shocked when they visited his residence and saw so many bowls that it looked like a pottery shop. Since a monastic needs only one bowl, all extra bowls should be given to the sangha or to another monastic. This enables others to use them and prevents a monastic from spending time worrying about and protecting her abundant belongings.

Although this precept concerns alms bowls, the principle behind it relates to our monastic life style in general. As those who have chosen to live simply, we should not accumulate extra or costly items, because doing so may make us attached to them or jealous of others who have more or better than we do. The Buddhadharma teaches us to be content and satisfied. We should use the objects we have until they are worn out. If we are not content and self-contained, but continuously seek more and better possessions, we will waste much time. In addition, our mind will be distracted, thinking, "I will use this one today and that one tomorrow." If we spend our time accumulating and protecting possessions, will we have time to practice and teach the Dharma? How can we advance spiritually if our mind is preoccupied with our belongings? Are we fulfilling the purpose of being a monastic? As monastic practitioners, our lives should be uncomplicated and our belongings simple. In this way we can devote our energy and time to enhance our practice so that we can benefit all sentient beings.

If a bhikshuni's alms bowl leaks but is still usable, and she obtains another one, she should give the new bowl to the assembly. Once the bowl is given to a representative of the assembly, it belongs to the sangha. The representative then returns the bowl to her, allowing her to use it. However, she must give one of her bowls away before the next day. If the representative of the assembly does not return the bowl, she commits a dushkrita offense.

The precept regarding extra bowls is slightly different for bhikshus, who are permitted to have an extra bowl for up to ten days. Once Ananda received an excellent bowl, which he wanted to offer to Mahakashyapa. Mahakashyapa was not there at the time, and Ananda was concerned about committing a transgression by keeping the bowl until his friend returned. He explained the situation to the Buddha, who inquired when Mahakashyapa would return and learned it would be after ten days. Thus he made the exception that a bhikshu may have an extra bowl up to ten days before transgressing this precept. However, for bhikshunis, the precept remained unmodified. Thus if a bhikshuni keeps an extra bowl overnight, she transgresses this precept.

Miscellaneous

Naihsargika-payattika 19: If a bhikshuni asks for one thing after another, she commits a naihsargika-payattika.

The incident leading to this precept occurred when one bhikshuni asked laypeople for cheese, and they got it for her. Later she changed her mind and said, "I don't want cheese. I need oil." The laypeople returned the cheese and bought oil. Again she changed her mind and asked for something else. This bhikshuni was being greedy and demanding, so naturally the laypeople were annoyed. For this reason, the Buddha established this precept.

Lodging

Initially bhikshus resided in forests, caves, glens, open spaces, cemeteries, or houses. Due to safety concerns, however, bhikshunis were not allowed to dwell in forests or in the open. As the sangha grew in number and the laity's respect for them increased, donors offered gardens, huts, meeting halls, and so forth to the sangha. At first these dwellings were used during the rains retreat only, for the sangha was to travel about during the rest of the year. Gradually, as years went on, more permanent dwellings were constructed, and over the centuries stable communities formed.

When a layperson offers land to a community, the monastic in charge of facilities may request assistance from the laity to construct buildings. The land and the buildings of a monastery belong to the entire sangha of the present and future. We must remember this, for when we are assigned a room in a monastery, we have the right only to use it. It does not belong to us, and while we live there, we must take good care of it, otherwise we deprive the future sangha of its resources. Similarly, we cannot build a house for personal use on land that belongs to the sangha. Doing so is regarded as stealing the sangha's property. However, we may build a house on the sangha's land and donate it to the community.

When living with others, we should endeavor to get along well with people who dwell in the area. Being mindful of our manners and behavior is important. Nowadays many people are aware of the environment and try to use resources wisely. As monastics, we must be especially careful in this regard. We should try to live a life of simplicity, not wasting or ruining resources that belong to the people and animals that will inhabit our planet in the future. Monastics in the past faced similar situations as the following precepts illustrate.

Prayascittika 77: If a bhikshuni relieves herself on living grass, she commits a prayascittika.

Shikshakaraniya 49: Do not relieve yourself, blow your nose, or spit on living grass, unless you are ill. This should be learned.

Prayascittika 77 originates due to the actions of bhikshunis, while shikshakaraniya 49 began due to bhikshus' actions. Regarding the former, many nuns at a monastery were practicing diligently, reciting the sutras, meditating, and doing walking meditation. In a large park with a beautiful lawn next to the monastery, laypeople would picnic everyday with their families and pets. They danced and sang, played games and enjoyed themselves. Sometimes, when they felt depressed, they cried. The noise disturbed the bhikshunis who meditated in the monastery. After a while, the bhikshunis asked the people to please keep the place quiet because they were meditating. But the laypeople replied, "This is our park." Having reached an impasse, the bhikshunis out of despair devised a plan and threw garbage, urine, and excrement on the lawn. When the laypeople came, their clothes got dirty, and their picnics were ruined. After a while, the grass died due to the garbage and filth everywhere. Unhappy about this situation, the laypeople criticized the bhikshunis. Thus, the Buddha set up a precept.

Nowadays, we would not relieve ourselves on grass unless we were traveling in distant areas of particular countries. Relieving ourselves, blowing our nose, or spitting on grass is not good hygiene. It disturbs the environment and other people living in it and is therefore improper behavior for bhikshunis.

This incident also concerns our interactions with others in the environment. Some Vinaya teachers explain that in ancient India, people regarded vegetation as the abode of certain spirits, so dirtying it would disturb those beings. Here we see the impact of folk religion. But from a different viewpoint, this story concerns bhikshunis having a disagreement with the surrounding community. Even now bhikshunis have similar experiences, and future practitioners will also encounter such predicaments. How should bhikshunis behave in such situations? What could they do to resolve the conflict? As bhikshunis, we need an environment conducive for practice; but we also need to take care of the people around us. How can we resolve such conflicts with the lay community when they arise? Please think about and discuss this.

Travelling

Several precepts concern travel, for example prayascittika 33-35, 51, 67, 79, 95-98, 100, and 161-163. In general, these precepts enable us to distinguish proper places to go, choose traveling companions wisely, travel at appropriate times and in an appropriate fashion, and go for a proper purpose. These precepts are for our safety and also help us not to waste time by wandering about or hanging out.

CHAPTER FIFTEEN

Organization in the Buddhist Community

All sentient beings are equal in that they want to be happy and to avoid suffering. Therefore, each person is worthy of respect, and we should endeavor to value one another. The Buddhist community has specific ways to bring about equality and mutual respect. For example, a person's social class before ordination does not make her either superior or inferior to other monastics. The Buddha frequently stated that a person is respected and noble, not because of her birth, but because of her behavior. Living in the precepts is a form of noble behavior, so those ordained longer are respected accordingly. For instance, one of the Buddha's disciples, Upali, who was of humble origin, joined the sangha just prior to five princes. The five princes gave up their royal status and social privilege when they were ordained, and since Upali was senior to them in ordination, they respected him.

Respecting those who joined the sangha before us is fundamental in the Buddhist community. We sit in ordination order in the prayer hall, we are served food according to our seniority. In ancient times in India and in modern times in

Thailand, the junior monastics prepare water for the senior to wash their feet upon returning from alms round. In both Chinese and Tibetan Buddhism, monastics no longer go on alms round. Nevertheless, the monasteries implement the principle of respecting and learning from those who are more experienced than we are in other ways.

This is not a rigid system of hierarchy, but a method for mental development. For example, when we are young, we are sometimes arrogant, and having to take the back seat helps us to calm our self-importance. In addition, it gives us the opportunity to rely on the energy and guidance of others who are more experienced. Thus, the system of seniority removes the stress of having to figure everything out for ourselves and opens us to learning from others. Receiving respect or going first reminds the seniors to be a good example and to extend their compassion and help to the newer members of the community.

In the Chinese Buddhist community, older people sometimes join the sangha. Because they had certain status and experiences in lay society, they sometimes want to be the leaders after they are ordained. This can cause difficulty in the monastic community because we must start at the beginning when we are trained as monastics, no matter what we have accomplished as laypeople. Sometimes those who ordain when they are older are used to certain social customs and want them to be regarded as Buddhist precepts. For example, children generally respect their parents. However, if a child is ordained before his or her parent, the child is senior in ordination and should be respected by her parent.

On certain occasions, however, order is not decided by ordination age. Spiritual achievement or knowledge of the Tripitaka may determine it. At other times, an individual's ability to serve to the community is the crucial factor, and people hold various offices in the monastery according to their skills. Depending on the situation, various ways of organizing and ordering monastics may be employed.

Serving the Sangha

The Vinaya tells a story about Bhikshu Dravyamallaputra. After attaining arhatship, he thought, "This body is impermanent. How can I use it to serve the sangha?" He asked the Buddha if he could hold the job of manager. The Buddha agreed, but asked the bhikshu to ask the assembly if it agreed with this. After one announcement followed by one proclamation, the monks remained silent, indicating their consent, and thus Dravyamallaputra took on the manager's job.

This job required much work. He assigned rooms to the monks according to their seniority. When laypeople requested a number of monks to come to their home for meals, he determined who would go. When new monks arrived at the monastery, he prepared rooms, bedding, and other facilities for them, took them around the monastery, and told them everything they needed to know to live there. As an arhat, Dravyamallaputra possessed superhuman powers, and one of his fingers radiated light. At night, when he led the guests to their rooms, he used his finger like a flashlight to guide them. Normally, an arhat deserves to be respected and served by others and should not have to serve the community. However, Dravyamallaputra acted with bodhichitta and wanted to serve the community regardless of his spiritual attainments. He was a model bodhisattva, and because of the excellent work he did for the sangha, the Buddha praised him.

Ananda, too, had an altruistic intention and wanted to serve the sangha. He held himself back from attaining arhatship so that he could serve the Buddha as his attendant. By listening to all of the Buddha's teachings, he was able to recite them at the First Council. His bodhichitta is evident: had he reached arhatship earlier, he might not have been able to offer as much service to the sangha.

Ananda's exceptional service as the Buddha's attendant becomes evident when compared to the actions of another bhikshu who once did that job. The Buddha said to the other bhikshu, "Please bring my garment. I feel cold." The attendant brought the Buddha's robe and covered him with it. Later, the Buddha again felt cold and asked for another garment, which his attendant brought. Around midnight the Buddha began to do walking meditation in the forest. Following him into the forest, the attendant sat under a tree. The Buddha practiced walking meditation the entire night. Exhausted, the attendant wanted to go to sleep and thought of a trick so the Buddha would stop walking and return to the monastery. Pretending to be a ghost, he screamed, made eerie sounds, and created shadows to terrify the Buddha. But the Buddha said to him, "You silly bhikshu. I have reached enlightenment and am not scared of ghosts at all!" From this, we can see that some people with high spiritual achievements hold office, while some officer-holders are not very smart.

Bodhichitta and Wisdom

To be an excellent office-holder in a monastery, we must cultivate the bodhichitta motivation. Wisdom is also required in order to serve the community. Using ordination age as the only criterion to determine position is not workable in a monastic community.

Similarly, any organization may use different ways to organize the people involved according to the particular mission to accomplish. Various positions and jobs are arranged in a hierarchical fashion, to facilitate people working together. In selecting people to fill these positions, the sangha must consider their knowledge and abilities, not their seniority in ordination. Someone young in ordination may be selected to lead the community in a specific area in which she has expertise. Although at poshadha, seniority in ordination is used to determine the seating arrangement, when the monastery holds an event for the public, those bhikshunis in charge of organizing it take the lead and are more visible.

In a community, the monastics do various jobs and have power in different areas so that activities function smoothly. When a person holds a particular position, we have to follow her instructions, even if we are senior in ordination. In my monastery, if a shramanerika is in charge of leading an event, even I have to listen and follow her directions. I have to be the model and follow the instructions of other nuns who are the leaders in a specific situation. By doing this, I encourage the other nuns to cooperate and do the same.

In our monastery, jobs are assigned once a year. However, another assignment of personnel is done for special events. By distributing the work and organizing ourselves in different ways according to the situation, we are more flexible and thus are able to accomplish our various purposes as an organization. For example, nuns from all over the world attended the three-week program in India, *Life as a Western Buddhist Nun*. Although all had different titles and responsibilities in their own countries—some were directors of centers or abbesses of temples—when they gathered together in Bodhgaya, they put aside their past positions and reorganized themselves for this specific event. We have to adjust when we go to different places for different purposes.

One day Bodhisattva Manjushri and Mahakashyapa went for a walk. Since Mahakashyapa was an arhat, Bodhisattva Manjushri asked him to go in front. But Mahakashyapa insisted that Manjushri go first because he had developed bodhichitta. In general, the sequence of order in a monastery is bhikshu, bhikshuni, shikshamana, shramanera, and shramanerika. However, on special occasions, a person who has developed bodhichitta will take the leadership role. Determining who should be first in any situation is not saying one is superior and the other inferior. Rather, it is a matter of who has the ability to serve the community at that time. In a Buddhist monastery, we do not emphasize superiority, for as Dharma practitioners, we should not be looking for fame, recognition, or power. Instead we emphasize how we can all serve the community. Such an attitude of mutual cooperation and respect is in harmony with the Dharma.

The Ch'an (Zen) monasteries in mainland China before the communist takeover had a special way to order the monastics. Before being allowed to hold an office, a person had to sit in the meditation hall for at least one semester (about six months), and sometimes for one year. There they received training and practiced intensively. Through the disciplined training of the meditation hall, a person developed the patience, endurance, and wisdom to hold a monastic office and provide service to the community.

Some positions in a monastery today are the same as those during the Buddha's time. For example, Dravyamallaputra's job, the manager of the monastery, has existed since ancient times. Another position existing since the Buddha's time is the person who leads the rituals. Usually this is the person most senior in ordination. She counts the number of people, states who is absent, maintains the order of the assembly, and leads the chanting.

Chinese New Year is a very special event in Taiwan, and the populace is very excited and active in celebrating it. Beginning on New Year's Day and continuing for about ten days, thousands of people come to the temple each day to pray and to celebrate. During this time the nuns in my monastery put aside our previous jobs and titles and organize ourselves especially for this period. Some sisters say that the laypeople have vacation while for us monastics, this period is the busiest time of the year and the one with the most work.

To create a festive atmosphere for the nuns, we decided to celebrate the New Year amongst ourselves a couple of weeks before its actual occurrence. Nevertheless, I remind my disciples that Chinese New Year is a secular holiday for laypeople, not a religious holiday for monastics. We have to distinguish between the two. Thus, while it is a time for the public to enjoy themselves, it is time for monastics to serve the community. As monastics our "holiday" time is *varshaka,* the three-month rains retreat. At its end is pravarana, the confession ceremony marking the completion of the retreat. After that, we can celebrate the great merit we accumulated by doing this retreat.

Many nuns say to me, "I came to the monastery to practice the Dharma. I didn't come just to work and serve." If you were in my position as the abbess, what would you say to them? In principle, a nun can only provide service to the community according to her ability and motivation. Since the community treasures the Dharma, if a bhikshuni is determined to focus on her practice, why shouldn't she be permitted to do so?

Sometimes everyone in the community wants to focus on her Dharma practice and studies, and finding someone to cook is difficult. This situation may be handled in a couple of ways. One is for everyone to cook for herself and eat whenever she is hungry. Another is to take turns cooking and eat together.

We should recognize that our service to the community and to the public is part of our cultivation and a manifestation of our Dharma practice. We must cultivate patience, compassion, and skillful means when we work with people. We may study and meditate on these, but through interactions with others we come to see if we have actually generated them. In addition, the sangha is a powerful field for accumulating great positive potential or merit. If we serve the community with a bodhichitta motivation and a happy heart, we enrich our minds with merit and thus create the causes to understand the Dharma better when we study and to gain realizations when we meditate. We should be broad-minded and create a good balance between service, study, and practice in our life.

CHAPTER SIXTEEN

Community Life

The Dharmaguptaka Vinaya contains twenty prescriptive precepts, called vastu or skandha, found in the part of the Vinaya called the Skandha. The most important of these will be discussed in this chapter. The term skandha means category, section, or chapter; in other words, things of a similar nature gathered together for easy reference. Unlike the precepts in the *Pratimoksha Sutra*, which list actions a monastic must avoid, the skandha describe the activities the sangha as a community must perform. These include the special observances or events of the community, such as ordination, the rains retreat, poshadha, and so forth.

One of the skandha describes the method of conducting the karma—the meetings or activities—of the sangha in a "legal" manner, i.e. an agreed-upon way. Here the requirements to conduct the above events are set out: the number of participants, the type of sima or boundary, the voting methods, and so forth. Different procedures are adopted according to the various matters that the sangha must handle.

To learn the prescriptive precepts, the "do's" as a monastic, we refer to the Skandha and to the Karma-vastu, the guidelines for conducting monastic procedures. For example, the Karma-vastu describes how monastics should conduct the ceremony to begin and end the rains retreat. But to know the types of rains retreat and what is to be done during them, we consult the rains retreat section of the Skandha, the Varsha-vastu.

The Buddha emphasized that working together and learning from each other are essential in the monastic community. One year, prior to the summer retreat, the bhikshus in one area discussed how to hold the retreat. They decided to observe silence for the three months of the retreat and only interact in the dining room. The first person to return from alms round would clean the dining room and prepare washing water for the other bhikshus. If he received more alms than he could eat, he would place the excess on the table, eat by himself, and return to his room to continue his practice. The second bhikshu returning from alms round would leave any excess alms he received on the table before eating, or if he did not receive enough, he could take what was left by the first bhikshu. After eating alone, he would return to his room to practice. The third bhikshu and all the rest would do likewise. The last bhikshu would clean the dining room and give any extra food to the animals. If their work required more than one person, they would use sign language to ask for help. After finishing their work, they would return to their own rooms and continue their practice.

After living in this way for the duration of the summer retreat, the bhikshus were very satisfied and reported to the Buddha. However, the Buddha responded in an unexpected way, saying, "How foolish! Why did you spend the summer retreat like a dumb sheep? You didn't talk to each other or teach each other! There is no purpose in remaining silent together."

The Buddha was not saying that we should never keep silence. Rather, he emphasized that when living together, we should use our speech productively. Monastics should use their speech not only to teach each other Dharma, but also to help correct each other's wrongdoings and give each other advice that aids our practice. In this way, all the sangha members will maintain their purity. In addition, they can discuss the best methods to accomplish the work they do together. For example, one function of the sangha is to teach the lay-people. We need to learn what to teach and how to teach skillfully. In addition, we are required to perform various activities together, such as ordination and poshadha. When these common acts, or karma, are virtuous, the members of a monastic community support the advancement of each other's practice. If the karma is not virtuous, the entire community, as well as the Dharma, will decline.

The monastic community performs five special observances:

1. Pravrajya: ordination
2. Poshadha: recitation of the *Pratimoksha Sutra*
3. Varshaka: summer retreat (also called rains retreat)
4. Pravarana: confession held at the end of the summer retreat
5. Kathina: receiving and giving away the "robe of merit"

The Summer or Rains Retreat and the Confession at Its Conclusion

Varshaka, *pravarana*, and *kathina* are three events done in conjunction with the summer retreat. In India the monsoon rains fall in the summer months. Rivers and streams flooded, and many monastics would lose their robes and bowls while crossing them. Some bhikshus even lost their lives. Moreover, walking into villages to collect alms during the summer would result in the accidental death of insects and the destruction of crops. Laypeople criticized the bhikshus for this, and in response the Buddha stipulated that instead of going from place to place without a fixed residence as they did in the rest of the year, monastics should remain in one place during the summer retreat. Gathering together, they should teach each other, clarify their doubts, and advance their practice. Living together gave them the opportunity to purify each other. The same holds true today.

Many Western nuns told me that they have done the summer retreat. During this time, they received more in-depth teachings on Vinaya, did individual retreats, studied the Dharma, or did ascetic practices. In ancient times, monastics recorded the Vinaya Pitaka and other scriptures during the summer retreat, and as a result, we now have these to read. Similarly, nowadays some monastics do works to sustain the Dharma, for example, compiling the Buddha's teachings, and writing, editing, and translating Dharma books. During the rains retreat, the community can also work together on important sangha issues by researching, discussing, and coming to a decision about them. For example, one rains retreat, the nuns in our monastery in Taiwan drew up guidelines on the usage of money and the community's method of bookkeeping. Last year we discussed our eating habits. We discovered that we have a lot of attachment to tasting good food and spend too much time thinking about what and how to cook. We made a decision during that summer retreat to simplify our life and our diet. These types of discussion are very beneficial for our individual practice as well as for community life.

Until recently Buddhism has existed only in the Northern Hemisphere. In the Southern Hemisphere summer is not during the same months, so the time in which the summer retreat is held should be different there. In China and Korea, the monastics have retreat not only during the summer, but also during the winter, for anywhere from one or two weeks to two or three months.[1]

The various Buddhist traditions begin the summer retreat on different days. For example, the Chinese tradition speaks of the rains retreat of the first, second, and third periods. The first begins on the sixteenth day of the fourth lunar month; the second begins any day after the seventeenth of the fourth lunar month until the fifteenth of the fifth lunar month; the third begins on the sixteenth day of the fifth lunar month. All are for three months' duration.[2] During this time, monastics do not leave the boundary, or sima, established for the retreat. If, for some urgent reason, they must go outside the boundary, they first state what they intend to do and request permission from the sangha to leave the site of the retreat. Every bhikshuni residing within the broad boundary of a monastery is required to do the rains retreat.

At the end of the summer retreat, another karma, pravarana, the confession at the conclusion of the summer retreat, is performed. Here, the community selects some senior bhikshunis to act as witnesses. Then each bhikshuni in the assembly kneels before one of these appointed bhikshunis and says, "Today everyone in the sangha purifies herself by confession. I, too, am doing this. Elder Sister, if you have seen, heard, or suspected that I have done any wrongdoing during the time of the rains retreat, please tell me." She repeats this three times. If the bhikshunis had not lived together for three months, they would not have observed each other's actions and would not be able to help each other purify their wrongdoings.

Kathina

During the rains retreat in ancient India, the monastics resided at one site, instead of going from place to place as they did during the remainder of the year. The laypeople had a chance to get to know them during this time, and witness their virtue and dedication to the Dharma. The laity would express their gratitude and respect for the sangha by offering cloth at the end of the rains retreat. Thus, this became the time monastics would make new robes.

Naihsargika-payattika 27: If a bhikshuni accepts an untimely garment as a timely one, she commits a naihsargika-payattika.

Here, "timely" refers to the time just after the rains retreat: either one month or five months, as described below.

The Kathina-vastu describes the kathina, or "robe of merit," a karma or activity occurring at the conclusion of the summer retreat. At this time those who successfully complete it receive five privileges to acknowledge their great accumulation of positive potential by doing the retreat. To qualify for these privileges, a bhikshuni must complete the summer retreat that begins on the sixteenth day of the fourth lunar month. In addition, she must engage in the kathina ceremony, in which the laypeople offer the bhikshunis cloth which they designate for one nun—usually a well-respected bhikshuni—and together make into a robe before dawn of the following day.

The privileges last for five months after the end of the summer retreat, during which time those bhikshunis are exempt from the offense of certain precepts. Some circumstances exist, however, in which the kathina period is shorter; for example, all the bhikshunis of a particular monastery may hold a formal karma or meeting in which they agree to voluntarily relinquish these privileges. The expiration or relinquishment of these privileges is called "giving away the kathina," an expression contained in some precepts. Other nuns, who participated in the rains retreat, but not during the first period, may enjoy the five privileges for one month. Some say that the Buddha encouraged monastics to begin their rains retreat early by enabling them to have this special reward. The five privileges are:

1. One may keep as many robes as one requires. See naihsargika-payattika 1, 3, and 17.

2. One may stay overnight without being with the three robes (for bhikshus) or five robes (for bhikshunis). See naihsargika-payattika 2.

3. One may eat apart from the assembly. See prayascittika 22.

4. One may eat out-of-turn meals. The original precept prohibiting out-of-turn meals[3] does not apply to bhikshunis.[4]

5. Having accepted an invitation to a meal, one may go to villages without telling other bhikshunis beforehand. See prayascittika 27.[5]

During the five months after the rains retreat, monastics would make new robes or to mend their tattered ones. To do this, sometimes they had to leave their old robes in the town and return to the monastery without them. For that reason, they could keep more than the usual number of robes during this time. Their new robes had to be completed before the merit robe was given away.

Because the living circumstances for monastics has changed so much from the Buddha's time, many monasteries no longer do kathina ceremony. Our monastery in Taiwan does not do it, nor do most Tibetan monasteries. In Singapore some Theravada bhikshus have enough robes and thus ask the laypeople to donate books to the Buddhist library or money to a Buddhist charity instead of robes to the monastics at the kathina ceremony. Two Western nuns from the Theravada tradition told me that both the monks and nuns in their community in England do this ceremony.

Poshadha

Poshadha (Pali: *uposatha*) was explained in chapter five. In brief it means "to purify," signifying the elimination of negativity and the accomplishment of what is good. By means of this ceremony, which involves the recitation of the *Pratimoksha Sutra*—in brief or in full—monastics purify and renew their precepts. Poshadha is held twice a month: on the full moon day (fifteenth of each lunar month) and the new moon day (thirtieth of each lunar month). All bhikshunis living within the broad boundary must attend unless they are ill or doing important work for the monastery, in which case they excuse themselves and express their willingness to attend. Prior to the recitation, each bhikshuni examines her own behavior to see if she has committed any offense. If so, she confesses in whatever way is suitable according to the type of offense she committed.

When only two bhikshunis are present on the premises, they confess to each other. If only one bhikshuni is there, she does self-examination in silence. She may also wish to do some purification practices and review her precepts. Although this is beneficial, it is not considered a full poshadha, for that requires the presence of at least four bhikshunis.

In our temple, we meet after the recitation of the *Pratimoksha Sutra* to discuss the precepts or to clear the air if anyone has perceived, heard, or suspected another bhikshuni of committing an offense. Twice a month, on the weeks when we do not do poshadha, the assembly gathers to purify and recite the bodhisattva precepts.

> Prayascittika 6: If a bhikshuni recites a sutra together with someone who has not received the (full) precepts, she commits a prayascittika.

The incident triggering this precept occurred when some bhikshus used a melody to recite a sutra with the laypeople. This disturbed people meditating nearby. Here the point is not which sutra was recited, but that when the monastics recited it with the laypeople, they used a melody which made the recitation seem more like entertainment than a religious activity.

In this precept and the precept prohibiting bhikshunis from eating garlic, the linguistic formation of the precept does not express its meaning directly. If the direct disciples of the Buddha had asked him to revise the language and make it clearer, he might have. Nevertheless, the Buddha was not in favor of monastics eating garlic: he told those who did to sit "down stream from the others so the smell did not disturb them."

In a similar way, the Buddha did not want bhikshunis to recite the *Bhikshuni Pratimoksha Sutra* with someone who is not a bhikshuni. In other words, only bhikshunis should attend the poshadha. However, they can recite other sutras—such as the *Heart Sutra* and so forth—together with laypeople.

Repentance

Repentance or confession is a necessary element for the sangha community to remain pure. The Vinaya speaks of two kinds of people. The first is ignorant in that they do not recognize their own wrongdoings. Nor do they know how to repent when seeing them. The second recognizes their offenses and knows how to purify them. A sutra says, "The previous way of thinking leads to evil actions, while the latter leads to virtuous deeds, like a torch clearing away the darkness." The Buddha emphasized the importance of repentance both in the Vinaya and in the sutras. Since many of us practitioners are unable to control our minds, we will violate precepts. Therefore, we must learn the method to purify and restore them.

The Vinaya speaks of six types of repentance:

1. Repentance of a parajika transgression: one is expelled from the order

2. Repentance of a sanghavashesha offense: one does the parivasa (if required), manatta, and abbhana

3. Repentance of a sthulatyaya: this varies according to the type of sthulatyaya committed

4. Repentance of a prayascittika
   - Repentance of a naihsargika-payattika: the bhikshuni gives the extra object to the sangha, confesses her offense, and a representative of the sangha returns the object to her
   - Repentance of a prayascittika: a bhikshuni confesses to another pure bhikshuni

5. Repentance of a pratideshaniya: a bhikshuni confesses to another pure bhikshuni

6. Repentance of a dushkrita
   - A bhikshuni confesses a serious dushkrita to another pure bhikshuni
   - She does self-confession in silence for a minor dushkrita, an error done unintentionally

A parajika transgression, in fact, cannot be repaired, and a bhikshuni who commits one is expelled from the order. At the time of violating a parajika, she automatically loses all of her bhikshuni precepts as well as her status as a bhikshuni. It is not the case that she still has the other bhikshuni precepts but in a degenerated form. She cannot live together with the assembly, perform karma together with them, or attend poshadha.

However, if the person, without wanting to conceal the wrongdoing for even a moment, expresses sincere regret and an earnest wish to remain a monastic immediately after committing a parajika for the first time, she can remain as a nun called a "learner of parajika." With sincere repentance, she saves herself from falling into the hell realm as a result of her action, but she will not be able to attain liberation from cyclic existence this lifetime. If she later commits another parajika offense, whether or not she immediately regrets it, she is permanently expelled from the order and loses her bhikshuni status forever.

In his commentary *The Brief Explanation of Karma*, Vinaya master Dauhai explains why one can still repent a parajika and become a learner of parajika although Theravada Buddhism does not contain this provision. This particular practice, he notes, enables sincerely reformed offenders to live with the sangha, learn the Buddhadharma, and legally share sangha materials. Therefore, although they may not repair the parajika offense, they can repent it and benefit from doing so.

Committing a parajika is not easy. Violating a prayascittika or shikshakaraniya is easier; because they relate to daily life activities that we frequently encounter, we are bound to break them accidentally. A parajika, on the other hand, is difficult to commit accidentally. Transgressing a parajika generally indicates that the person lacks a sincere and strong determination to be a bhikshuni.

To repent a sanghavashesha offense, one needs to perform three acts sequentially: parivasa, manatta, and abbhana.

However, when wishing to express this sequential process simply, the term "manatta" is used to indicate the entire repentance. Parivasa occurs only if one has concealed the fault. Here one remains alone to contemplate one's wrongdoing for as many days as one concealed it. Manatta is the service that the bhikshuni offers to the assembly for a half-month, during which time the thirty-five rights of bhikshunis listed in the Vinaya are suspended. For example, she may not ordain others, vote during karma, or point out the wrongdoings of others. She performs service to the community by doing such things as cleaning the hall daily, preparing the hall prior to the recitation of the *Pratimoksha Sutra*, serving meals, and cleaning up after them. If a guest monastic comes to the community, she must tell the guest she is performing manatta. She sits at the end of the row of bhikshunis, just before the shramanerikas. During these two weeks, the offender confesses in front of the assembly daily, saying, "Elder Sisters, I have committed a sanghavashesha. Now I am performing manatta. Today is the (give the number) day of my manatta." At the end of manatta, the assembly eliminates the remaining fault accrued from breaking this precept by performing abbhana, the rehabilitation rite. This karma is one announcement followed by three proclamations, and it must be done in an assembly of forty monastics—twenty bhikshus and twenty bhikshunis.

Sthulatyaya means "great offense," "gross wrongdoing," or "big hindrance to the virtuous path." According to the *Commentary to the Brief Explanation of Karma*, two types of sthulatyaya exist:

1. An independent sthulatyaya is an action that by nature is a big hindrance to the root of virtue
   * First degree: breaking up the Dharma (e.g. spreading wrong views), stealing objects worth four units of ancient currency, stealing the sangha's objects, and so forth

- Second degree: breaking up the harmonious sangha, stealing objects worth two or three units of ancient currency, having physical contact with the opposite sex with or without a cover, and so forth.
- Third degree: viciously slandering the sangha, stealing objects worth one unit of ancient currency, using wigs made of human hair, eating newly slaughtered meat, and so forth.

2. A dependent sthulatyaya arises when one has done some, but not all, of the branches of a parajika or a sanghavashesha.
    - First degree: committing some branches of a parajika in a heavy way. To repent this, the offender confesses to a pure bhikshuni in an assembly consisting of at least five bhikshunis.
    - Second degree: committing some branches of a parajika in a light way or some branches of a sanghavashesha in a heavy way. To repent this, the offender confesses to a pure bhikshuni in an assembly of four bhikshunis outside the sima, or boundary.
    - Third degree: committing some branches of a sanghavashesha in a light way. To repent this, one confesses to another bhikshuni.

The repentance required for each of the six subdivisions of sthulatyaya offense is different.

Three steps exist to repent a transgression of a naihsargika-payattika. First the offending bhikshuni gives the extra object to the assembly. Second, kneeling in front of the assembly, she says, "I am guilty of possessing an extra object and will now correct myself." The representative tells the assembly, "Bhikshuni So-and-so has committed the offense of possessing an extra object and has given it to the assembly." The representative says to the bhikshuni, "It is good that you acknowledged your mistake and are determined to change." Third, the representative returns the object to that bhikshuni. Although the bhikshuni possesses the extra object again at the conclusion of the meeting, she has purified her mistake by admitting it and relinquishing the object in front of the assembly.

To confess a prayascittika offense from the 178 prayascittika precepts, a bhikshuni kneels in front of another pure bhikshuni and admits her mistake.

A pratideshaniya offense usually occurs if a bhikshuni is healthy, yet she begs for some special food. In this situation, she confesses to another pure bhikshuni.

Two different dushkrita offenses exist. The heavier one is created if a bhikshuni intentionally violates any of the one hundred shikshakaraniya, or training rules. To purify, she confesses to another pure bhikshuni. A minor dushkrita occurs if a bhikshuni unintentionally does any of the shikshakaraniya. She confesses this to the Buddha by herself.

Bhikshus and bhikshunis are not allowed to confess to each other. They confess to members of their own sangha. If a bhikshuni commits a sanghavashesha, she goes to the bhikshu sangha only to ask for rehabilitation at the completion of manatta. She does not confess the wrongdoing before the monks.

Karma

An official meeting or action of the sangha is called a karma. Monastic affairs have to be resolved by monastics themselves, and meetings occur for various purposes. According to the purpose, the sangha considers the kind of activity or meeting to hold, the procedure to adopt, the number of participants required, and the place where that activity is done. Each type of karma must be done in a specific way in order for the proceeding to be legal and therefore acceptable to the entire community. The democratic nature of the sangha and its harmonious spirit are reflected in these karma. Sometimes the specific voting procedures are also called karma, although in this case, they have adjectives adjacent to them describing their particular nature.

A sangha carries out two kinds of karma: the karma for purifying wrongdoings and the karma for carrying out good deeds. To perform a karma to purify wrongdoings, the entire community gathers together and carefully examines the situation. They decide the type of offense committed by a particular bhikshuni and the method to employ to purify it. The karma to carry out good deeds includes ceremonies such as ordination, poshadha, and the confession ceremony at the end of the summer retreat.

Learning the principal terms used in describing a karma is helpful. An "announcement" is a motion presented in verbal form, in which an issue and the suggestion for its resolution are announced to the assembly. For example, in sangha-vashesha 10, a bhikshuni capable of conducting a meeting (hereafter called "the presenter") will present a motion to the bhikshuni who has tried to break up the harmonious sangha as well as to the assembly, saying, "Listen Elder Sister, Bhikshuni So-and-so tried to use various ways to break up the harmonious sangha, insisted on doing so, and refused to desist. Now the assembly is here. With patience please listen to me, Elder Sisters. I would like to admonish her for the purpose of stopping this negative behavior. Bhikshuni So-and-so, you should not break up the harmonious sangha, nor should you insist on doing so. Bhikshuni So-and-so, to benefit from practicing the Buddhadharma, you should live harmoniously with the assembly with joy and without dispute, like water in milk. This is the announcement."

A "proclamation" is a repetition of the announcement with a call requesting disagreeing opinions from the assembly at the end. Usually there is a pause between each proclamation so that any disagreeing opinion may be expressed. For example, in the above case, the presenter says to the assembly, "Elder Sisters, please listen to me. Bhikshuni So-and-so tried to break up the harmonious sangha, insisted on doing so, and refused to desist. The assembly admonishes her now for the purpose of stopping this negative behavior. Bhikshuni So-and-so, you should not break up the harmonious sangha, insist on doing so, or refuse to desist. Bhikshuni So-and-so, to benefit from practicing the Buddhadharma, you should live harmoniously with the assembly with joy and without dispute, like water in milk. Those who agree with the admonition (to stop Bhikshuni So-and-so from continuing her negative behavior), please remain silent. Those who disagree, please speak up (and express your opinion). This is the (say the number: first, second, etc.) proclamation."

A "resolution" is achieved when the number of proclamations required for a specific issue is completed. The resolution is announced after the last proclamation. To continue with the example: After the third proclamation which is required to settle this particular issue, the presenter says, "All the Elder Sisters have agreed by remaining silent. The admonition of Bhikshuni So-and-so (to stop her from continuing that negative behavior) is complete. Please observe the resolution accordingly."

Four major elements constitute a karma:

1. The type of karma. To conduct a karma, the assembly gathers and is informed of the specific reason for the gathering. In that way, the members know if an ordination, confession, poshadha, or other karma will be performed and thus will know the type of karma required to accomplish that. Three types of karma are mentioned: proceedings done alone, through thought; proceedings carried out by two bhikshunis; proceedings carried out by four or more bhikshunis; and so forth.

2. The matter to be resolved

3. The number of participants. The number of participants determines the issues that can be resolved:
   * Proceedings done through thought alone, by reminding oneself
   * Proceedings carried out by two people, in which one confesses to the other
   * Proceedings carried out by a sangha of at least four bhikshunis

* Proceedings carried out by a sangha of at least five bhikshunis. These include pravarana at the conclusion of the rains retreat and ordination in remote areas.
* Proceedings carried out by a sangha of at least ten bhikshunis. These include ordination in a central area where Buddhism flourishes.
* Proceedings carried out by a sangha of at least twenty bhikshunis. These include abbhana which rehabilitates a bhikshuni after she completes manatta to purify a sanghavashesha offense.

There are three types of the proceedings done by a sangha of four or more bhikshunis: those with

1. One announcement (39 types)
2. One announcement followed by one proclamation (57 types)
3. One announcement followed by three proclamations (38 types)

4. The place. Depending on the type of karma to be done, different boundaries are needed to make it legal:

* Broad boundary. This delineates the complete area within which a sangha dwells. For example, the broad boundary encompasses all the buildings and surrounding land owned by the monastery. The boundary may be marked in each direction by a natural object—a tree, river, or mountain top—or an artificial boundary, such as a fence or ribbon. On poshadha days, everyone within a broad boundary who is qualified to attend poshadha must be present.
* Ordination boundary. This is a specific place, usually an enclosed or indoor area where only qualified monastics can enter. The purpose for setting up this boundary is to give ordination. This may be set up within a broad boundary.
* Small boundary. This is used, for example, when the bhikshuni sangha gathers to recite the *Pratimoksha*

Sutra in a place where no broad boundary has been previously established. At the end of poshadha, the small boundary is dissolved.

Two additional sima are:

- The boundary within which monastics should be with their robes, especially overnight. We should not be separated from our three robes overnight, but should have them in the same room with us.
- The boundary delineating the place where the sangha's food is stored. Since monastics are not allowed to keep food with them overnight, it is kept in a designated area that is separate from where they sleep, within a boundary set up for that purpose.

In the example of giving full ordination, the type of karma is one announcement followed by three proclamations; the matter is full ordination; the number of participants in a central land is three bhikshuni masters (a preceptor, instructor, and supervisor), and seven witnesses—ten bhikshunis in total—plus the ordinands. The bhikshu sangha that gives the ordination later in the same day is also composed of ten bhikshus. In an outlying area where there are fewer monastics, the bhikshuni and bhikshu sangha may each consist of five members. The place is designated by the boundary the sangha sets up at the beginning of the proceedings.

To eliminate the offense of a sanghavashesha, the karma is one announcement followed by three proclamations. The matter is to eliminate the fault of the sanghavashesha offense. Four or more bhikshunis must be present. If a bhikshuni commits a shikshakaraniya intentionally, a procedure carried out by two people is needed, for she confesses to another pure bhikshuni. If the offense was done unintentionally, a proceeding done alone through thought is sufficient.

Depending on the type of karma and its purpose, various numbers of participants are necessary: one person, two people, four people, or the entire assembly. If a confession through thought is necessary, only one person is required. If a bhikshuni has to confess to another bhikshuni, two people are required. For ordination, ten bhikshunis are required, although in a remote area, only five are needed. To perform the confession ceremony at the end of the summer retreat, five people are required. To remove the wrongdoing of a sanghavashesha at abbhana, twenty bhikshunis and twenty bhikshus are required. To perform poshadha, the entire sangha must be present. Besides the cases just mentioned, other events are done by four or more bhikshunis.

Initially, during the Buddha's time, all monastics returned to one place to do poshadha on new and full moon days. Monastics who lived far away had to walk a long time to get to the place of poshadha. They were tired and sometimes did not arrive in time for the ceremony. Due to this, the Buddha allowed monastics to set up a boundary in their own areas. Thus, on poshadha days, monastics within each broad boundary gather together to purify and restore their vows.

The purpose of setting up a small boundary when reciting the *Pratimoksha Sutra* is to avoid the offense of performing a karma without the agreement of the entire assembly. When the small boundary is set up, only the people qualified to attend poshadha may participate. Those who are outside the boundary, such as shramanerikas, commit no offense if they do not come. If the small boundary is not set up, both the bhikshunis and the shramanerikas commit an offense because those who are not fully ordained should leave the area where poshadha is held. All those qualified to attend poshadha—in other words, all bhikshunis in the area—should attend. If someone cannot attend, she must express her willingness and request to be absent to another bhikshuni before poshadha begins. In that case, during the ceremony, when the leader asks, "Are there any absent bhikshunis who wish to be present and are pure?" the other bhikshuni reports, "Bhikshuni So-and-so is pure and requests to be excused because (and gives the reason why she cannot attend)."

Precepts Related to Sangha Karma

Since the sangha is to resolve its own affairs, certain attitudes and methods are to be followed by the members. An essential attitude is the willingness to cooperate with others.

> Prayascittika 39: If a bhikshuni does not accept admonition, she commits a prayascittika.

Many precepts were triggered by a bhikshu who had a bad temper. One time, when he was about to do a misdeed, the assembly tried to stop him by giving advice. Because he refused to accept their advice, the Buddha set up this precept. When a person commits a misdeed after being admonished, she commits two transgressions: the first is the misdeed itself; the second is not listening to admonition. As a community, we have the responsibility to help purify each other, and each individual has the responsibility to receive admonition graciously.

> Prayascittika 52: Suppose a bhikshuni says, "I understand the Dharma taught by the Buddha. To indulge sexual desires is not a hindrance to the path." Another bhikshuni admonishes her, saying, "Elder Sister, do not say such a thing. Do not slander the World-Honored One. It is not good to slander the World-Honored One. The World-Honored One never said such a thing. With innumerable skillful means the World-Honored One taught that sexual desire is a hindrance to the path, and that to commit sexual offenses is a hindrance to the path." If that bhikshuni persists in her misconduct when admonished by this bhikshuni, this bhikshuni should admonish her up to three times, so that she may give up her misconduct. If she refrains from her misconduct after the third admonition, good; if not, she commits a prayascittika.

This bhikshuni has committed the wrongdoing of wrong view, which is especially pernicious because by holding onto such a view, she not only harms herself but also can also adversely influence the direction of the entire community.

For these reasons, the community has the responsibility to correct her wrong view.

In the situation described by this precept, the assembly admonishes the bhikshuni, but she refuses to listen. She does not violate the precept prohibiting sexual conduct because she has not engaged in sexual activity. Her offenses are wrong view and not accepting admonition. The Buddha repeatedly said that sexual desire is an obstacle to the path. This bhikshuni is confused about the meaning of unwise sexual behavior. Laypeople can have sexual relationships with their spouse and have a family. As long as they do not engage in unwise sexual behavior such as adultery, they do not create negative karma that blocks their attaining higher realizations. However, monastics follow a different code of conduct. For them, all sexual contact is prohibited. Here, distinguishing the fine line between the Dharma and the Vinaya is helpful. One behavior, in this case, sexual relations, is accepted by the Dharma for laypeople but prohibited by the Vinaya for monastics. This bhikshuni has confused these two, with potentially dire consequences for the sangha. The assembly has the responsibility to advise her and encourage her to give up her wrong view.

Along this line, we must distinguish four activities:

1. Violating a precept
2. Holding wrong views
3. Behaving in a way improper for monastics
4. Wrong livelihood

Each of the four has particular criteria associated with it. For example, to determine if a particular action violates a precept, we need to know the status of the person doing the action: is he or she a Buddhist, non-Buddhist, lay disciple, novice monastic, or fully ordained? In addition, we must consider the motivation, the action taken, the method of doing it, and the result. For example, having sexual relations is not in violation of a precept for laypeople, but it is for monastics.

Wrong views are disastrous because they steer us away from the correct path. Someone holding wrong views will follow an unwise path, thinking it is correct. To distinguish if a view is right or wrong, we have to consider the object, the universality or limitation of the action viewed, and whether it concerns the conventional or ultimate nature.

To determine if a behavior is improper for monastics, we must consider the person, situation, motivation, degree of impropriety (i.e. is the action naturally negative or simply bad manners? Is one behaving like a fool? A degraded person?). Similarly, wrong livelihood is determined by one's status, motivation, and so on. For example, doing business is fine for laypeople but in violation of precepts for monastics.

In conclusion, to evaluate a specific situation concerning any of these four, many factors need to be taken into consideration. To enhance our understanding, we can think of examples of each of the four and evaluate them using the various criteria. Here again, we see the dependent nature of things the Buddha's advice is not rigid dogma, but has various meanings and methods of implementation according to the person and the circumstance. Ignoring any of the related factors could lead to making a wrong statement or judgment.

> Prayascittika 54: Suppose a shramanerika says, "I know the Dharma taught by the Buddha. To indulge sexual desires is not a hindrance to the path." A bhikshuni admonishes the shramanerika, saying, "From now on, you are no longer a disciple of the Buddha. You cannot follow bhikshunis around. Shramanerikas may sleep together with bhikshunis for two nights. Now, there is no such thing for you. Get out. Be gone. You should not live here." If a bhikshuni knows a shramanerika to have been thus expelled and yet stays together with her, she commits a prayascittika.

Although this shramanerika has not committed a root downfall, she holds a serious wrong view, and the community has the right to expel her. The bhikshuni involved commits an offense because she has disobeyed the decision the assembly

made to expel the shramanerika by still maintaining relations and living with her.

> Prayascittika 58: If a bhikshuni, after performing a karma
> with others, later says, "The bhikshunis give the possessions
> of the assembly to those they are close to," she commits a
> prayascittika.

This incident involved an arhat who volunteered to serve
the sangha by managing sangha property and assigning
rooms to the monastics. Because his work was demanding,
he had no chance to accept invitations to laypeople's houses.
Those monastics who visited laypeople's homes often received robes in addition to food, and because this arhat
worked so diligently, his ragged robe which barely covered
his body was the worst among all the monastics. One day, a
layperson offered a nice robe to the community. In general,
the person managing sangha property would decide who
would receive the robe, but because he was the manager and
needed a new robe himself, he asked the assembly to decide
who would get it. During a meeting, the assembly agreed—
by performing an announcement followed by one proclamation—that he deserved it because he worked so hard
serving them.

Later, thinking that if he objected to the sangha's decision
he might get part of the nice robe himself, another bhikshu
began a rumor that the arhat received the expensive robe
because he was well-liked by the monks in the assembly.
Accusing the sangha of being partial and making decisions
unfairly, he tried to stir others up. For this reason, the Buddha set up this precept. If an issue has been settled in the
community according to the Dharma and the Vinaya, we
have to abide by that decision. If we later have doubts or
disagree with a decision, we should not gossip or spread ru-
mors in private. Rather, we should express our opinion
openly during a gathering of the assembly.

Prayascittika 59: If a bhikshuni gets up and leaves during a karma of the sangha, she commits a prayascittika.

A group of six bhikshus committed several offenses. One day a sangha meeting was called. Although the purpose was to discuss the monks' practice in the Dharma and Vinaya, these six bhikshus thought it was to censure their wrongdoings. Everyone within the broad boundary who was qualified to attend the meeting came, but to inhibit the proceedings, these six bhikshus stood up and left. Without their presence, the assembly was incomplete and could not perform the karma to admonish them. The Buddha established this precept to prevent monastics from interrupting karma for their own selfish purposes. However, if a bhikshuni is occupied by an important matter, such as taking care of an ill nun or doing work for the sangha, she can express her willingness to attend the meeting and ask to be excused. She should not just say, "I don't like what you're talking about," and leave.

Prayascittika 60: If a bhikshuni asks another bhikshuni to explain her absence and her wish to be present (at a karma), and later reprimands her, she commits a prayascittika.

In another situation similar to the one above, this group of six bhikshus expressed their willingness to be present at a karma to another bhikshu and asked to be excused. The bhikshu relayed their message to the assembly, which thus was able to perform the karma without these bhikshus' presence. Later on, because the six bhikshus did not like the decisions the assembly made, they regretted not being there. They complained that because they thought the meeting was for another purpose, the decisions the sangha made without their presence were not valid and they would not follow them. Thus the Buddha set up this precept.

Whenever a monastic is required to be present at a karma and asks to be excused, he or she must express willingness to accept the decisions made by the assembly as long as they are made according to the Dharma and the Vinaya. If for personal reasons, a bhikshuni later disagrees with a decision and tries to make excuses for not following it, she commits a prayascittika. When the assembly meets, each bhikshuni has the right to express her opinion and to vote. If we give up this right by not attending the meeting, we must cooperate with resolutions the assembly makes. We should not disrupt the community by later complaining because we do not like the decisions.

Observing precepts purely requires not just one person. We live the precepts in our daily lives in the context of our interactions with others, that is, in a community. Sometimes because of an individual's personality or temperament, he or she will reject admonition, refuse to accept advice, or not follow a decision the community made. Such behavior has a harmful influence on the entire community. Caring about the effects of our actions on other individuals and on the sangha, we should resolve to support our communities in performing virtuous karma, so that as a group we can protect and sustain the Dharma.

Resolving Conflicts

As ordinary human beings, we have the Buddha nature as well as defilements obscuring it. Thus, conflict arising within a community is natural and to be expected. We must learn to resolve these conflicts wisely and completely, not only for the peace of mind of the individuals and the community involved, but also for the preservation of the Dharma. The Buddha talked of six causes of disputes:

1. Being overwhelmed by anger and refusing to speak
2. Maliciousness and the wish to harm others
3. Envy and holding grudges
4. Deceit
5. Lack of a sense of personal integrity and consideration for others

6. Evil desires and wrong views

Being aware of how and in what situations these attitudes arise can help us prevent disputes. Disputes are of four types:

1. Oral disputes. These arise when monastics hold differing views regarding Dharma practice.

2. Disputes arising from censure. If a bhikshuni commits a transgression, the assembly must eliminate her mistake. Once this is done, however, disputes may arise if the past is brought up again or if offenses which were resolved are brought up for review.

3. Disputes arising from different views regarding offenses

4. Disputes arising from the previous three

The Buddha prescribed seven ways to end disputes:

1. *Sammukha-vinaya.* The dispute is resolved in the assembly, with the presence of the parties involved.

2. *Smirti-vinaya.* The case is resolved by remembering events: the accused bhikshuni publicly recalls her innocence, and the accusation is removed. When Bhikshu Dravyamallaputra was wrongly accused of committing a parajika (see sangha-vashesha 2 and 3), many bhikshus kept asking him to remember the transgression. Although he expressed his innocence repeatedly, saying that in this life he could not remember doing anything of that nature even in a dream, the bhikshus persisted in asking him to think harder. Not knowing what to do, Dravyamallaputra talked to the Buddha. The Buddha told the assembly to perform the *smirti-vinaya* karma, which requires one announcement followed by three proclamations to reach a resolution. They did; the dispute was settled, and the case closed. A situation in which a monastic remembers his or her guilt is dealt with by the sixth method of ending disputes.

3. *Amudha-vinaya.* A bhikshuni states that her offense was committed due to insanity.

4. *Tatsvabhavaisiya-vinaya.* A bhikshuni voluntarily admits her wrongdoing. Others should not force her to confess.

5. *Pratijnakaraka-vinaya.* The dispute is settled by majority vote, those voting being knowledgeable in the Dharma.

6. *Yadbhuyasikiya-vinaya.* Evidence is presented so that the person accused can remember and admit her mistake.

7. *Trinastaraka-vinaya.* This is called "covering the mud with straw." In protracted disputes, an elder is appointed to counsel each side and to spread the "straw" of the Dharma over the "mud" of the dispute.

These methods to settle disputes are practical guidelines set out by the Buddha. They can be of great help when you begin monasteries in the West. Please learn them in more depth by studying the Vinaya.

EPILOGUE

Teachers who practice and understand Vinaya well are not afraid of change. They allow their students to experiment. However, they supervise and guide their students so that they do not go astray or get sidetracked.

Master Yin-shun said that teaching Vinaya is not setting restrictions, telling students, "Don't do this; don't do that." Rather, a good teacher activates students' potential so that they have a clear understanding of the path to follow. Vinaya is not meant to confine people, but to give them an indication of what they can do and the type of people they can become. He distinguished intellectual concepts from the practical reality of implementing the principles they describe in daily life. Implementation is about opening up potential, and to do this, a teacher must understand the student's background and abilities.

Although I have not been able to go into depth in this book, I have explained the general principles to be aware of in monastic life. You can put the Vinaya into practice in your daily life right now, and in the future continue to study and think about it. Reflect on the meaning of each precept and how you can use it to become more aware of your thoughts, words, and deeds. As your bring your speech and deeds in line with the meaning of the pratimoksha, your mind will automatically become calmer and clearer, and the gross disturbing attitudes will not arise as often. Such study, reflection, and mindfulness of the precepts are helpful for monastics and laypeople alike.

The Buddha took care of and continues to take care of his followers by teaching the Dharma and the Vinaya. When I joined the sangha, my teachers taught me continuously, and I now want to repay their kindness by contributing to the welfare of the sangha and the Three Jewels. I ask you, too, to use your talents with love to benefit the sangha.

When the Buddha accepted women into the sangha, he confirmed women's ability to attain liberation and enlightenment. After Mahaprajapati, the first bhikshuni, passed away, the Buddha held her relics in his hand and said to the assembly, "This bhikshuni has fulfilled the meaning of being a great human being." He praised and admired what Mahaprajapati had accomplished, for she was not only a bhikshuni who lived in pure ethical discipline, but also a great human being who benefited others. Being a great human being is not related to gender; it depends on caring about the well-being of all our fellow sentient beings.

Now let us dedicate our positive potential. We have read the *Pratimoksha Sutra* and the teachings for the assembly are completed. We now offer the positive potential of our reading the *Pratimoksha Sutra* to all sentient beings so that they may attain Buddhahood all together.

APPENDIX

Preliminary and Concluding Rituals for the Recitation of the *Bhikshuni Pratimoksha Sutra*[1]

Preliminary Ritual

Two bhikshunis, having been appointed as ritual conductors, invite the Eldest Bhikshuni into the meditation hall on behalf of the assembly.

Setting the Boundary[2]

Facing the Buddha, all bhikshunis bow three times (half-bow, full bow, half-bow).

Sutra Reciter: Is the sangha assembled?

Respondent: The sangha is assembled.

Sutra Reciter: Is it in harmony?

Respondent: It is in harmony.

Sutra Reciter: Have all those who are not fully ordained left?

Respondent: *(After sending them out:)* They have left. *(If there are none:)* There are none.

Sutra Reciter: What is the purpose of this harmonious assembly now?

Respondent: To set up the boundary.

Sutra Reciter: Elder Sisters, now we have an assembly of bhikshunis. Since it is time to have the gathering to set up the boundary, please listen with patience. This is the statement for setting up the boundary.

Elder Sisters, now we have an assembly of bhikshunis to set up the boundary. Whoever disagrees, please say so. Those in this assembly of bhikshunis who want to set up the boundary, please remain silent. Speak if you disagree.

(Wait a moment.)

Since the assembly has shown its silent approval, this assembly of bhikshunis has completed setting up the boundary. The assembly has agreed. Please follow through this resolution.

Establishing the Purpose

Facing the Buddha, all bhikshuni bow three times (half-bow, full bow, half-bow).

Sutra Reciter: Is the sangha assembled?

Respondent: The sangha is assembled.

Sutra Reciter: Is it in harmony?

Respondent: It is in harmony.

Sutra Reciter: Have all those who are not fully ordained left?

Respondent: *After sending them out:* They have left. *If there are none:* There are none.

Sutra Reciter: What is the purpose of this harmonious assembly now?

Respondent: To confess wrongdoings.

Sutra Reciter: Elder Sisters, now we have an assembly of bhikshunis. Since it is time to have the gathering to confess wrongdoings, please listen with patience. This is the statement for confessing wrongdoings.

Elder Sisters, now we have an assembly of bhikshunis to confess wrongdoings. Whoever disagrees, please say so. Those in this assembly of bhikshunis who want to confess wrongdoings, please remain silent. Speak if you disagree. (Wait a moment.)

Since the assembly has shown its silent approval, this assembly of bhikshunis has agreed to confess wrongdoings. The assembly has agreed. Please follow through this resolution.

Confession

Sutra Reciter: Elder Sisters, for whoever has committed any offense, now is the time to have this gathering. Please listen with patience. Whoever has committed any offense must confess. This is the statement for confession.

Together:

For all the wrongdoings I have done in the past
Based on beginningless attachment, anger, and
    ignorance,
And created by body, speech, and mind,
I now regret and confess all of them.

(Recite three times, bowing once after each recitation.)

Actual Bhikshunis' Poshadha

Sutra Reciter (standing in front of her seat and facing the assembly): I pay homage to the Elder Sisters. The assembly has assigned me to recite the Pratimoksha Sutra. If I make any mistake, please be kind and point it out to me.

Sutra Reciter: Homage to our teacher Shakyamuni Buddha.[3]

Assembly: Homage to our teacher Shakyamuni Buddha.

Repeat a second and third time.
Assembly and reciter do a half-bow to each other. Everyone sits down.

Sutra Reciter: The *Pratimoksha Sutra* is very rare to encounter. It is hard to encounter even during numerous eons. It is even harder to observe it, and it is much harder to practice it.

Now the Sutra Reciter begins reciting the Pratimoksha Sutra.

Concluding Ritual

When she has finished, she waits a minute before giving a sign. Everyone then stands.

Sutra Reciter (*facing the assembly*): I have finished sincerely reciting the *Pratimoksha Sutra* which the assembly assigned me to recite. However, due to my physical, verbal, and mental laziness, the recitation was not fluent. I made you sit here for a long time, and this may have disturbed you. Elder Sisters, please be generous and extend your compassion to me.

Reciter and assembly make a half-bow to each other. The reciter walks around her seat and faces the Buddha.

Dissolving the Boundary

Sutra Reciter: Is the sangha assembled?
Respondent: The sangha is assembled.

Sutra Reciter: Is it in harmony?
Respondent: It is in harmony.

Sutra Reciter: What is the purpose of this harmonious assembly now?
Respondent: To dissolve the boundary.

Sutra Reciter: Elder Sisters, now we have an assembly of bhikshunis. Since it is time to have this gathering to dissolve the boundary, please listen with patience. This is the statement for dissolving the boundary.

Elder Sisters, now we have an assembly of bhikshunis to dissolve the boundary. Whoever disagrees, please say so.

Those in this assembly of bhikshunis who want to dissolve the boundary, please remain silent. Speak if you disagree.

(Wait a moment.)

Since the assembly has shown its silent approval, this assembly of bhikshunis has completed dissolving the boundary. The assembly has agreed. Please follow through this resolution.

Dedication

The reciter bows three times to the Buddha while the assembly recites:

> I have recited the *Pratimoksha Sutra* and the poshadha for the assembly is completed. I now offer the merits of my reading the *Pratimoksha Sutra* to all sentient beings so that they may attain Buddhahood all together.

Then everyone bows three times together.

Respondent: Thanks to the Reciter.

Sutra Reciter: Everyone do a half-bow to the Buddha.

Everyone does a half-bow and then leaves the hall in order of seniority.

In Luminary Temple after the recitation ceremony, the bhikshunis meet together. The disciplinarian invites the assembly to point out the improper acts or attitudes either in individuals or in the group. If necessary, individuals may explain their situation or express their willingness to correct a wrongdoing. The assembly may decide how to improve the community life.

NOTES

Editor's Preface

1 This topic is explored in more depth in Thubten Chodron, "Western Buddhist Nuns: A New Phenomenon in an Ancient Tradition," *Women's Buddhism, Buddhism's Women*, ed. Ellison Findly (Boston: Wisdom Publications, 2000).

Introduction

1 The number of bhikshu and bhikshuni precepts varies according to the Vinaya tradition. In the Theravada tradition, there are 227 bhikshu precepts and 311 bhikshuni precepts. In the Dharmaguptaka there are 250 and 348 respectively; in the Mulasarvastivada there are 253 and 364 respectively.

Chapter Two

1 Upali recited the Vinaya at the First Council in seventy parts. Later it was condensed into ten parts, five parts, four parts, and so on. In his *Collection of Selected Speeches*, Vinaya Master Hong-yi briefly mentions the history of the Vinaya practiced in China: "Regarding the Vinaya of specific schools, the earliest one translated into Chinese was *Shi-song-lu (Ten-part Vinaya* from the Sarvastivadin School) in the fourth or fifth century CE. Its primary translator was Kumarajiva. Master Hui-yuan, the first patriarch of the Pure Land School, enthusiastically promoted this

Vinaya. At the time of division of North and South (420-588 C.E.), this Vinaya was widely practiced in southern China. The next Vinaya introduced into China was the *Four-part Vinaya* (from the Dharmaguptaka School). The time of its appearance in China was not far from that of the *Shi-song-lu*, but not many people practiced it until the Sui Dynasty (589-618). At the beginning of the T'ang Dynasty (618-907), this Vinaya reached the peak of its popularity. The third one translated into Chinese in the Eastern Tsin Dynasty (317-419) was *Mahasangha-vinaya* (*Mahasamgika Vinaya*). During the time of division of North and South, some people in northern China tried to promote it. After the *Mahasangha-vinaya*, the *Five-part Vinaya* came to China during the Dynasty of (Liu) Song (420-477). Since its style was concise and simple, Vinaya Master Dao-xuan greatly praised it. Unfortunately, not many people spread it. After that, the *Mulasarvastivadin-vinaya* arrived, which was originally practiced mostly in the Tibetan area. Its translator was Tripitaka Master Yi-jing who lived during the era of Empress Wu in the T'ang Dynasty (684-703). Master Yi-jing had been in India for over twenty years. With his diligence and talent, he mastered the details of Vinaya in a way unsurpassed by other contemporary foreign monks in India. He was the greatest Vinaya master in China both before and after that time."

2 When the sangha first split into different groups during the Second Council (116 years after the Buddha's parinirvana), Aryasthaviranikaya was the conservative group. One subdivision of this general category was the Samghika Vinaya of the Sarvastivadins.

3 The word "vastu" that appears in the following list refers to a basis of ethical training.

Chapter Three

1 This does not mean that any particular individual is more important than another. Rather, because they hold more ethical precepts and have dedicated their lives to the Dharma in a way that the others have not, bhikshus and bhikshunis as a whole are more capable of sustaining and passing on the Dharma.

2 "Mara" refers to all forces opposed to liberation, be they external beings or internal mental states.

3 As the story illustrates, the purpose of this precept is to protect bhikshunis from embarrassing or uncomfortable situations and to prevent laymen from losing respect for them. Other precepts also concern a couch or bed and illustrate different aspects of a bhikshuni's relationship with laypeople.

> Prayascittika 84: If a bhikshuni enters a layman's house and without telling the householder, sits on a couch, she commits a prayascittika.

Although this precept appears similar to the previous one, the reason behind it is different. In this case, Bhikshuni Sthulananda went to the house of a high minister who was not Buddhist. He had a large beautiful couch on which only he was allowed to sit. Thinking it was lovely, Sthulananda sat on it without asking permission. Although his servant explained that she was not allowed to sit there, the minister was upset when we saw someone sitting on his seat.

However, what followed made him even angrier. The bhikshuni had her period, and because she was careless, she dirtied the couch and left, without taking care of it. When the man saw this, he rebuked her, saying, "She is like a thief and a prostitute. I don't respect bhikshunis at all." Due to this incident, the Buddha established the above precept, which concerns manners. If we wish to use things owned by others, we should ask their permission first. The reason behind this precept is clearly different from the previous one.

Other precepts, for example prayascittika 83, 85, and 116, were established so that bhikshunis would be mindful of basic manners when relating to the public.

> Prayascittika 83: If a bhikshuni sits in a layperson's house and then goes away without telling the owner, she commits a prayascittika.

A bhikshuni visited the house of a layman, who was happy to see her and asked her to be seated outside on a nice cushion he placed there for her. Later, he went to do his work, and after a while, she left without telling him. Seeing the cushion, a thief stole it, making the householder unhappy. He said to the bhikshuni, "Why didn't you tell me you were leaving? I would have put the cushion inside the house, and it wouldn't have been stolen." Due to this situation, the Buddha established the above precept.

> Prayascittika 85: If a bhikshuni makes her bed and stays over-
> night in a layperson's house without telling the owner, she
> commits a prayascittika.

A group of bhikshunis walking on a road to Kosala came across
an empty house in a village. Tired, they made their beds and
slept there without talking to the owner. Some laypeople saw
and asked, "Who arranged for you to stay here?" to which the
bhikshunis responded, "No one did. We let ourselves in." The
people criticized the bhikshunis as shameless, saying, "How can
you claim to be knowledgeable of the Dharma while behaving
like thieves?" Because of this incident, the Buddha established
this precept.

> Prayascittika 116: If a bhikshuni enters a layperson's house,
> asks the owner to prepare bedding for her to stay overnight,
> and then goes away the next day without informing the owner,
> she commits a prayascittika.

A bhikshuni went to a layman's house, stayed the night there,
and departed the next day without telling him. Later, due to an
accident, the house caught fire and burnt down. Unhappy over
the loss of his property, the householder said to the bhikshuni,
"I thought you were still looking after the house. Had you told
me you were leaving, I would have taken care of the house."
Thus, Buddha set up this precept. While the above precepts were
established to remind bhikshunis of basic manners, other precepts came into being to ensure bhikshunis' safety, to prevent
stubbornness, and so on.

4 The listing of the eight gurudharma varies in the various Vinaya schools. The following is according to the Dharmaguptaka.

5 This reflects the view that men are more susceptible to pride,
while women have more difficulty with attachment.

6 Situations exist, however, in which a bhikshuni is prohibited
from showing respect to a bhikshu due to his misconduct.

7 Manatta is a temporary suspension of the normal privileges
to which each bhikshuni is entitled in the sangha. It occurs when
a bhikshuni commits a sanghavashesha offense. When she completes the period of manatta, abbhana, a rehabilitation ceremony,
is held by both bhikshus and bhikshunis. At this time her normal privileges are reinstated.

8 Although in general, monastics may point out the faults of other members of their community with a kind attitude in order to help them, during the rains retreat, this is not permitted. At the close of the retreat, they may speak of any mistakes that they have been seen, heard, or suspected were made.

Chapter Four

1 The listing of the six regulations for a shikshamana varies according to the various Vinaya schools. The one here is according to the Dharmaguptaka tradition. Also see Kabilsingh, Chatsumarn. "From Sikkhamana to Silsdhara" in *Yasodhara*, Vol. 15, No 4 (No. 60), July-September, 1999.

2 The requisites are food, clothing, medicine, and shelter, which includes a bed and bedding.

Chapter Five

1 The ceremony to set up the boundary and other preliminary and concluding rituals are found in the appendix.

2 This and the following verses are as translated by Karma Lekshe Tsomo and Heng-ching Shih in *Sisters in Solitude* (Albany N.Y. State University of New York Press, 1996).

3 In Tsomo's work, the Sanskrit diacritics are included. The editor apologizes for not including them here. Also, Tsomo uses slightly different spelling for some of the Sanskrit words than the editor does.

4 This and the following verses are from the *Bhikshuni Pratimoksha Sutra* of the Dharmaguptaka school. Ibid.

5 That is, poshadha.

Chapter Six

1 Manatta lasts six nights for bhikshus.

2 Please note that "vow" indicates one's level of ordination, for example, as a bhikshuni, shramanerika, or upasika. Each vow has a different number of precepts. For example, the bhikshuni entails following 348 precepts, the shramanerika vow ten precepts, and the upasika vow five precepts.

Chapter Thirteen

1 Since the Vinaya would indicate the needed object to be excessive for a normal monastic, a procedure called "assignment" is done to enable a needy monastic to receive extra requisites with purity. Here the person who needs the extra object gives it to another bhikshuni, who then returns it to her and briefly explains that by means of this back and forth process, she may keep the object with purity.

2 Bhikkhu Thanissaro, ed., *The Buddhist Monastic Code* Valley Center CA, (Metta Forest Monastery, 1994), p. 165.

3 This is a ritual of placing the cloth under shared ownership. Ibid. pp. 165-172, 415-9, 534-6. There may be differences between the Theravada and Dharmaguptaka Vinaya on this point. It needs further research.

Chapter Sixteen

1 Some communities of Western monastics who reside in the cold climates of Europe and North America hold a three-month retreat in the winter months when activities naturally slow down due to the weather. This enables them to have programs for laypeople in the summer months.

2 In the Tibetan tradition, the rains retreat begins on either the sixteenth of the sixth month or sixteenth of the seventh month. It too lasts for three months, although doing an abbreviated six-week retreat is possible.

3 The bhikshu precept dealing with this is:

> Prayascittika 32: Suppose a bhikshu eats out-of-turn meals, he commits a prayascittika unless it is at special times. By special times it is meant when he is ill or when the donor also offers robes in addition to food.

This precept was made to prevent bhikshus from eating a meal just before going to the home of a donor who had invited them for a meal, thus offending the host because they were too full to eat very much. Since monastics had difficulty receiving enough cloth and thread, and these goods were usually given together with a meal, they were exempt from not eating out-of-turn meals during the kathina time.

4 According to Master Shu-ming, some precepts in both the naihsargika-payattika and prayascittika categories are applicable only to one gender because the necessary conditions have not ripened, the situation for monastics of the other sex to engage such acts is rare, or the public is more tolerant of monastics of the other sex who engage in such behavior. However, this does not mean that the same act committed by monastics of the other sex is totally free of transgression: it could result in a dushkrita offense.

5 This precept and the story behind it are:

> Prayascittika 27: If a bhikshuni has already accepted an invitation to the main meal, yet goes to another house during the period from dawn to the time of the meal or from the time of the meal to noon without informing other bhikshunis, she commits a prayascittika, unless it is an allowable time. Allowable times are when she is sick, when she is sewing robes, and when she is traveling. These are the allowable times.

In the Buddha's time a wealthy man in Shravasti had a dear friend named Barnanto who became a monk. He thought, "When Bhikshu Barnanto comes to our village, I want to offer food to the sangha for his sake." One day, when the man heard that Barnanto was in Shravasti, he sent a messenger to the monastery inviting the bhikshus to a meal at his house the next day. The bhikshus arrived, and after sitting down said, "All the monks are here. Food can be served now." The wealthy man asked that they wait until Barnanto arrived. The bhikshus again said that all monks were there and food should be served quickly since they had to finish their meal before noon. The man again requested them to wait. Meanwhile, after having breakfast, Barnanto visited other households. By the time he arrived at the man's house, it was almost noon. As a result, the bhikshus did not have enough food due to having had little time to eat.

Another time a friend of Barnanto brought his newly harvested fruit to the monastery and asked the assembly to wait for Barnanto before sharing it. Again Barnanto was visiting other households. He returned after noon, and thus all the bhikshus could not have the fruit. Because of these incidents, the Buddha said that, having accepted an invitation, bhikshus should not stay long in other households after breakfast or after the main meal.

After that, many bhikshus dared not go to the village if more than one donor had invited them. The Buddha therefore revised the precept allowing the bhikshus to visit other households if they had told a monk in their monastery beforehand. Later illness, making garments, and accepting offered robes were added to the list of exceptions.

Appendix

1 This was translated by Bhikshuni Jendy Shih from the Chinese text under the instruction of Venerable Bhikshuni Wu Yin at Bodhgaya, in 1996, prior to the poshadha of the Western bhikshunis during *Life as a Western Buddhist Nun*. It corresponds to the way poshadha is conducted at Luminary Temple in Taiwan.

2 The boundary for poshadha is the hall in which the gathering is held. Since everyone doing poshadha is already there, speaking about absent bhikshunis is not necessary at this point.

3 In Chinese: *Namo bentse tsay ta muni fo.*

GLOSSARY

abbhana Absolution. The formal procedure of the monastic community for rehabilitating and restoring the rights of a suspended monastic, i.e. one who has committed a sangha-vashesha.

adhikarana-shamata Modes of handling disputes mentioned in the *Pratimoksha Sutra*.

announcement A motion presented in verbal form, in which an issue and the suggestion for its resolution are announced to the assembly during a formal meeting.

arhat A person who is free from samsara and has attained liberation.

bhikshu (Pali: *bhikkhu*) A fully ordained Buddhist monk.

bhikshuni (Pali: *bhikkhuni*) A fully ordained Buddhist nun.

bhikshuni-upadhyayini One's bhikshuni preceptor with whom a newly ordained bhikshuni trains for at least two years.

bodhisattva A person who has the firm altruistic intention to become a Buddha to benefit sentient beings.

Buddha A fully enlightened being. "The Buddha" refers to the historical Buddha of this age, Shakyamuni Buddha.

Dharma (Pali: *Dhamma*) True paths and true cessations; the Buddha's teachings.

Dharmaguptaka The Vinaya school prevalent in China, Korea, Taiwan, and Vietnam.

dushkrita (Pali: *dukkata*) Light offense.

gurudharma (Pali: *garudhamma*) Eight rules regarding the relationship between bhikshus and bhikshunis.

karma (1)Volitional action, as in karma and its results. (2)An action taken by an assembly of monastics; a meeting of monastics done for a specific purpose.

kathina The robe of merit. At the kathina ceremony after the rains retreat, the sangha receives and distributes offerings of cloth to be used to make robes.

learner of parajika A bhikshu or bhikshuni who, upon committing a parajika offense, immediately has sincere regret for the wrongdoing and does not wish to conceal it even for a moment. The person may continue to live with the sangha, although he or she is not considered an actual bhikshu or bhikshuni.

Mahaprajapati (Pali: Mahapajapati) The Buddha's aunt and stepmother, who became the first bhikshuni.

manatta The period of pennance, repentance, and suspension of monastic privileges for one who has committed a sanghavashesha.

Mulasarvastivada The Vinaya school prevalent in Tibet.

naihsargika-payattika (Pali: *nissaggiya pacittiya*) Lapses with forfeiture. A category of precepts found in the *Pratimoksha Sutra*.

nirvana (Pali: *nibbana*) Liberation from cyclic existence.

ordination (Skt: *pravrajya*) The ceremony through which one becomes a monastic.

parivasa Probation. A time in which a bhikshuni who has committed a sanghavashesha lives apart from the community to contemplate her misdeed.

parajika Defeat or root downfall. The most serious category of precepts. The offense committed when a parajika precept is completely transgressed.

poshadha (Pali: *uposatha*) The twice monthly purification and restoration ceremony of the bhikshus and bhikshunis.

prayascittika (*also Skt: payattika*. Pali: *pacittiya*) Lapse. A category of precepts in the *Pratimoksha Sutra*. The offense committed when a naihsargika-payattika or prayascittika precept is transgressed.

pravarana (Pali: *pavarana*) The ceremony concluding the rains retreat.

pratideshaniya (Pali: *patidesaniya*) An offense requiring confession. A category of precepts in the *Pratimoksha Sutra*.

pratimoksha (Pali: *patimokkha*) Individual liberation, the goal of the practice. The code of monastic precepts leading to this liberation.

Pratimoksha Sutra The texts containing monastic precepts: the *Bhikshu Pratimoksha Sutra* with the monks' precepts and the *Bhikshuni Pratimoksha Sutra* with the nuns' precepts.

pravrajya The ordination procedure.

proclamation A repetition of the announcement made at a karma with a call requesting disagreeing opinions from the assembly.

rains retreat (summer retreat) The three-month period of the summer monsoon rains in India, during which the sangha lives within a restricted boundary in order to avoid unnecessary movement that could harm crops and insects prevalent during this season.

resolution The conclusion reached by the assembly during a karma when the number of proclamations required for a specific issue is completed.

samsara Cyclic existence. The suffering cycle of rebirth under the control of disturbing attitudes and karma.

Sangha An individual who has attained the path of seeing and above.

sangha A community of four or more monastics.

sanghavashesha (Pali: *sanghadisesa*) Remainder, an offense requiring suspension; the second most serious category of precepts.

shikshakaraniya (Pali: *sekhiya, skyhya*) Training rules. A category of precepts in the *Pratimoksha Sutra.*

shikshapada (Pali: *sikkhapada*) Precept of training.

shikshamana (Pali: *sikkhamana*) A probationary nun.

shila Ethical discipline.

sima The boundary within which a particular karma of the sangha is performed.

skandha (Pali: *khandhaka*) Groups of similar teachings prescribing religious rituals and practices that the sangha is to do.

shramanera (Pali: *samanera*) A male novice monastic.

shramanerika (Pali: *samaneri*) A female novice monastic.

sthulatyaya (Pali: *thullaccaya*) A grave offense, usually one in which either a parajika or sanghavashesha precept was partially, but not fully, transgressed.

stupa (Pali: *thupa*) A Buddhist reliquary or monument.

sutra (Pali: *sutta*) A discourse given by the Buddha; the text containing such a discourse.

tathagata "One thus gone (to enlightenment)," i.e. a Buddha.

Three Higher Trainings (Skt: *trisra-shiksha*; Pali: *tisso sikkha*) The higher trainings in ethical discipline, concentration, and wisdom.

Theravada (Skt: *Sthaviravada*) The Vinaya school prevalent in Southeast Asia and Sri Lanka.

upasaka A male Buddhist who has taken refuge and some or all of the five lay precepts.

upasampada (Pali: *upasampanna*) Full ordination as a bhikshu or bhikshuni.

upasika A female Buddhist who has taken refuge and some
or all of the five lay precepts.

varshaka (Pali: *vassa*) The rains retreat.

vastu Bases for ethical training.

vihara A monastic dwelling, an early monastery.

Vinaya The ethical discipline, precepts, and guidelines for
training for the monastic community. The scriptures explaining these.

FURTHER READING

Vinaya

Bhikkhu Thanissaro. *The Buddhist Monastic Code*. 1994. For free distribution, write to: The Abbot, Metta Forest Monastery, P.O. Box 1409, Valley Center, CA 92082, USA.

Chodron, Thubten, ed. *Preparing for Ordination· Reflections for Westerners Considering Monastic Ordination in the Tibetan Buddhist Tradition*. Seattle: Life as a Western Buddhist Nun, 1997. For free distribution, write to Dharma Friendship Foundation, P.O. Box 30011, Seattle, WA 98103, USA.

The Daily Requisites of Vinaya, English translator unknown. Taiwan: The Committee of Religious Affairs Fo Kuang Shan Buddhist Order, 1998.

Dhirasekera, Jotiya. *Buddhist Monastic Discipline*. Sri Lanka: Ministry of Higher Education Research Publication Series, 1982.

The Essentials of the Rules of Discipline for Sramanera and Sramanerikas. English translator unknown. Taiwan: The Committee of Religious Affairs Fo Kuang Shan Buddhist Order, 1998.

Gyatso, Tenzin. *Advice from Buddha Shakyamuni Concerning a Monk's Discipline.* Dharamsala: Library of Tibetan Works and Archives, 1982.

Hirakawa, Akira. *Monastic Discipline for the Buddhist Nuns.* Patna, Tokyo: Kashi Prasad Jayaswal Research Institution, 1982.

Horner, I. B. *Book of the Discipline (Vinaya-Pitaka).* Pts. 1-4 of *Sacred Books of the Buddhists.* London: Routledge & Kegan Paul, Ltd., 1982.

Kabilsingh, Chatsumarn, trans. *The Bhikkhuni Patimokkha of the Six Schools.* Bangkok: Thammasat University Press, 1991.

Kabilsingh, Chatsumarn. *A Comparative Study of Bhikkhuni Patimokkha.* Varanasi: Chaukhambha Orientalia, 1984.

Miao, Shu-lien, trans. *The Dharmagupta-Bhiksuni-Karman,* Taiwan: Chinese Buddhist Association, 1983.

Miao, Shu-lien, trans. *The Model Transmission of the Shramanerika Ordination.* Taiwan: Chinese Buddhist Association, 1983.

Mohoupt, Fran, ed. *Sangha.* Kathmandu, Nepal: International Mahayana Institute. (P.O. Box 817).

Nhat Hanh, Thich. *For a Future to Be Possible.* Berkeley: Parallax Press, 1993.

The Profound Path of Peace, no. 12 (Feb. 1993). Write to: International Kagyu Sangha Association, c/o Gampo Abbey, Pleasant Bay, N.S. BOE 2PO, Canada.

Provisional Version of Regular Monastic Rites for Nuns. Contact Bhikshuni Jampa Tsedroen, Tibetisches Zentrum e.V., Herman-Balk-Str. 106, D-22147 Hamburg, Germany.

Rhys Davids, T. W. and Herman Oldenberg, trans. *Vinaya Texts.* Pts. 1-3. New Delhi: Atlantic Publishers and Distributors, 1990.

Roth, G. *Bhiksuni-Vinaya, Manual of Discipline for Buddhist Nuns (Arya-Mahasamghika-Lokottaravadin)*. Tibetan Sanskrit Works Series, 12. Patna: K.P. Jayaswal Research Institute, 1970.

Tegchok, Geshe. *Monastic Rites*. London: Wisdom Publications, 1985.

Theravada Bhikkhuni Vinaya. Vol. 3 of *Vinaya Pitaka*. Pali Text Society.

Tsedroen, Jampa. *A Brief Survey of the Vinaya*. Hamburg: Dharma Edition, 1992.

Tsering, Tashi and Philippa Russell. "An Account of the Buddhist Ordination of Women." *Cho-Yang* 1.1 (1986): 21-30. Dharamsala: Council for Religious and Cultural Affairs.

Tsomo, Karma Lekshe. *Sisters in Solitude: Two Traditions of Monastic Ethics for Women*. Albany: State University of New York Press, 1996.

—— ed. *Buddhist Women Across Cultures: Realizations*. Albany: State University of New York Press, 1999.

—— ed. *Sakyadhita: Daughters of the Buddha*. Ithaca, N.Y.: Snow Lion Publications, 1988.

—— ed. *Swimming Against the Stream: Innovative Buddhist Women*. London: Curzon Press, 1999.

Upsak, C. S. *Dictionary of Early Buddhist Monastic Terms*. Varanasi: Bharati Prakashan, 1975.

Wijayaratna, Mohan. *Buddhist Monastic Life According to the Texts of the Theravada Tradition*. Trans. Claude Grangier and Steven Collins. Cambridge: Cambridge University Press, 1990.

Wu Yin. *Teachings on the Dharmagupta Bhikshuni Pratimoksha*. Given at *Life as a Western Buddhist Nun*. For audio tapes, write to Hsiang Kuang Temple, 49-1 Nei-pu, Chu-chi, Chia-I County 60406, Taiwan.

Women and Buddhism

Allione, Tsultrim. *Women of Wisdom*. Ithaca: Snow Lion, 2000.

Arat, Paula. *Zen Nuns: Living Treasures of Japanese Buddhism*. Ann Arbor: University of Michigan, 1993.

Bartholomeusz, Tessa. *Women Under the Bo Tree, Buddhist Nuns in Sri Lanka*. Cambridge: Cambridge University Press, 1994.

Batchelor, Martine. *Walking on Lotus Flowers*. San Francisco: Thorsons/HarperCollins, 1996.

Cabezón, José Ignacio, ed. *Buddhism, Sexuality and Gender*. Albany: State University of New York Press, 1992.

Chang, Pao. *Biographies of Buddhist Nuns*. Trans. Li Jung-hsi. Osaka: Tohokai, Inc., 1981.

Chodron, Thubten, ed. *Blossoms of the Dharma: Living as a Buddhist Nun*. Berkeley: North Atlantic Books, 1999.

Chodron, Thubten. *Spiritual Sisters*. Singapore: Dana Promotion, 1995.

Falk, Nancy Auer. "The Case of the Vanishing Nuns: The Fruits of Ambivalence in Ancient Indian Buddhism." In *Unspoken Worlds: Women's Religious Lives in Non-Western Cultures*. Edited by Nancy Auer Falk and Rita M. Gross. Harper & Row Publishers, 1980.

Findlay, Ellison, ed. *Women Changing Tibetan Buddhism*. Boston: Wisdom Publications. (forthcoming).

Gross, Rita. *Buddhism After Patriarchy: A Feminist History, Analysis, and Reconstruction of Buddhism*. Albany: State University of New York Press, 1993.

Havnevik, Hanna. *Tibetan Buddhist Nuns: History, Cultural Norm, and Social Reality*. Oslo: Norwegian University Press, 1989.

Horner, I. B. *Women Under Primitive Buddhism*. Delhi: Motilal Banarsidass Publications, 1990.

Kabilsingh, Chatsumarn. *Thai Women in Buddhism.* Berkeley: Parallax Press, 1991.

Khema, Ayya. *I Give You My Life: The Autobiography of a Western Buddhist Nun.* Boston: Shambhala Publications, 1998.

Klein, Anne. *Meeting the Great Bliss Queen.* Boston: Beacon Press, 1995.

Mackenzie, Vicki. *Cave in the Snow.* London and New York: Bloomsbury Publishing, 1998.

Man Giac, Thich. "Establishment of the Bhiksuni Order in Vietnam." *Dharma Voice (Quarterly Bulletin of the College of Buddhist Studies)* 3 (1988): 20-22. Los Angeles.

Murcott, Susan, trans. *The First Buddhist Women: Translations and Commentary on the Therigatha.* Berkeley: Parallax Press, 1991.

Norman, K.R., trans. *The Elders' Verses II Therigatha.* London: Luzac and Co. Ltd., 1966.

Paul, Diana Y *Women in Buddhism.* Berkeley: University of California Press, 1985.

Piyadassi, Thera. *The Virgin's Eye.* Singapore: Samadhi Buddhist Society, 1980.

Rhys Davids, Caroline, trans. *Psalms of the Sisters.* London: Oxford University Press Warehouse, 1909.

Sakyadhita newletter. Past issues available from: Ven. Lekshe Tsomo, 400 Hobron Lane #2615, Honolulu, HI 96815, USA.

Tsai, Kathryn. *Lives of the Nuns: Biographies of Chinese Buddhist Nuns from the 4th to 6th Centuries.* Honolulu: University of Hawaii Press, 1994.

Tsomo, Karma Lekshe, ed. *Buddhism Through American Women's Eyes.* Ithaca, N.Y.: Snow Lion Publications, 1995.

Willis, Janice D., ed. *Feminine Ground, Essays on Women and Tibet.* Ithaca, N.Y.: Snow Lion Publications, 1989.

Women and Buddhism. Spring Wind - Buddhist Cultural Forum. Vol. 6, nos. 1-3 (1986). Toronto: Zen Lotus Society.

Yasodhara (formerly *NIBWA*) newsletter. Past issues available from: Dr. Chatsumarn Kabilsingh, Faculty of Liberal Arts, Thammasat University, Bangkok 10200, Thailand.

History

Dutt, N. *Early History of the Spread of Buddhism and the Buddhist Schools.* New Delhi: 1930.

Warder, A. K. *Indian Buddhism.* Delhi: Motilal Banarsidass, 1980.